W9-BZM-131

PEOPLES OF THE WORLD
Africans South of the Sahara

PEOPLES OF THE WORLD
Africans South of the Sahara

Joyce Moss • George Wilson

The Culture, Geographical Setting, and Historical Background of 34 African Peoples

FIRST EDITION

 Gale Research Inc. • DETROIT • LONDON

Joyce Moss
George Wilson

Illustrator: Lynn Van Dam

Gale Research Inc. staff

Coordinating Editor: Linda Metzger

Production Manager: Mary Beth Trimper
Production Associate: Mary Winterhalter

Art Director: Arthur Chartow

10 9 8 7 6 5

The paper used in this publication meets the minimum requirements of American National Standard for Information Sciences--Permanence Paper for Printed Library Materials, ANSI Z39.48-1984.

Printed in the United States of America
Published in the United States by Gale Research Inc.
Published simultaneously in the United Kingdom
by Gale Research International Limited
(An affiliated company of Gale Research Inc.)

Contents

The New Africa: African Countries Today

Preface

Human history began in Africa. Discoveries by Mary and Richard Leakey, along with Glynn Isaac and many others, show that the earliest ancestors of modern humans, the Australopithecines, inhabited the Great Rift Valley from the Danakil region of northern Ethiopia to central Tanzania more than three million years ago. By two million years ago, a new species Homo habilis had developed. These hominids made the first stone tools.

The first human ancestors to spread beyond Africa were of the species Homo erectus, who expanded to southern Europe and southern Asia before 500,000 years ago. A number of recent discoveries now make it probable that the modern variety of human species, Homo sapiens, to which all the people of the world belong, also originated in Africa between 100,000 and 50,000 years ago. Assuming this view is correct, less than 50,000 years ago human beings like ourselves spread out of Africa to the rest of the world. Africa, then, was the cradle of present world civilizations.

Africans of the Sudan were among the early farmers and herders in the world. From before 5000 B.C., they domesticated crops such as sorghum, cotton, and sesame and contributed them to world agriculture. As early as 1000 years B.C., commerce began to grow in many parts of Africa and ironwork technology began spreading across the continent. The early kingdoms of Napata and Meroe ruled the middle Nile River region. From 100 to 600 A.D., the powerful kingdom of Aksum controlled trade in gold, ivory, frankincense, and myrrh in the Red Sea region, where Ethiopia appears today. Far away in West Africa, the gold-trading kingdom of Ghana ruled a vast area between the 4th and 11th centuries A.D.

During the centuries before 1500, a variety of different kingdoms arose in many parts of Africa. Two great commercial systems grew up, the trans-Saharan trade to North Africa and the Mediterranean, and the Indian Ocean trade to the Middle East and South Asia. In the 15th century, European merchants began to travel to Africa, opening up a third great system of commercial relations for Africans, the Atlantic trade. While many Africans prospered, the trans-Saharan and Atlantic trades added a tragic dimension to commerce, the selling of many Africans into slavery in the Arab countries and in the Americas. Finally in the 1880s and 1890s, Europeans set up colonial rule over African countries, only to give back independence to most regions in the 1950s and 1960s.

Modern Africa combines the old and new. It is old in the history of human life and new in political adjustment. Most of the countries from the Sahara Desert south are new and often not clearly defined political entities. Given boundaries during the short colonial era, they struggle with ethnic accommodation and great economic problems. In these struggles, they are guided by the elements. Divided by the equator, the continent follows a pattern of rain forest, savannas, grassland, and deserts as one moves both north and south from the equator. Nations strive to control water and other natural resources. Meanwhile, their boundaries make for strange configurations: long, thin nations that are essentially single river valleys, countries consisting of desert and semidesert or of rain forest with fingers of territory extending toward water sources or outlets to the sea.

This book is an exploration of peoples south of the Sahara and their relationships with the political areas in that region of Africa.

Acknowledgements
and a Note about Sources

African studies is an evolving field of research. Without written records about early life there, scholars have had to piece together information from linguistics, blood typing, and archaeological finds. Their conclusions sharpen as evidence mounts, and some sources become unreliable as new information surfaces. Therefore, the presence of a working specialist is invaluable in providing corrected information for such a source as *Peoples of the World.*

The authors are particularly indebted to Dr. Christopher Ehret, professor of African history at the University of California at Los Angeles, who reviewed the entire book and provided valuable criticism and suggestions for improving the manuscript.

The authors appreciate the research and writing aid provided by Colin Wells, Paulett Shapiro, and Lisa Velarde; also appreciated is the careful editing of the manuscript provided by Linda Metzger of Gale Research.

Gratitude is extended to Barbara Neibel, Monica Guylai, and Shiva Rea Bailey for many of the book's photographs, which were contributed from their private collections.

Introduction

Cave and rock paintings and artifacts left by ancient people trace movements of African groups from the north to the south over thousands of years. Settling near the water sources, these ancients were building great societies while Europe was engulfed in serfdom. Trading in salt, copper, gold, cattle, farm products, and for a time, slaves, African states grew in wealth and in their awareness of their counterparts particularly in the east. States such as Great Zimbabwe, Nok, Mutapa, Mali, Ghana, and Songhai rose to be centers of trade, then fell to be replaced by kingdoms of the Don, Hausa, and others. Hundreds of societies, their relationships often suggested by common languages, arose before the first Europeans had any knowledge of the African continent.

Africa and Europe

After the early 1400s, these societies also traded with sailors and business people from Europe. Stimulated by the search for gold and the need for shipping ports and supply stations on trade routes to the east, this association resulted in a rush by the Europeans to divide the spoils of Africa. In the 1700s and 1800s many of the European countries claimed colonies in the new-to-them land.

Often the colonies were formed with little regard for the boundaries of old societies. People within a single society might find themselves ruled by more than one European overseer, while others were suddenly required to share power with different groups--sometimes with their old enemies.

Europeans brought positives and negatives to the new land. European languages gave divergent groups greater ability to carry on dialogue. European tools increased production of some natural resources. On the other hand, Europeans greatly increased a trade in human slaves that had gone on in a low-keyed manner for centuries. Increasing the spiritual variety on the continent, Europeans added another religion to the ancient beliefs, and to the Muslim religion that had already been introduced to Africa by the 800s.

Africa today is a result of the European and Arab influences, and of the African people's struggle to maintain their old identities. The struggle is reflected in the cities, where change is slowly forming national identities along the lines of the earlier European colonies. In the cities newly formed governments share influence with leaders of each society in the city. In communities like Benin City, Nigeria, official city governors share responsibilities with traditional chiefs who preside over sections of the city settled by various ethnic groups. Some African clothing leans toward European styles. At the same time, other Africans take pride in wearing customary apparel. Africa is a continent in transition, particularly in the region south of the Sahara Desert.

Coverage of a Changing Africa

African societies of the past often grew by assimilation of nearby peoples. Traditionally, those societies south of the Sahara most often were tolerant of the people they absorbed and even allowed some self government in exchange for tribute from the conquered. Time shifted the balance of power and the influence of trade; old empires were replaced by new ones throughout the region or contracted to become lesser kingdoms. The pattern of change is reflected in the rise of the great empires in the savanna region of West Africa.

The people of Africa are divided into hundreds of societies. While these societies are sometimes related by language, forming a few major language groups such as the Bantu and Khoisan, each society has its own traditions and customs. These traditions are much guided by the environment and show a long and exceptional skill in adjusting to the range of topography and climate of the continent. The variety among these traditions is one of the distinguishing qualities of Africa.

North of the Sahara, Arab traders and religious leaders dominated the societies beginning in the 700s and 800s A.D. Arab merchants established routes through the Sahara Desert and gradually influenced the south. However, the state of governmental divisions in southern Africa today is largely due to 18th and 19th century claims by European nations.

These three phases of history are reflected in the state of African development today—the rise, fall, and division of old empires, the resulting myriad of relatively independent societies, and the often new configurations imposed largely by European colonization.

Format and Arrangement of Entries

Reflecting these three influences on modern Africa, this book is divided into three sections—The Old Cultures, African Societies Today, and The New Africa: African Countries of Today. The Old Cultures provides a brief overview of the change in leadership in one region of Africa as an example of a pattern of growth and change throughout the south.

Organized alphabetically by culture names, African Societies Today includes a sampling of hundreds of societies giving color and variety to Africa. Each entry is arranged as follows:

A dictionary-style definition introduces the entry, pronouncing the people's name, describing the group in brief, and furnishing the key facts of population, location, and language.

Following this introduction are detailed descriptions under three main headings: Geographical Setting, Historical Background, and Culture (for the old societies) or Culture Today.

For quick access to information, subheadings appear under main headings. The Culture Today section, for example, may include the following categories—Food, clothing, and shelter; Religion; Education; Business; Family life; The arts. (Due to the unique experience of each group, the subheadings vary somewhat across the entries.)

The entries conclude with a section headed For More Information, which is a selective guide for readers wanting to conduct further research on the featured group.

Each entry includes a map showing the location of the society within the array of political states in Sub-Saharan Africa. Line drawings and photographs illustrate the entries and assist the reader in understanding cultural differences.

The country briefs in The New Africa section include two maps, one to locate the country on the continent of Africa and another to show some geographical features and to indicate the country's relationship to some of the societies living there. The briefs contain information about population, languages and cities as well as a description of the topography of the nation and current events and issues within each country.

Other Helpful Features

A Bibliography of sources used to compile this work is included in the back matter. Although every effort is made to explain foreign or difficult terms within the text, a Glossary has been compiled to further aid the reader. A comprehensive Subject Index provides another point of access to the information contained in the entries.

Comments and Suggestions

Your comments on this work, as well as your suggestions for future *Peoples of the World* volumes or future editions of *Africans South of the Sahara*, are welcome. Please write: Editors, Peoples of the World, Gale Research Inc., 835 Penobscot Bldg., Detroit, Michigan 48226-4094; or call toll-free 1-800-347-4253.

Table of African Countries and Societies

The table below illustrates the relationship of African countries to the societies described in this book.

Country	Societies Within the Country
Angola	Chokwe, Herero, Kongo
Benin	Ewe, Fon, Fulani, Yoruba
Botswana	Khoisan, Tswana
Burkina Faso	Fulani, Hausa, Malinke
Burundi	Tutsi
Cameroon	Fang, Fulani
Central African Republic	MButi
Chad	Fulani
Congo	Kongo, MButi
Djibouti	Afar
Ethiopia	Afar, Amhara, Falasha
Gabon	Fang
Gambia See Senegal and Gambia	
Ghana	Ashanti, Ewe
Guinea	Fulani, Kru, Malinke
Guinea-Bissau	Fulani, Malinke
Ivory Coast	Ashanti, Kru, Malinke
Kenya	Kamba, Kikuyu, Maasai
Lesotho	——
Liberia	Kru, Malinke
Madagascar	Betsileo
Malawi	——
Mali	Fulani, Malinke, Tuareg
Mauritania	Fulani
Mozambique	——
Namibia	Herero, Khoisan, Tswana
Niger	Fulani, Hausa, Tuareg
Nigeria	Fulani, Hausa, Ibo, Yoruba
Rwanda	Baganda, Tutsi
Senegal and Gambia	Fulani, Malinke, Wolof
Sierra Leone	Fulani, Malinke
Somalia	——
Sudan	Baggara, Dinka
Swaziland	——
Tanzania	Maasai
Togo	Ashanti, Ewe, Fon, Hausa
Uganda	Baganda

Union of South Africa	Afrikaners, Cape Coloured, Khoisan, Tswana, Zulu
Western Sahara	——
Zaire	Bemba, Chokwe, Kongo
Zambia	Bemba, Chokwe
Zimbabwe	Ndebele

The Old Cultures

The history of Africa is long, and the movements of the peoples of Africa wide-ranging and varied. Kingdoms arose and grew to absorb their neighbors. Eventually, other kingdoms expanded to clash with existing ones, or leaders of conquered peoples appeared who were strong enough to challenge their rulers. Over and over, this scenario was repeated throughout Africa south of the Sahara. The events in western Africa, which are described in the following pages, illustrate how kingdoms rose and fell.

NOK
(knock)

The earliest known empire of West Africa.

Population: Unknown.
Location: Nigeria.
Languages: Unknown.

Geographical Setting

Extending from the coast of present-day Nigeria 60 miles inland is swamp and mangrove forest. Beyond that lies 150 miles of tropical forest reaching to the intersection of the Niger River and the Benué River. Inland from this junction, along the Benué, the land rises to a 2000-foot-high plateau, and the dominant plant life becomes the tall grass of the savanna. Here on the Jos Plateau in the middle of Nigeria is the site of the earliest known major ironworking culture of West Africa.

Historical Background

Evidence of cultures that, for their time, may have been as sophisticated as any in Europe exists in many places in Africa. Beautiful murals on cave walls and rocks, painted in bright and enduring colors, attest to civilizations as far south as the Cape of Good Hope. Both east and west of Lake Chad in central Africa remnants of early peoples suggest complex societies well adapted to the conditions bordering the Sahara Desert. Many present-day societies are the remains of past kingdoms replaced by other African groups or displaced by European intervention. Malinke, Hausa, Maasai, Ashanti, Yoruba, Ibo, and other peoples were once powerful rulers in their areas and contributed much to the spoken literature and beautiful art of parts of Africa. One of the earliest known societies that may have formed an ancient kingdom lay north of the Benué River in what is now Nigeria. Its culture is known to historical archeology as Nok.

In the time of Nok, there were no written records kept in West Africa. Therefore, the knowledge of the people who lived then must be gathered from remnants of ancient buildings and from bits of tools and pieces of art able to withstand the climate for thousands of years. Recovered artifacts indicate that farming people lived on the savanna before 1000 B.C. Around 500 B.C., these agriculturists began to be organized into a society with villages and a strong interest in art. The society, known as Nok, came into being and lasted until nearly 200 A.D. After that the region began to lose its cultural and economic unity, and the old Nok society faded.

Culture

Artifacts found in Nigeria indicate that the people of Nok were peaceful farmers who built small communities consisting of houses of wattle and daub. That their society was advanced is indicated by their crafts skills. These artifacts include tools that are the earliest evidence of ironworking in West Africa. The Nok made jewelry of iron and of tin. Beads of tin have been found, indicating Nok interest in beauty and decoration.

Perhaps the most revealing artifacts are the terra cotta figurines the Nok left. The nearly life-sized figures of people and animals required considerable skill to create and a knowledge advanced for that period of firing clay objects.

The Nok society gave way to new social organizations with the coming of hunters and herders into their agricultural community. However, the Nok heritage of craftsmanship carried over into recent centuries and shows probable linkages between these early people and the Yoruba craftsmen of today (see YORUBA) and those among the Fon of Benin (see FON).

For More Information

Africa—From Early Times to 1800. Edited by P. J. M. McEwan. London: The Camelot Press, Ltd., 1968.

Oliver, Roland and J. D. Fage. *A Short History of Africa.* New York: New York University Press, 1964.

GHANA
(gah' nah)

Early people who established a great kingdom
that became the western and southern trading stop for
travelers crossing the desert of Africa.

Population: Unknown.
Location: North of the Senegal River in Mali and Mauritania.
Language: Soninke, a Mande-related language of the Niger-Congo
family.

Geographical Setting

The ancient society of Ghana was established in the semidesert and
steppe region of southern Mauritania and eastern Mali. Here the
rainfall is low, ranging from 8 to 30 inches annually as one moves
from north to south across the region. The countryside is sandy, but
not so hot as in the central African desert. Because of its nearness to
the Sahara, the state that arose there was well suited to become a
western and southern terminus for traders from the east and north.

Historical Background

Myths. So little is known of the origin of the ancient kingdom of
Ghana, which was located nearly 500 miles from the present country
of Ghana, that many speculations and myths have grown up around
it. Earlier writers speculated that the kingdom was created by white
migrants from the north who won the rule of the blacks already in
the area. Others writing at the same time disavowed this claim and
laid the foundation of Ghana to the black people who were already
in the area. These people appear to have been ancestors of the Soninke

and to have spoken a Mande language. Present-day Mande languages include Malinke, Mende (of Sierra Leone), and Kpelle (of Liberia).

Early empire. What is really known about the kingdom has come from Arab visitors and traders. Perhaps the first to describe the kingdom for the outside world was Al Fazari, an Arab merchant of the 8th century. Al Fazari and others described a great kingdom with its base at the city of Kumbi, whose wealth lay in gold deposits found to the south of Ghana and that carried on a brisk trade with Berber merchants from the east and north. It was a kingdom that, as told by the Arab and Berber visitors, had been in existence for a long time—long enough to have had a succession of 40 or more kings before 1000 A.D.

Some reports held that the king was able to mount a hundred thousand warriors on fine horses and camels, as the people of Ghana sought to expand their territory. In time, the Kingdom of Ghana grew by absorbing smaller realms around them, until Ghana ruled over a region as big as modern-day Morocco. By 977 A.D., Ghana occupied much of the land around and west of present-day Timbuktu. In that era, Ghana expanded northward to include the Berber city-state of Aoudaghost, a state the Ghana king continued to rule until 1054.

Muslim domination. With the rise of the Berber "Almoravid" movement in the western Sahara and its conquest of the Maharab between 1054 and 1076, Muslim influence in Ghana grew, and trans-Saharan traded entered a new phase. The Kingdom of Ghana began a second period of prosperity. For a century, the country flourished under the new religion. Well-constructed stone houses began to replace the older wood and thatch homes for the wealthy. Muslim mosques appeared at the outskirts of Ghana villages. A large cemetery used by practicing Muslims at that time gives today's students much of the information we have about Ghana. In the 1200s another empire conquered the old kingdom, and the country of Ghana disappeared. Even as its origin is obscure, so is its death. Its demise began when King Sumaguru Kante of Sosso defeated Ghana in 1203 and took some of its citizens into slavery. Sundyata, King of Mali, completed the task when his troops captured the capital city of Ghana and destroyed it entirely around 1240.

Culture

The royal court. The king encountered by Al Fazari was a king who might well have illustrated the style of kings throughout the West

Africa Sudan belt. Claiming almost divine right to rule, this king exacted exceptional respect from his people. Calling his subjects to audience with his *daba,* a giant drum made from a tree trunk, the king, sitting on a throne surrounded by his chosen nobles and be-decked with gold jewelry, required visitors to kneel and sprinkle their heads with dust before being allowed to address him. Further attesting to the king's importance, even the court animals were arrayed in gold. To protect his claim to divinity, no one was allowed to see the king eating or performing any other earthly duties except during an annual initiation of the crops.

Ornamentation of the king, his nobles, and their animals indicate a society in which metal crafting had become an important art form.

The people. Most of the people of the kingdom were farmers, who raised bulrush millet, black-eyed peas, and other crops, and tended cattle, goats, sheep, camels, and horses. Others were conscripted to work in the gold fields, and mine gold for the ruling classes. They traded the gold with Berber merchants from the north and east, who bought salt from Saharan mines to be then traded to peoples farther south.

The peasant people of Ghana were poor, farming to earn a living and paying taxes to the king. Common dress was made of leather from the animals that were hunted or tended in the savanna. These people lived in rounded earth or thatch huts, as do poorer people in Africa today. But around each town or city where trade with the Arabs was carried out, stone houses and mosques arose to accom-modate the traders. In time, these structures and contact with the visiting merchants persuaded most of the rulers to adopt the Muslim religion in word, if not entirely in deed.

Religion. The early religion, as in other parts of Africa where people spoke Niger-Congo languages, especially observed veneration of ancestors and of animals and plants in the local environment. As the king became stronger, this religion came to focus on the king as a divine ruler with magical powers. Even after the Muslim religion began to be more widely accepted by the people, it was often blended with earlier beliefs. Trade with the Arabs had long been important. Now this exposure caused some to turn to Islam. Still, it was not until the jihads, or holy wars, of the 18th century that the Muslim religion made great inroads against the older religions.

For More Information

Davidson, Basil. *Africa, History and Achievement*. Stains, England: The Commonwealth Institute, 1984.

Oliver, Roland and J. D. Fage, *A Short History of Africa*. New York: New York University Press, 1964.

MALI
(ma'lee)

An ancient kingdom of the Sudan ruled by
Mande-speaking peoples.

Population: Unknown.
Location: Parts of present-day Mali, Mauritania, and Senegal.
Languages: Mande, also Arabic.

Geographical Setting

Surrounding the Senegal and Gambia rivers and extending inland in
a large bulge that included the sites of today's Timbuktu and Gao
along the Niger River, the Kingdom of Mali lay mostly on the savanna bordering the Sahara Desert. This kingdom was so large that
it encompassed a wide variety of climates and terrains. Reaching
1,000 miles eastward from the Atlantic Ocean, the nation extended
from the edge of the Sahara Desert on the north to the forest land
on the south, and included richly fertile river areas as well as the
early gold mining areas of the upper Senegal River country.

Historical Background

Origin. About 1203 A.D., their realm decimated by attacks from the
north, the old Kingdom of Ghana had become a vassal to the Sosso
King Sumaguru. This king also ruled over the Mandinka kingdom
located near the Niger River south of Ghana. In the African tradition
of authority, which changed with the power and ruthlessness of rulers,
Sumaguru sacked the principle city of Kumbi and proved to be a
brutal ruler. In order to protect the land he had acquired, this king
decreed that all the sons of the Mandinka ruler be put to death. The

exception, as the story is told, was one crippled son who Sumaguru believed to be no threat.

That boy, Sundyata, outgrew his weakness and became a strong leader of his people. In 1235 Sundyata defeated Sumaguru, and in 1240 he added all of the old kingdom of Ghana. In order to build a governing structure based on the existing clans, Sundyata circulated his capital from one clan's influence to another—from Naini to Jeriba, to Maui-Kousa, to Kangala. In the process, he built the most powerful kingdom in the savanna, eventually controlling the trade routes of the western Sudan and southern Sahara. Some of these routes passed through Gao, a Songhai city through which Sundyata was able to command free passage. However, Timbuktu was to become the thriving center of culture. Traders had made it into a city of half a hundred thousand, with stone houses, shops, libraries, and mosques.

Conversion to Islam. Although Sundyata professed to be Muslim, he in fact mixed this religion with other ideas to accommodate his own desires and the beliefs of his people. A later king (*mansa*), Musa, who ruled from 1312 to 1337 strongly followed the Muslim tradition, and in 1324 even undertook a pilgrimage to Mecca. The reports of this trip underscore the accumulation of wealth and the power of the Mali kings. It is reported that Mansa Musa began his pilgrimage escorted by 500 slaves, each carrying a gold staff, and by 160 camels, each carrying 300 pounds of gold. Mansa Musa brought back with him Arab scholars and their books and housed them in fine quarters in Timbuktu. This civilization was to exist for many years.

Fall of Mali. In the 1300s, questions of succession to the throne began to weaken the kingdom. By the end of this century, neighbors were invading lands held as vassal states by the Mali, and one of these vassals, Macina, had succeeded in regaining its independence. In 1433 and 1434, Tuareg raiders occupied Timbuktu and Walata, another most important Mali trading center. By 1468, Mali was so weakened that Sunni Ali, the ruler of the Songhai based in the old city of Gao, was able to capture Timbuktu and later to defeat the Mali at Jenne. Mali power eroded in the east, and future Mali rulers moved farther west. By the mid-1600s, even the western Mali fell to the Bambara states in that area. The remnants of the once powerful state were the small Mandinka kingdoms of the 19th century on the upper Niger river. The strength and size of the Mali kingdom had allowed it to endure for 400 years.

Culture

Economy. Rooted in the farming activity that had long existed in the region of old Ghana and inland, the Mali society was based on farming and tending animals. To this they added mining for gold and copper in the south and for salt in the west. These three products were the center of a brisk trade set up with traders from the east. Buildings of stone arose in the principle cities such as Timbuktu, in sharp contrast to the wattle and thatch homes of the surrounding farm communities.

Muslim influence. In the trading centers, the Muslim religion, although claimed by the Mali rulers, lived side by side with ancient traditions. If Muslim practices interfered with trade, such as by slowing gold production, other beliefs were quickly endorsed. The Mali kings held power in part through respect of the local chieftains, and these subrulers were free to practice the religion of their communities.

Life in Mali. Under Mali rule, Muslim schools began to appear in the Sudan, and a class of educated and literate people arose in the cities. And even though people outside the city were farmers and loyal to local chieftains, the rulers were able to establish an atmosphere of safety and tranquility. Ibn Battuta, an Arab traveler in 1352–3 wrote (Oliver and Fage 1989 p. 89):

> [These people] are seldom unjust, and have a greater horror of injustice than other people. . . . There is complete security in their country. Neither traveller nor inhabitant has to fear robbers or men of violence.

However, even the Mali rulers were reluctant to give up their people's belief in royal magic, and the acts of subservience by their subjects that full adherence to the Muslim religious law would have required. In the end, after much erosion of the central power and the establishment of many lesser kingdoms on land once held by Mali, the kingdom fell to the ruler of a vassal state who had gained his rank partly by professing great skills in sorcery.

The Kingdom of Mali was founded by Mande-speaking people. Today the Mande languages include Malinke, Bambara, Soninke, and Kpelle-Mende.

For More Information

Niane, D.T. *Sundiata: An Epic of Old Mali.* Translated by G.D. Pickett. White Plains, New York: Longman, 1960.

Oliver, Roland and J.D. Fage. *A Short History of Africa.* New York: New York University Press, 1964.

SONGHAI
(song'hi)

Black people of the Niger River area whose principle city was Gao.

Population: Unknown.
Location: From east of the ancient city of Gao on the Niger River westward to the mouth of the Gambia River.
Languages: Songhai, a Nilo-Saharan language, and Arabic.

Geographical Setting

The old Kingdom of Songhai lay in the steppe and savanna region south of the Sahara Desert. Here the Niger River scribes a long arc as it turns south toward the Gulf of Guinea. Farther west, the Senegal and Gambia Rivers water fertile valleys on their way to the Atlantic Ocean. Much of the land is brush and grassland. Rainfall comes mainly in July and August and ranges from 10 to 30 inches a year on average. The Niger River frequently floods the surrounding countryside. The easiest route of transportation in the days of the Songhai Empire was by river.

Historical Background

Trade routes. For hundreds of years, a society of farmers and fishermen lived along the Niger River south of Timbuktu. In time they migrated northward and established their principle towns at Kuka and Gao. Their tradition tells of visits from people of the north, some of whom came to stay and establish a terminus for trade traffic across the Sahara and from the east. This mix of peoples built a trading center at Gao, and by the 11th century had been influenced by the eastern and northern visitors so that the leaders of the people had adopted the Muslim religion. Trade routes crossed at the city of Gao, and the Songhai prospered. Prosperity and power brought surrounding communities into allegiance with the rulers of the Songhai.

Mali and Songhai. As the kingdom of Mali, whose rulers did not adopt the new religion, grew, the small chiefdom of the Songhai was threatened. For a time (1335–1345 A.D.) it became a vassal state, paying tribute to the king of Mali. However, by the 1400s, Mali had begun to weaken, and Songhai citizens who adhered to the Sunni division of the Muslim religion had gained control of the government. These Sunni leaders were able to gain independence from the decaying Mali state and began to conquer neighboring groups of Bambara and Macina. Under the rule of Muhammed Da'o and Suliaman Dama, Songhai began to build an empire.

Sunni Ali. The major growth of this empire, however, came after 1464 A.D., when a master of witchcraft, Sunni Ali, took control of Songhai. Ruthless in his actions, Sunni Ali devoted most of his 27-year reign to warfare. He gained a reputation of invincibility and expanded the influence of Songhai through Mali to the west and into the land of the Hausa to the east. When scholars at Timbuktu questioned his authority, Sunni Ali suppressed them with stern measures. One unsupported Muslim account tells of his taking 30 of the scholars' daughters as his wives and then having the wives killed.

Despite his cruelty, Sunni Ali established a system of government that was to endure for a hundred years. At that time, it was not uncommon for a defeated people to submit so completely to a conqueror that the losing army almost immediately joined the victors in other conquests. In this way, Sunni Ali was able to mount armies for whatever adventure he chose. He divided the conquered land into provinces over which his followers presided, governing through the traditional clans and cults.

Muhammed Toure. Sunni Ali professed to be Muslim, but refused to let Muslim practice interfere with the expansion of his empire. He ruled as a magician-king, claiming the right to rule through his heritage. Mysteriously, Sunni Ali died in an accident in 1492. One of his governors, Muhammed Toure, took over the crown and continued the expansion of Songhai. This ruler became a devout follower of Islam and in 1495 upon his return from a pilgrimage, began to centralize the government of Songhai and to appoint Muslim followers as governors and tax collectors. He brought efficiency to the government, but in so doing destroyed the linkage with the old clan structures. Nevertheless, Muhammed Toure was able to rule and build the Songhai Empire for more than 30 years. Finally, in old age, he was deposed by his own son. There followed a series of upheavals in government during which eight rulers (askias) governed during a 60-year period. By the last decade of the 1500s, Songhai's power had weakened.

The fall of Songhai. Meanwhile, people from the east had begun to explore the possibility of claiming the gold and salt deposits of Songhai. Invaders from Morocco, armed with muskets and cannon, descended upon the land, and the rulers of Songhai were forced to flee east of the Niger. There they broke into two groups, held together feebly for a time, then fell apart into the various communities that had been conquered to form the Songhai Empire. The market city of Gao retained some economic importance but no longer was a center of the empire.

As Songhai decayed, new kingdoms were growing in strength: the several Hausa city-states to the east, the Fulani in the area of Macina and Dirma, and the Bambara in the west.

Culture

Early inhabitants. The people of Songhai were in the beginning farmers and fishermen. They built large canoes to patrol and fish the Niger River. As Songhai grew to be a thriving market town, a class of merchants developed. Then, as Sunni Ali expanded the empire, many of the men were conscripted for the armies, resulting in too few workers to take care of the fields. It was necessary to assign people from the conquered chiefdoms to duty in the fields. This added to the blending of peoples in the Gao region.

River economy. The chief builder of Songhai, Sunni Ali, was originally from Kuka. One of his first conquests was of the Dende, a Songhai fishing society along the Niger. These people added shipbuilding skills to the economy. Large canoes were made from logs when these were available, or by lashing together smaller pieces of wood in areas where there were no large trees. The river people, some of whom lived on islands in the river, were skillful net makers for their work as fishermen. They were also skillful river navigators and in demand to move trade goods and the large array of materials needed for army activities.

Houses. One result of trade and conquest was a capital city of mixed structure. The traditional domed, thatch homes were joined by stone houses, shops, mosques, and burial sites of the rulers. Today little is left of the old Gao near the site of the town of that name today. Only a tower of one of the burial sites and a piece of a Mosque remain of the mostly wood and thatch city.

Religion. Religious practice was also mixed. The ruling class claimed at least to follow the Muslim religion brought to them by traders in whose custom it was good business to follow. However, most of the farmers and laborers stayed instead with their older beliefs in the power of spirits of various sorts and in sorcery.

Language. The original people of Songhai had no written language of their own. As their kingdom grew, some of the leaders sought to persuade Berber and Arab scholars to live among them. So the earliest records of Songhai that exist are records in Arabic of the Berber and Arab scholars and merchants. The Songhai Empire was never able to build the standard of scholarship that was found farther up the Niger River at Timbuktu.

The downfall of the Songhai came in large part because of their use of outdated weapons. The iron-headed spears and bows and arrows used by the Songhai defenders were no match for the guns introduced by the Moroccan invaders.

For More Information

July, Robert W. *A History of the African People.* New York: Charles Scribner's Sons, 1970.

McEwan, P. J. M., editor. *Africa—From Early Times to 1800.* London: The Camelot Press, Ltd., 1968.

Oliver, Roland and J. D. Fage. *A Short History of Africa.* New York: New York University Press, 1964.

BANTU
(ban' too)

A grouping of numerous black peoples inhabiting equatorial eastern Africa and southern Africa.

Population: 100,000,000 (est.).
Location: From southern Cameroon east to the Kenya coast and south to northern Namibia, Botswana, and South Africa.
Language: Bantu.

Geographical Setting

Cutting through Gabon, Congo, Zaire, Uganda, Kenya, and the southern tip of Somalia, the equator divides Africa. At the equator and for some distance north and south, the climate is warm and humid and tropical forests grow from Liberia to the Great Rift Valley in which lies Lake Victoria. North and south of this tropical forest area, the land changes to steppes and savanna where rainfall is more moderate and grasses and scrub brush are the dominant plants. Still farther north and south, deserts provided barriers across which early settlers found it difficult to move: the Sahara in the north and the Kalahari and Namib deserts in the south. While kingdoms and chiefdoms rose and fell in the savanna regions and along the coasts, other societies were growing and changing in the rain forests.

Historical Background

Finding facts about ancient cultures is like treasure hunting. Those who pursue this treasure search for clues in many forms: artifacts often in the form of pottery or sculpture or tools, geography for the most hospitable environments for development, and language. Tracing the language back in time provides information about which societies preceded existing ones. Looking for the oldest words in the language suggests where the people lived and how they earned a living. For example, a language that lacked words for grains but included words for such wet area plants as yams might suggest that the speakers did not live in grasslands where grains would grow easily. Old words that dealt with fishing and boat building suggest life along a water way. From these clues, anthropologists try to determine where people originated, how they moved, and the forms of their daily lives. Such detective work suggests that the early Bantu societies lived in tiny chiefdoms which grew and threw off other small groups as the society expanded. These groups developed their own versions of the original Bantu language. Tracing and relating these languages has drawn this picture of the early Bantu.

Origin. Beginning in the third millennium B.C., from a homeland in Cameroon, Bantu peoples spread east and south into the rain forest region of equatorial Africa. Then between 1000 and 100 B.C. Bantu communities began to spread beyond the rain forest into the savanna country all around the south and east sides of the forest. Finally, between 100 B.C. and 500 A.D., a further large expansion spread Bantu peoples all across eastern Africa and into southern Africa.

Movement and assimilation. As they moved, they encountered other peoples who would influence the Bantu. Groups moving eastward in the first few centuries A.D. encountered in East Africa people from the Nile region and from Arabia. In southern Africa, Bantu settled among Khoisan peoples, such as the San ("Bushmen") hunters and gatherers and the Khoikhoi ("Hottentots"), who raised cattle and sheep. One coastal Bantu people, the Swahili, became important merchants from the 9th century onward, trading to the Middle East with Arabs, Persians, and Indians, and becoming Muslim in religion themselves.

Instead of one Bantu people, they divided and redivided into a great number of distinct societies sharing some common forms of government and religious belief, and related languages. The different conditions of life for the various societies, and their interaction with different non-Bantu peoples, resulted in a great variety of cultural practices and livelihoods.

Gradually, the Bantu people spread throughout the central, eastern, and southern regions of Africa, becoming more fragmented along the way. Instead of one language-speaking group, they divided into a number of peoples who shared the same base language but spoke a range of offshoots that developed from the language. The conditions of life, and associations with others near the various subgroups produced many different Bantu-based languages, including Swahili, a mixture of the Bantu language and Arabic.

Bantu today. Bantu languages are spoken by Chokwe, Kuba, Luba, Kikuyu, Swazis, Venda, Xhosa, Zulu, Ndebele, and many other groups in the vast third of Africa extending from Cameroon, Zaire,

1 **Bantu before 3000 B.C.**
2 **Bantu about 2500 B.C.**
3 **Bantu about 1500 B.C.**

Uganda, and Kenya in the north, southward to the Cape of Good Hope.

Culture

Political organization. The Bantu originally were organized under a system of local clan chiefs. As groups grew and expanded, new groups were created and new kings and chiefs put in place. Then, as these kingdoms gained power, they became independent of their original rulers, sometimes separating their subjects so that different dialects of the Bantu language became separate languages whose speakers lived slightly different lifestyles. In the period after 1000 A.D., the policies of Bantu leaders sometimes worked against them. It was common practice for dominant rulers to leave local leaders in place over the people they conquered. As the ruling chief's government tended to age, and local leaders proved strong, the governments were overthrown and new kingdoms established.

Hunters and warriors. The earliest Bantu societies arose before the use of iron had come to this region, but they had learned to use stone tools and to fashion clay pottery and art objects.

Much later some Bantu groups were users of iron and frequently became feared by other peoples because of their iron-headed hunting spears. Such tools helped greatly as the Bantu societies expanded and increased their needs for food and living space. By the 1100s, Bantu societies in several areas, notably in the western parts of the Congo basin, in western Uganda, among the Luba, and in Zimbabwe, were beginning to grow in size and complexity. In these areas chiefs began to evolve into kings. In Luba country evidence for this belief lies in the graves of the supreme kings, who were frequently buried with considerable worldly goods made of copper, iron, and ivory. Some kingdoms developed strong centers of their society. One of those is Great Zimbabwe, a walled city built of stone that was a trading center, providing gold and ivory to Swahili merchants at the Indian Ocean Coast.

Bantu life. The early Bantu had words for plants such as palms, and knew how to use the products of the palms for food and drink. They also knew of yams and of groundnuts. These foods grow in the tropical areas or in the most rainy of the savanna areas. These early societies also had words to describe fishing and boating. These activities, along with farming, were probably part of the daily lives of the early forest and wet savanna people.

As the societies grew and expanded, they learned other skills: using grasses to build houses instead of the forest branches and palm leaves and, when rock became the dominate building material, constructing villages of stone, and planting new grassland crops such as sorghum and bulrush millet.

Examination of their language also tells us that some of these early residents of the equatorial zone knew about cattle and sheep.

Arts. At a time that fiefdom was the way of life in Europe, the early African societies had developed great social skills and craftsmanship. Their artisans created fine jewelry in copper, gold, ivory, and iron. They also created bells used in royal ceremonials, fine pottery, bark and raphia cloth, and in some areas, notably Zimbabwe and the Maravi Kingdom, cotton cloth.

Bantu languages. Today, descendants of the first Bantu make up many of the peoples we identify as separate groups. For the most part, relatively new groups in the chain of history, these are some of the peoples of Africa who show their Bantu ancestry through their use of a form of the Bantu language:

Bantu woven papyrus.

Bemba*	Kuba	Ndebele*
Fang*	Lesotho	Ngundi
Ganda*	Loangos	Nyika
Here	Lunda	Ovambo
Kamba*	Makua	Ovimbundu
Kikuyu*	Maravi	Pondo
Kimbundu	Maasai*	Tsonga
Kongo*	Mbundu	Tswana*
	Mukande	Zulu*

* See more about these societies in this book.

For More Information

Dictionary of the African Continent. London: Europa, 1981.

July, Robert W. *A History of the African People.* New York: Charles Scribner's Sons, 1970.

Osae, T. S., S.N. Nwabara, and A. T. O. Odunsi. *A Short History of West Africa—A.D. 1000 to the Present.* New York: Hill and Wang, 1973.

African Societies Today

AFAR
(uh far')

People of Arabic descent living on the border of
Ethiopia and Djibouti.

Population: 350,000 (1985 est.).
Location: Northern Somalia, Djibouti, southern Ethiopia.
Language: Afar, a Cushitic (northeastern African) language.

Geographical Setting

The country of Ethiopia is a divided land. The western two-thirds of the country is highland with an average elevation of 3,000 feet but with mountain peaks rising much higher. This part of the country is a high plateau with two branches: the major part extends north and south while the other bends eastward to the "horn" of Africa. The two branches of the highlands isolate a low, flat basin along the southern edge of the Red Sea, the Afar Plain. The Afar Plain extends along the coast through the country of Djibouti and blends into a larger plain in the south, the Somali Plain. This lowland is desertlike, dry and hot, with rainfall less than 7 inches each year and temperatures that have reached 135 degrees Fahrenheit. Some of the land lies below sea level. Lake Assal, in the middle of the plain, is filled partly by sea water that percolates into the depression then evaporates to leave mounds of salt. Another lake, Abbe, is fed by the Awash River, which is rapidly drying up near the lake as Ethiopian farmers farther up the river dam it for irrigation.

Historical Background

Origin. The ancestors of the Afar people have lived in the Afar plains region for thousands of years, possibly as far back as 3000 B.C. The modern Afar society began to form between 1000 and 1500 A.D. Some intermarriage of Afar with Arab immigrants from across the Red Sea took place during this period, but the most important influence of the immigrants was their role in gradually spreading the Islamic religion among the Afar. In the flatlands along the Red Sea, the Afar established themselves as sheepherders, camel raisers, and salt miners, with little government except for local chiefs. One Afar sultanate, with the Oasis of Aussa as its base, arose as early as the 1600s, but its influence over most Afar areas was weak.

Camel raisers, shepherds, and traders. The austere desert with few oases supported a limited number of sheep and many camels, which grazed on desert bush. The only natural resource available to the Afar was the salt that hardened into large cakes in the marshlands along the sea. To the north, the people living in the Ethiopian highlands were dependent upon the Afars for salt supplies. In turn, the Afars looked to the Ethiopians for farm products they could not grow in the desert. When the Oromo of the mountains and flatlands of southern Ethiopia threatened Afar territory, the Afar accepted the overlordship and protection of the king of Ethiopia, who reigned from the northern highlands.

Relations with other peoples. Afar law was as harsh as the land. While living harmoniously with their trading neighbors, the traditional law among these nomads often treated a misdeed among their own people or unfriendly neighbors harshly. Young Afar men gained status by killing other men as long as this occurred in war or against enemy neighbors. This aggressive nature helped isolate the Afar from nearby people who feared their violence. It was not until the 1800s that one sultan ruled over a significant part of the Afar people. He was the Sultan of Aussa, who controlled the bit of fertile land at the mouth of the Awash River. Still, the Afar were and are divided into a number of local chieftaincies, with each chieftain (known as a *dardar*) having loose authority over a small group of villages.

French rule. In the late 1800s, the French came to the port of Djibouti and took control over the Afar who lived nearby. The land north of Djibouti was at first named French Somaliland, but in the 1970s became known as the French Afar and Isaas Territory. The Afar, because of their cooperation with the French, were the dominant force in the government. In the 1940s, the French threatened to withdraw from the area, opening a debate about who should take over the country—the Somalis to the south or the Ethiopians to the north. The debate was resolved in 1977 by the creation of the French Afar and Isaas Territory, and subsequently the independence of this territory as the country of Djibouti.

Independence. The Afars and Isaas now compete for seats in the parliament of Djibouti. In 1985, the Afars held 30 seats in the parliament while the Isaas held 33 seats. The great majority of Afar people, however, live in Ethiopia and have long been reluctant to accept highland rule. The Afar have their own political bodies: the Afar National Liberation Movement, formed in 1974 by Sultan Ali Mirah, whose chief objective has been an independent Afar nation, and the Afar Liberation Front, with the same objective but with Marxist, or Communist, supporters. The Afar are divided among at least a dozen organized groups at civil war with the Ethiopian government at Addis Ababa.

Culture Today

Appearance. With little government, independence and local justice have been the rule for the Afar. This fierce independence and warlike attitude is often accentuated by the decorative habit of the men, who dye their beards bright red. The Afar are a dark-skinned people with narrow noses.

Social structure. Afar people are distinctly divided into two groups named for colors: Asiamara, the reds, claim to have descended from the people of the Ethiopian Highlands and to have the right to dominate the people and hold title to the lands. This "patron" group lives together with a group called whites, the Adiomara. The white "clients" recognize this historical right and live and graze goats on the land at the discretion of the reds. Both groups can still be seen in their flowing white robes or skirts, which are traditionally smeared with *ghee* (clarified butter) for beauty. Both groups claim Arab ancestry: the Reds as descendants of the Yemenite Har-El-Mass, and the Whites as descendants of the Arab patriarchs, Halbay and Ankala.

Food, clothing, and shelter. Some Afar live on the coast of the Red Sea and are fishermen and salt miners. In the inland both "patrons" and "clients" live in tent communities in the Dankali Desert, herding their animals from one grazing land to the next and mining salt slabs from salt deposits to trade with their neighbors.

The basic food of the Afar is the milk and meat of the sheep, goats, and camels they herd. Other foods include vegetables grown in the limited fertile area near the Awash River or acquired through the salt trade. A most popular food acquired through trade is the red pepper, an ingredient in many Ethiopian dishes. Ghee, made by boiling and refining butter into a golden liquid, is used as part of the diet, in religious rites, and as an important Afar cosmetic.

In the few spots where the soil is fertile, men and women, barefoot and wearing single-cloth costumes, can be seen tilling the soil with short, hand hoes. Except in the cities, the Afar dress remains the traditional single cloth wrapped around the waist and reaching to the knee—white for men and brown for women. An important part of the clothing for men is the *jile,* a long knife worn across the stomach. In addition, warriors display amulets around their necks, and married women cover their hair with a black kerchief called the *shash.* European-style clothing and industrialization are changing these traditions as cities grow in Afar land.

Today Afar workers are employed at the seaport of Aseb, one of three ports available to Ethiopians. Two of these ports are in the disputed territory of Eritrea along the coast of the Red Sea. The third port is in the independent country of Djibouti in the Afar region. Ethiopia maintains a naval station in the port of Aseb. At this port in Afar territory, the people wear European style clothing and live in concrete-block homes.

Religion. The ancient religions, in which sacred trees and groves play important roles, are still part of the daily life of the Afar. However, lying along the coast of Africa at one of the points nearest to the Arabian peninsula, the land of the Afars was early influenced by Islam, and in fact, the Afar claim to be of Arab descent. Today the Afar people follow the Muslim faith, but blend that religion with their earlier religious beliefs, which include more gods and greater association with the environment. Some tribes are known for their elaborate tomb structures such as the tomb of the Sheik Abba Yeddidi on Mount Gouda. The religion is celebrated in an annual feast of the dead, *Rabena*, and in the *jenile*, an oracle-dance. On a national scale, religion is another divisive force, since the rulers of Ethiopia have long been adherents of a unique Christian faith, the Ethiopian Orthodox Church.

Values. Today most of the Afar tend goats, sheep, and camels and drive caravans loaded with salt to market in Ethiopia or to ships at the Red Sea ports. Courage and fierceness for men and modesty for women are strongly held values among the Afar. In the past, a boy among the traditional Afar was considered a man when he killed his first victim, received increasingly higher regard for killing others, and won the right to wear an iron bracelet after killing ten or more people. Today the fierce form of Afar justice is gradually giving way to rule by the national governments of Somalia, Ethiopia, and Djibouti.

In the 1980s the Afar people began to unite under the two political organizations and to press the Ethiopian government for independence. In this struggle, they have often aligned themselves with their northern neighbors in Eritrea in the continuing civil war. Isolated from the rest of Ethiopia, unable to control rescue foods and medical supplies sent to that country, and suffering from a series of recent droughts, the Afar are caught in a cycle of starvation and bitter war.

For More Information

Dostert, Pierre Etienne. *Africa 1989.* Washington, D.C.: Stryker-Post Publications, 1989.

Englebert, Volctor. "The Danakil: Nomads of Ethiopia's Wasteland." *National Geographic,* February 1970, pp. 186–211.

Gibbs, James Lowell, editor. *Peoples of Africa.* New York: Holt, Rinehart and Winston, 1965.

Nelson, Harold D. and Irving Kaplan, editors. *Ethiopia, A Country Study.* Washington, D. C.: U. S. Government Printing Office, 1981.

Prouty, Chris and Eugene Rosenfeld. *Historical Dictionary of Ethiopia.* Metuchen, New Jersey: Scarecrow, 1981.

AFRIKANERS
(af'rih kah'ners)

Descendants of Dutch Boers who arrived in
South Africa in the 17th century.

Population: 2,600,000 (1988).
Location: South Africa (Cape Province, Orange Free State, and
Transvaal).

**Once Afrikaners were concentrated in the region shown. Now they
are spread throughout South Africa.**

Languages: Afrikaans, a Dutch dialect influenced by Malayan and French; English.

Geographical Setting

The southern tip of Africa is a coastal plain of broad, grassy plateaus, fertile rolling uplands, and a southeastern crescent-shaped ridge, the Drakensberg Mountain. North of the Cape that separates the Indian and Atlantic oceans, the southern Transvaal and Orange Free State provinces rise to a 4,000-6,000-foot-high region known as the High Veld. The Veld becomes an undulating pastureland that slopes gently toward the Orange River. North of the Orange and Vaal Rivers lies a ridge known as the Witwatersrand, an area rich in gold mines and the home of the country's industrial cities. To the west of this region, a "Middle Veld" of scrub brush and scattered trees extends toward the Kalahari Desert. Below the Drakensberg Mountains in the east, a subtropical farmland and forest area borders the northeast coast.

Historical Background

The Afrikaners are a white population who have had many difficulties working and living with the black populations among them. This tension has been with the Afrikaners nearly since their first arrival in Africa and was once the cause of a migration of the white people to relatively uninhabited African territory, a journey the Afrikaners speak of as the "Great Trek."

Origin. The first Afrikaners were Dutch sailors and settlers who visited the Cape of Good Hope on the southern tip of Africa in the 1600s. In 1651, the Dutch East India Company sent Commander Jan Van Riebeek to set up a midpoint supply station between Europe and India. One year later his party of 200 men and 4 women rounded the Cape of Good Hope and dropped anchor at Table Bay, a port at which Portuguese and English merchant ships had stopped for many decades. These sailors had established a trading community on the Cape among the Khoikhoi and San who lived there. The Dutch settlers were soon living alongside the Khoikhoi cattle herders. As more migrated not only from Holland but also from France, England, and Germany, their need for farmland grew. Consequently, the San and Khoi people were pushed farther away from land near the Cape. In 1659 Dutch settlers defied their own government and attacked the Khoikhoi, using cattle theft as an excuse to seize land and subjugate the native cattlemen. The Dutch then instituted a policy that placed the former Khoi and San landowners into the status of noncitizens. Encouraged by promises of free land, the number of Dutch farmers grew to 600 by 1687 and to well over 1,000 by 1700. Most of the Khoikhoi lost their land and became servants. The Dutch also imported slaves from West Africa, India, Ceylon, and the Dutch East Indies.

Migration. In the early 1700s, the ancestors of today's Afrikaners (Boers) faced the strict rule and economic controls of the Dutch East India Company as well as harassment from the San and the Xhosa, a larger black African group, who were aided by British settlers. Because of these factors, they began to spread eastward from Cape Town. In ox-driven covered wagons, and with their Khoikhoi servants and slaves, these settlers established themselves all across the areas south of the High Veld. This is recorded in Afrikaner literature as the Great Trek.

British rule. In 1795, France occupied Holland. Britain took this opportunity to secure its claim on the Cape, ruling an area that had become one-third white with the rest mostly Khoikhoi and San. However, the Afrikaners had become accustomed to the loose rule of the Dutch and faced many economic and political conflicts with their new government. Finally, following the easing of restrictive laws on servants in 1828 and the freeing of slaves by the British in 1834, more than 5,000 Afrikaners elected to move farther north into the High Veld region of the Orange and Vaal rivers. Some moved into Zulu territory in what is now eastern Natal (see ZULUS). In 1838 they seized the land at the Battle of Blood River and proclaimed Natal an Afrikaner republic.

Diamonds. The discovery of diamonds (1867) and gold (1886) in the High Veld and Middle Veld regions encouraged British political and economic expansion into those regions, which resulted in war with the Boers. The Anglo-Boer War began in 1899, and by 1902 the British had gained control after thousands of Boers had died in prison camps and 7,000 had been killed in battle. Five years later, the British granted limited self-government to the Transvaal and Orange River Afrikaners.

Afrikaner dominance in South Africa. Having lost some claim to the land, the Afrikaners moved in greater numbers to the cities and eventually outnumbered the British. In 1910, they created the Union of South Africa with a white minority and a black African majority. The new country was headed by Louis Botha, an Afrikaner. Gradually, the Afrikaners won influence in the government from the British. By 1948 the Afrikaner National Party had won a political victory over the British, and by 1961 the Afrikaner government had become strong enough to leave the British Commonwealth of Nations.

Changes in apartheid. The tensions between the Afrikaner-led South African government and black groups such as the Zulu, Lesotho, and Xhosa increased as the black population grew to be 75 percent of the country. To retain control and to encourage dissension among the black groups, the government established "homelands", areas set aside for the different black groups. Blacks were excluded from government and elections and were restricted in their movements. In recent years, international pressure on the South African government to abandon the policy of racial segregation has grown. The Afrikaners, long in control of the country, have been forced to relinquish some of their power. South Africa has meanwhile embarked on changes that will allow blacks and coloureds to share in business and in government with Afrikaners.

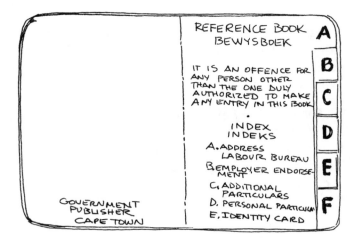

South African passbook.

Culture Today

Economy. The first Afrikaners were traders, farmers, and cattle ranchers in the European tradition. They rapidly changed the agriculture of the Cape from one of subsistence farming (farming for family food) to a plantation and ranch life that supplied the growing trade needs of west-to-east travelers. The Afrikaners carried the ranching life to their new land in the Transvaal. The dispute over land ownership is still a dominant force in South Africa. However, the discovery of gold and diamonds has led to the establishment of large cities and the development of an industrial economy. Today, many Afrikaners live in cities and work in industries of which mining is the single most important. Afrikaners have moved into all levels of government, become leaders in business management, and emerged as entrepreneurs.

In the early days of settlement, Afrikaners adhered to a policy of subjugation of other peoples, which they felt was important to their security. They were a minority surrounded by black peoples, a situation that continues today. To control the situation, the Afrikaner government forced black South Africans to carry an identifying card that indicated where they lived and where the government permitted them to travel. Today, however, this policy is under increasing attack. Black groups are pressing for greater freedom and economic stability. The 22 percent of the population of South Africa that is of Afrikaner or British ancestry claims 86 percent of the land but is being forced to yield to the demands of other groups. About 89 percent of the Afrikaners have moved to the cities, where they own or work in factories producing such items as food, metal products, clothing, and machinery. Drought has been a factor in reducing the number of farmers to 11 percent of the Afrikaner population. In the cities, employers rely on blacks for low-cost labor, paying them less than is demanded by white laborers. This policy led to widespread white unemployment in the early 20th century, but the problem was dealt with by great expansion of employment in government jobs and other efforts by the Afrikaner-dominated governments on behalf of their own people.

Religion and holidays. The Afrikaners brought their traditional beliefs from their European homeland. Most are members of the Dutch Reformed Church, a form of Calvinist Christianity. Next to political meetings, religion is a most significant institution in Afrikaner life. The strict Calvinist teachings of the Dutch Reformed Church are an integral part of all cultural, educational, and political activities. The Calvinists place great value on hard work and landownership. To insure the survival of their religion, the people use the Bible in schools to reinforce government policies. Young people are encouraged to attend school camps for further instruction in Christian responsibilities.

Afrikaners observe religious holidays such as Christmas and Easter. The most important nonreligious holidays are Republic Day on May 31, Settler's Day on September 7, and Kruger Day on October 10th, a celebration of the political and cultural history of the Republic from the Afrikaner point of view.

Community life. Physically separated from the black African majority and the Cape Coloured and Asian communities, the Afrikaner enjoys a high standard of living. The segregated Afrikaner sections of the

A copper mine in South Africa. *Photo by Eliot Elisofon. Courtesy of National Museum of African Art.*

South African cities are modern and resemble European communities. Beside them, lower-quality housing in separate communities isolates the blacks who make up much of the working class of South Africa.

The well-to-do Afrikaners live in spacious single-family homes with lush wooded gardens and swimming pools. State-assisted housing, subsidized single-story houses and apartments, is provided for lower income whites. Afrikaners live in a range of well-ordered white neighborhoods; from the stately manor houses of upper-income Pretoria and northern suburbs of Johannesburg, to the chic "yuppie" enclave of Hartford Village outside of Cape Town, to the unpretentious white suburbs and small cottages of less prosperous communities.

Inside the home Afrikaners enjoy every conceivable modern convenience and Western habit. From a cultural standpoint their lifestyle resembles that of middle-class Americans. The average working-class Afrikaner is largely concerned with his or her job, home, children, car, sports, and vacations, and is reluctant to see political change because it threatens the current lifestyle.

Clothing. The average working-class Afrikaner commutes to his or her job in a compact car imported from Europe, the United States, or Japan, wearing Western-style work clothes and business suits. The younger Afrikaner generation is indistinguishable, except for language, from its American counterpart. They favor the latest designer-inspired fashions advertised in magazines and television commercials. When not in school uniforms, young people wear the latest casual clothes: blue jeans, sweatshirts, T-shirts, high-top sneakers, mini-skirts, and so on.

The older generation tends to be more conservative. Housewives wear simple dresses, blouses, and skirts, and often wear hats and gloves when they go into town. Men wear open-collar shirts and trousers, work clothes, and casual jackets.

Recreation. Afrikaners are avid sports fans. Rugby (a sport played like a mix of soccer and football) is a national pastime enjoyed by almost everyone. One popular outdoor sport is *jukskei*, more a social gathering than a game. As in tennis and cricket matches, jukskei players wear white clothes while they heave wooden cylinders across green playing fields into a sandy area.

Afrikaner leisure time tends to be family oriented. Families attend rugby matches, outdoor barbecues, and public celebrations together. They take family vacations at beaches such as Durban.

Food. Despite the international menus enjoyed in restaurants, the Afrikaner has a sentimental attachment to the foods that originated in the kitchen-garden economy of the Dutch Boer and French Huguenot immigrants. Complex specialties, influenced by Malayan-Cape cuisine, remain favorites. A purely Afrikaner dish is *bobotie*, minced meat baked with garlic, chopped onions, and spices, covered with beaten egg, and served over cold rice or mashed sweet potatoes. A Dutch-pot stew called *Bredie* consists of meat or fish cooked in butter with highly seasoned regional vegetables. The *braaivleis*, or outdoor barbecue, is a national institution for Afrikaners, and no cookout is complete without grilling *Sosaties*, tender cubes of skewered mutton, over hot coals. The Afrikaners are internationally famous for their preserved fruits and vegetables and seasonings, which are prepared with chilies, turmeric and many Indian spices. Among the favorite dishes that date back to the founding of Cape Town are suckling pig, grilled *boere-wor* sausages, a fish stew called *smoor-vis*, pumpkin, pancakes and waffles, and a crusty bread called *rooster-koek*. For beverages, Afrikaners are reknowned for their excellent Constantina wines, sherries, and brandies.

Language. Afrikaners are best known for their lively language and humor, which is often directed at differences with English-speaking South Africans. There are Afrikaans-language newspapers published under government control, presenting highly censored news. In contrast to this is the new *Vrye Weekblad*, a weekly paper that rejects white domination and presses for racial democracy. However, the press in South Africa is highly controlled. In 1974, the Newspaper Press Union amended its codes relating to security matters and stirring up racial discontent. In 1982 the Steyn Commission recommended compulsory registration of journalists. This recommendation was abandoned, but the Protection of Information Act of 1982 defined penalties for publishing materials endangering the national security. All media has been censored in South Africa since 1986.

Arts and culture. Widespread use of the Afrikaans language began to wane in the 1920s, but folk-tradition lives on in songs, music, poetry, history, and the Bible of the early days. Contemporary writers published in English include novelists I. D. du Plessis, Laurens van der Post, Alan Paton, historical novelist D. F. Malherbe, dramatist J. F. W. Grosskopf, as well as Afrikaans-speaking Coloureds such as Peter Abraham.

Storytelling along with writing is a great source of entertainment among Afrikaners. Jan Spies was a popular storyteller in the 1980s, appearing on television both in his own country and abroad.

Architecture in the colonial Cape Dutch style is represented by many fine examples of the period in homes and churches. Afrikaner painting, sculpture, and music prevail in folklore about the founding of the Cape Colony. Popular Western music and dance are performed on the stages of South Africa's many concert halls and opera houses.

In the late 20th century there has been a growing antiapartheid movement among Afrikaner artists and performers. Theater director Chris Pretorius, a descendant of Andries Pretorius, who led the battle at Blood River in 1838, is among the group of artists who are rebelling against the racial policies of the government. Individuals like Pretorius, artist Braam Kruger, choreographer Marlene Blom, dancer Robin Orlin, the rock group GBB (Die Gereformeerde Blues Band), and poet Breyten Breytenbac have been the spiritual leaders of the Afrikaner counterculture.

For More Information

Brink, André. "The Afrikaners." *National Geographic*, October 1988, pp. 556–585.

Elphick, Richard. *Kraal and Castle: Khoikhoi and the Founding of White South Africa.* New Haven, Connecticut: Yale University Press, 1977.

Harrison, David. *The White Tribe of Africa.* Berkeley: University of California, 1981.

Lacour-Gayet, Robert. *A History of South Africa.* London: Cassel & Co., 1977.

Powel, Ivor and Philip Brooks. "The Other Afrikaners." *Vogue Magazine*, July 1990, pp. 196-230.

AMHARA

(am ha' ra)

African peoples with slender builds and Mediterranean features who practice an agricultural economy in the central highland plateau of Ethiopia.

Population: 12,000,000 (1989 est.).
Location: The central and northern highlands; Begemdr, Gojjam, Shoa and Wallo provinces of Ethiopia.
Language: Amharic, the official language of Ethiopia since the 13th century.

Geographical Setting

The Ethiopian highlands consist of tablelands, steep mountain ranges, fertile plateaus, and lowlands with relatively mild climate. Dividing them is the Great Rift Valley, which bisects the entire country. The once lush forests of the high plateaus, rich in flora and fauna, have been cleared and transformed to pastureland through centuries of intensive agricultural use. Overgrazing and deforestation have resulted in soil erosion and flooding during the rainy seasons. Between December and February the central plateau experiences a mild rainy season of about 40 to 50 inches. Annual rainfall in the low-lying arid Ogaden plateau, however, decreases to as little as four inches. The Great Rift Valley cuts through the provinces of Tigre, Wallo, and Shoa, separating the highlands of the north and west from those of the south and east. The Amhara live in the north central highlands from Addis Ababa to Lake T'ana, Ethiopia's largest lake and the source of the Blue Nile.

Historical Background

Origins. The people who later came to be known as the Amhara, the founders and rulers of Ethiopia, had their beginnings in the mixture of Abyssinians (early Ethiopians) and immigrant traders from southern Arabia. Before 500 B.C. the Cushitic and Omotic-speaking peoples of Ethiopia had established trade with the people who lived near the Red Sea.

Centuries of continuous migration by Arabic traders who crossed the Red Sea had a profound influence on the native population. As early as the 6th century B.C. Sabaeans from southwest Arabia and Semitic peoples from the Yemen areas settled northern Abyssinia and mixed with the local people. This mixture produced a new civilization that combined South Arabian and African traditions.

The kingdom of Aksum. Among this new group in the Tigre region there arose the state of Axum, or Aksum, in the 1st century A.D. By 350, the kingdom of Aksum had become the strongest state in the area of the Red Sea and northeast Africa. The Aksumites spoke the Ethio-Semitic dialect called Ge'ez, first introduced by the Arabic immigrants. They flourished for centuries by means of long-distance trade, principally through the port of Adulis on the Red Sea.

Traders from many ports of call, including Christian missionaries from the Eastern Roman Empire, visited and settled in the Aksumite kingdom among the Ge'ez-speaking people who called themselves Habesha. These peoples were known to be successful traders whose caravans traveled far and wide inland in search of gold and ivory.

Christianity. Sometime in the 4th century, King Ezana of Aksum was converted by the missionaries to Christianity, founding the Christian state of Ethiopia. This gave Ethiopia its distinctive religious identity among the predominantly Muslim states to the north and east and the African peoples to the south.

At its height, the power of the Christian Aksumite kingdom reached far and wide in the region, but in the 7th century its power declined, largely because of its struggles with the surrounding Muslim and African states. By the 10th century, the kingdom was confined to a small core area.

Aksum began to recover in the 12th century when the Zagwe people occupied the throne and re-established a powerful state. The Zagwe kings, committed to Christianity, were responsible for building great churches at Aksum, using as their models those built in the Holy Land. Christianity became a source of unity to the Ethiopian people and helped preserve their national existence.

The first Amhara emperor, Yenuno Amalak (1270 A.D.), of the restored Aksum began a succession of rulers who claimed divine rights by virtue of direct descent from the royal couple Solomon and Sheba. This line of rulers survived until the fall of Haile Selassie in 1974.

Portuguese intervention. In the 1530s, Muslims led by Ahmed, who was nicknamed "the Left-handed," invaded and nearly destroyed the Ethiopian kingdom. In desperation, Emperor Galawdewos appealed to the Portuguese for help. The combined forces defeated the Muslims and killed Ahmed in 1543. Thereafter, a permanent capital formed at Gondar in the 1630s and marked the continuation of the Amhara empire, which remained safe for another three centuries.

The period between 1779 and 1855 saw the erosion of central power, the decline of the church, and a degree of anarchy that split the kingdom into powerful substates. In the early 1850s, after considerable skirmishes with the substates, Theodore II proclaimed himself king and undertook a campaign to reunify Ethiopia. He was successful in establishing a new dynasty.

Other European influences. At about the same time, interest in Ethiopia developed among the European powers because of its access to the main route to India. British, French, and Italian missionaries began to arrive. Unfortunately for Theodore, European intervention in Ethiopian affairs grew. This encouraged opposition of Ethiopians to Theodore, becoming a permanent crisis. Theodore earned a reputation for being oppressive and cruel in his ceaseless efforts to maintain his sovereignty of Ethiopia. In 1868, British forces allied with the opposing Ethiopian forces to defeat Theodore at Magdala, his fortress capital.

The opening of the Suez Canal in 1869 led to the Italian purchase of Assab, and to French (1883) and British (1884) possession of Somalia. Menelik, the king of Shoa, strengthened his position by signing a treaty in 1889 with the Italians, giving them sovereignty of the Eritrean highlands. In 1896, after defeating the Italians decisively at the Battle of Adowa, Menelik signed a treaty which clearly defined the Italian regions of Ethiopia. This consolidated Menelik's power and helped his conquest of Ethiopia. Menelik claimed to be restoring the rule of the house of Solomon.

20th century. After Menelik's death in 1913, his daughter Zauditu was proclaimed Empress. Upon her death in 1930, she was succeeded by a distant relative, Haile Selassie.

Selassie initiated a new governing class and centralized governmental authority. Italian occupation of Ethiopia in 1936 by Mussolini forces sent Haile Selassie into exile. In 1941 British forces drove the Italians from Ethiopia and Haile Selassie was restored to the throne at Addis Ababa. Cooperation with the British resulted in a convention between the two countries in 1944 that placed them on a level of equality. In 1952, Britain and the United Nations agreed to the return of Eritrea, which gave Ethiopia direct access to the Red Sea and the port of Massawa.

In 1960, an attempted coup d'etat by the Imperial Guard failed. Disagreements continued however and opposition between rebel and loyal factions polarized the country. This threw Ethiopia into a period of economic and political upheaval. The government's failures combined with Haile Selassie's concealing of disastrous famines in Welo and Tigre, where an estimated 100,000 to 300,000 Ethiopians died of starvation, led to the revolution of 1974. Haile Selassie was overthrown in September of that year.

Under the military rule of Mengistu, chairman of the Provisional Military Administrative Council, PMAC, the Amhara lost their privileged status as a ruling class in Ethiopia. Today the language of the Amhara is the official language of the country, but the Amhara people now share the government with other Ethiopian groups.

Culture Today

Land distribution. While the Amhara no longer control the government, they are considered the socially dominant group of Ethiopia. Amhara comprise 25 percent of the population and remain rural and agricultural despite the increasing influence of the Western world in the modern cities such as Addis Ababa and Asmara.

Life for today's Amhara is relatively simple and still depends upon land tenure. The principal of *Gult* and *Rist*, although abolished in 1966, is retained by Amhara descendants. A *gult*-holder was typically a member of the ruling group who received land from the Emperor as reward for his service; he could demand tribute and labor from those over whom he held gult rights. *Rist*, land-use rights, could be claimed by any descendant, peasant or noble, male or female, of the original holder of rights to an area of land.

Social structure. Amhara social structure is based on a feudal class society. At the top of the social order, until recently, was the emperor, followed by the landed elite, clergy, the merchant class and farmers, then lower status artisans, lower caste tanners, potters, and metalsmiths. Below this social order were the freed slaves. There was no social mobility among the minority castes, and interaction was restricted to business. Amhara groups function mostly as landholding groups, attending to the business of watching over and allocating the land.

Government. The Amhara live in separate hamlets in the rural highlands. Provincial governors, those hereditary male leaders once appointed by the Emperor, play the role of village chief, the *cheqa sum*, and their power is limited to presiding over village council meetings and acting as judges. Often they mediate disputes involving land transfers. The village council, the *kebele*, is responsible for the order of the community, and is in turn responsible to the central Ethiopian committee, the *Derg*, which presently rules Ethiopia under a military government.

Religion. The Coptic Christian church of Abyssinia, a unifying force for the Amhara, plays an important role in daily life. Its laws, considered to be those of the land, and virtually unchallengeable, are a blend of older beliefs and Christian doctrines. Divorce is forbidden. Church liturgy is known to have influenced Amharic literature, most notably the traditional poetry called "wax and gold."

An estimated 10–20 percent of Amharan males are lay priests, the *kes* or *kahen*, and represent the more educated members of the rural society. These priests marry and live in their own family homes on church land. Priests are also farmers, tilling the land around their churches. In the rural areas they perform ceremonies rather than preach and are considered to set the example for villagers by living a holy life.

Agriculture. More than 90 percent of the Amhara rely on farming and raising stock for survival. Farming is considered men's work, and even men who live in the cities are said to be part-time farmers. Agricultural technology consists of the wooden scratch-plow, supplemented by irrigation and terracing tools. Amhara farmers, who represent a wide cross section of the social order, grow mostly cereal grains: teff, barley, millet, corn, wheat, hops, beans, chickpeas, and lentils. Teff is ground into the flour for a flat bread, *injera*, the mainstay of the Amharan diet.

Village life. Amhara towns, small kin-based hamlets with market centers and surrounding farmland, are in stark contrast to the modern urban cities. South of the old capital of Aksum is Addis Ababa, which means "new flower," situated in what is regarded as the invigorating and healthful climate of the highlands. Founded in 1887, Addis Ababa is a mixture of the old and new; modern hotels, foreign embassies, government ministries, universities, high-rise buildings, and luxury apartments often sit next to simple dwellings—huts with grass roofs and earthen floors. Smaller cities such as Gondar, the "walled city" of Harer, and Asmara are evolving into modern centers of commerce linked by communications, railways, and highways.

Food, clothing, and shelter. Amharan diet is considered to be poor in proteins and vitamins because farm animals are used primarily for raising stock and as beasts of burden; cows and bulls are slaughtered only when they become too old to be used for farming. Normally, the diet consists of two meals: a daylight lunch and a heavier evening meal. *Injera*, the main staple is a flat slightly sour bread that resembles a huge pancake and covers the entire surface of a small table. It is commonly served with a layer of *wot,* which is a puree of chickpeas, minced onion, and *barbare*, the famous red cayenne pepper of Ethiopian cuisine. Sometimes finely sliced meat is added, but this is most often reserved for Sundays or special feasts. The overall culture of the Amhara is most evident in the affairs surrounding the church. Obligatory fasting is observed two days out of the week and is limited to one meal a day with no meat, eggs, or dairy products. Ghee, clarified butter, is almost always present in the diet and is made by shaking milk in a gourd until it turns to butter. The substance is then boiled and refined to the consistency of clear oil.

Amharan foods are highly aromatic and prepared with liberal use of spices, including coriander, wild thyme, fenugreek, garlic, and mustard seed. Vegetables such as cabbage and pumpkin are also consumed, and the daily drink is *talla*, a slightly fermented barley beer.

Clothing plays an important role in the life of the Amharan and is a sign of wealth and status. Both men and women wear the *shamma*, a shawl draped over the shoulders and arms like a toga. Underneath, women wear a long loose dress, the *kamis*, and the men wear narrow white trousers or khaki shorts. In colder weather they add a woolen cloak called *barnos*. Western clothes are generally worn by the men in the cities, but the *shamma* is used like a jacket over suit pants.

For the rich and poor alike, traditional housing in the rural areas is a cone-shaped hut called the *tukul*. The walls of the dwellings are made of clay and straw with a thatched roof; sometimes the houses are built of woven bamboo strips. Furniture consists of a few stools, rugs, and animal furs for sleeping. All cooking takes place on a fireplace made from three stones. In the cities the *tukul* is replaced by one-room houses constructed of plaster-covered wood with corrugated metal roofs. These houses generally have earthen floors and no running water or electricity. Wealthier people live in high-rise apartment buildings complete with air conditioning and modern conveniences. However, only the very wealthy or government officials in Addis Ababa and Asmara can afford to live in Western-style homes.

Family life centers on ownership of land. Extended families, the kinship group, tend to live in the same community. The family is the only social unit to which a person belongs, and life within the family is polite but strict. The typical family is patriarchal, with women in a subordinate role. The women, however, are not as oppressed as their counterparts in other ethnic groups. Today their rights have expanded so that they can take grievances to the kebele and own land.

Arranged marriages and long engagement periods are observed. In the cities, marriage involves some degree of choice but divorce is forbidden by the church. Children are baptized, and upon puberty, girls are guarded and not allowed to leave the house alone.

Arts. Painting, music, and literature are influenced by the Coptic church. Most writing done in the ancient Ge'ez language is now being translated into Amharic and English, producing a rich store of plays, poetry, and novels. Crafts include wooden sculpture, pottery, and metalsmithing in gold and silver. Painting is generally religious in nature. Both ancient and modern works usually depict stylized figures of saints, animals, and hunting scenes. Many frescos and friezes can be found in the churches. Fewer works are produced today. Along with poverty and illiteracy, which have deeply affected the standard of living, has come a decline in the practice of craft skills.

For More Information

Buchholzer, John. *The Land of the Burnt Faces.* New York: Robert M. McBride Co., 1956.

Caputo, Robert. "Ethiopia: Revolution in an Ancient Empire." *National Geographic*, May 1983, pp. 614–645.

Gailey, Harry A. *History of Africa from 1800 to the Present.* New York: Holt Rinehart and Winston, 1972.

Lands and Peoples of Africa. Vol. I. Danbury, Conn.: Grolier, Inc., 1983.

Levine, Donald N. *Wax and Gold: Tradition and Innovation in Ethiopian Culture.* Chicago: University of Chicago Press, 1965.

The World and Its Peoples: Africa North and East. Vol. 2. New York: Greystone Press, 1969.

ASHANTI
(ah shan'tee)

A black African people who migrated from open country to the forest regions of central and southern Ghana.

Population: 1,000,000 (1980).
Location: South-central Ghana and the Ivory Coast.
Languages: Twi, one of the Niger-Congo language family; English.

Geographical Setting

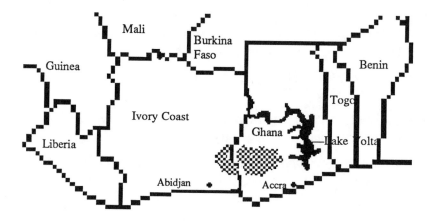

The sloping terrain of the Ashanti uplands dips gently in a southerly direction and meets a belt of tropical rain forests that extends inland from the Ivory Coast on the west and travels eastward to the Volta Basin. South of the basin is a 2500-foot horizontal plateau of sandstone that divides Ashanti into a southern and northern forest zone. The northern forest is a savanna woodland with large expanses of low grasses and short, stubby evergreen trees. This section is subject to the *harmatten*, a hot and dry desert wind. In contrast, the warm and humid southern zone is subject to monsoon winds. A damp and fertile high forest with tall grasses and trees, this equatorial zone receives 70–85 inches of rainfall annually.

The city of Kumasi in the Ashanti heartland of the southern zone is situated some 20 miles from Lake Bosumtwi, Ghana's largest natural lake, and receives an annual rainfall of 73–87 inches. Overall temperatures average around 80 degrees Fahrenheit. The northern zone is typically hot in the day and cool in the evenings. Slash-and-burn agriculture, deforestation, and overcultivation of the cleared land for cash crops has caused extensive damage to the once fertile and deciduous forests.

Historical Background

Origin. The Ashanti comprise a large branch of the Akan peoples whose ancestors are believed to have settled the basin of the Black Volta, the area west of the Ivory Coast, in 10th century A.D. Oral history indicates that these ancestors of the Ashanti migrated to the forest regions more than 2,000 years ago.

Much mixing of different peoples is believed to have taken place during the centuries of continuous migration northward and southward. Immigrants mingled with pre-existing groups and produced the Akan, the people who developed the Twi language. They continued to migrate farther north and south to lightly inhabited, yet fertile and safe, forest zones, where they founded the first Akan states of Twifo, Adansi and Denkyira.

At about the same time, the Mande-speaking immigrants from the nearby Empire of Mali had discovered gold in the region and had established trade routes. The Akan settled directly on the trade route to the gold fields in the southern forest zone and divided themselves into clans and closely knit lineage groups under the leadership of capable and shrewd rulers. Here they enriched themselves with trading and agricultural activities, prospering and establishing powerful states.

Contact with Europeans. Recorded history began in 1471 with the arrival of Portuguese sailors and traders in search of gold, ivory, and spices. The Portuguese landed on the coast and discovered the willingness of local tribes to trade gold for European goods. In 1492 the Portuguese built Fort Elmina on the coast and developed it into a gold trading market. Soon rival traders from Spain, France, and England followed suit and established trading posts. The area became known as the Gold Coast.

Sometime before 1600 a group of the Akan, farmers of the Oyoko clan, grew restless and began to move northward in search of more land on which to grow their crops. Moreover, they wanted to share in the gold and kola-nut trade. The Oyoko clan, led by their shrewd and skillful ruler, Obiri Yeboa, settled the forest area in the vicinity of Lake Bosumtwi and established the core of what later became the town Kumasi. The hardworking Oyoko cultivated the land, built a town, and became involved in the production and sale of gold and kola nuts to northern and coastal merchants. Before long the pioneering clan was joined by other clans, whom they absorbed without difficulty. As they grew in size and became prosperous, the various families banded together; they called themselves Ashanti and named their town Kumasi.

Founding the Ashanti kingdom. At its outset, the first Ashanti state, a league of five or six clans each with its own chieftain, was weak and small. Facing competition for land and trade from the other Akan states, the Ashanti were under constant pressure from their powerful overlords, the Denkyira. The Denkyira demanded that the Ashanti pay tribute and taxes in gold and slaves. In order to secure the land and secure his position as leader, the politically astute King Yeboa closed ranks among the clans by engaging in attacks on neighboring states that refused to recognize his rule. Yeboa was killed in the 1670s in a war against the Domaa tribe.

The loose Ashanti alliance, subject to the tyrannical rule of the despised Denkyira, were consolidated into a powerful union under the leadership of Yeboa's nephew, Osei Tutu of Kumasi. Tutu proved to be even more formidable than his uncle. Together with his close adviser and priest, Okomfo Anokye, he played on the chieftains' common fear and hatred of the Denkyira and on the use of magic.

He devised a constitution for the union and developed a strong army. Under Tutu's brilliant administration and his policies of expansion, the capture of slaves from weaker tribes, and the mining of gold, the union thrived and became the leading force in the region. Proclaiming himself king, Tutu asserted that a golden stool had magically tumbled onto his lap from the sky. This event was viewed as a sign of divine election and the golden stool thereafter came to represent the spirit of the Ashanti union—the symbol of the political and religious head of the kingdom. Subsequently, all Ashanti rulers, called Asantehene, came from the Oyoko lineage and were "en-stooled" on the golden throne.

Golden era. The Ashanti's reputation for being fierce and warlike was further enhanced by the next Asantehene, Opoku Ware, a far-sighted ruler and energetic military strategist. The conquests of his reign brought Kumasi into its period of glory. The Ashanti kingdom became a center of political, intellectual, and religious life. All manner

Ashanti stool makers. *Photo by Eliot Elisofon. Courtesy of National Museum of African Art.*

of important figures visited and paid tribute: chiefs and soldiers, envoys and traders from many forest states, merchants, and educated Muslims. The Muslims, first introduced to the region by the immigrant traders who had hired them as scribes, clerks, and accountants, brought with them their considerable skills and the Islamic religion. They introduced the sciences and the Arabic language, staffed the Asantehene's court as civil servants, and had a deep influence upon the Ashanti culture.

By the 17th century the Gold Coast had attracted more Europeans. Dutch adventurers, followed by the British, Danish, and Swedish, arrived and built trading posts. The Dutch captured Fort Elmina, and in 1642 ousted the Portuguese from the Gold Coast. They then tried to eliminate the other foreign competitors and captured all but one of the British posts.

The trade in slaves, which was a commercial sideline until the 1640s, came to surpass gold as the primary export from the Gold Coast. The incessant demand for slaves made the trade very profitable for both the European dealers and their suppliers, the strong coastal societies like the Fante and Ga and the Denkyira who controlled the interior. The Denkyira controlled all trade with the wealthy Dutch market at Elmina. In order to maintain their power over other tribes, the Denkyira needed guns and gunpowder. They obtained the weapons from the Dutch and paid for them with gold and slaves, which they demanded as taxes from the Ashanti.

The Ashanti, also dependent on firepower, felt the weight of taxation and decided to do away with the obstacle that prevented them from trading directly with the Dutch. In 1701 they defeated the Denkyira and came into possession of the rent agreement to Fort Elmina. This piece of paper gave them control of Elmina and the castle was on Ashanti soil. The victory brought them into direct contact with the European traders.

Intergroup warfare. Now the steady supply of slaves bound from the Gold Coast to Brazil, to the European sugar plantations in the West Indies, and to North America was mainly controlled by the Ashanti. The monopoly of the slave trade caused friction with the competing coastal societies and resulted in several wars. But the Ashanti continued to have a major stake in the kola trade to the north and engaged in campaigns in those regions to solidify their control of that commerce. Having welded themselves into a powerful military confederacy, the Ashanti expanded their control to most of the interior. With their increased wealth from the slave trade, they built an empire that reached far beyond the core of Kumasi.

Recurrent conflict between the Ashanti and Fante in the 18th and early 19th centuries not only disrupted trade but caused the British to intervene and restore order. The British outlawed the slave trade in 1807, and the other European nations followed suit. Thereafter, the Europeans were drawn into continuous conflict with the Ashanti empire. In 1874 the British invaded and burned Kumasi to the ground, then imposed a peace treaty on the Ashanti chiefs. Despite being shattered, the Ashanti entered into a period of civil wars. The British finally re-entered Ashanti affairs because of the pressures of colonial competition with France and concern over trade disruption.

In 1895 the British "de-stooled" the Asantehene Prempeh and exiled him and the royal family to an island in the Indian Ocean. The Ashanti's refusal to accept British occupation led to another revolt against them. In 1900 the British demanded the Ashanti surrender the symbolic golden stool to them. More than anything else, this act enraged the Ashanti. In 1902, after a period of bitter fighting, the Ashanti were finally subdued and their land became a British colony.

In 1924 the British permitted the return of Prempeh I, the exiled Asantehene, and two years later he was allowed to resume authority, but only over the town Kumasi. In 1935, because of continued A-shanti nationalism, the British decided to restore the confederacy with Prempeh II as the Asantehene.

A 1946 constitution gave the Africans a measure of self-government and an elected majority on the legislative council. For the first time the Ashanti and the European people of the Gold Coast Colony sat on the same assembly.

In 1957 the Gold Coast was the first colony to gain independence. The Convention People's Party headed by Kwame Nkrumah came into conflict with Ashanti desires for self-government. Nkrumah unseated two important Ashanti chiefs in 1958 and moved to destroy opposition to central power. In 1960 the nation became the republic of Ghana, with Nkrumah as its president.

Nkrumah became a dictator and was overthrown by a military coup in 1966 that was begun in Kumasi, the Ashanti capital. Today Ashanti is one of Ghana's federal regions and enjoys a large measure of self-rule. Each of its districts is headed by a chieftain.

Culture Today

Politics. The descendants of the Ashanti empire, which once dominated the vast reaches of Ghana with its military might, are today dispersed among the many towns and small villages in the districts of the Kumasi region. The period of transformation that began with Ghana's independence has slowly exposed both the rural and urban Ashanti to new economic activities and modern education. Today they maintain a highly visible political identity.

Government. For the Ashanti, religion and politics overlap. Because of this their towns and villages, headed by their chieftains, are semi-independent political and religious units. The desire to keep their economic and political independence has led to the rise of Ashanti nationalism, particularly among the more educated town dwellers.

City life. Today the town of Kumasi, Ghana's second city, is the country's largest market and an important business center. Western-style institutions, such as the university and National Cultural Center, with its museum and galleries, exist alongside the Asantehene's palace and the home of its religious relics and artistic heritage. Kumasi's roads and railway links to the capital city of Accra have made it the leading communications center of the country.

Village life. In contrast to the Ashanti who live in modern apartments in the larger towns and city, the majority of Ashanti are rural people who cultivate the land for cash crops such as cocoa. In the villages, the traditional way of life is dictated by a clan organization based on matrilineal descent (descent through the mother's lineage). The clan, or *Abusua*, is a group of families who trace their heritage to a common female ancestor. These units regulate social behaviors, chiefly marriage. The land, which is owned by the clan, is worked by the lineage members and is administered by the clan elders. The head of the group is the chieftain, a male elder who is elected by a male majority. He determines who will farm the land and where to build houses, and arbitrates all disputes brought before him.

Religion. Religious rituals play a major role in Ashanti life and are based on the worship of the spirits of the dead. The Ashanti make use of a great many spiritual items, often embellished liberally with gold. The supreme symbol of authority, the Golden Stool, is the spirit of the union. Likewise, the local symbol of authority is the highly decorated wooden stool of the chief. The most important duty of this chieftain is to guard the seats of the ancestors, which represent the spirits of past chiefs.

Food, clothing, and shelter. Generally, living conditions in the rural areas are better than in the urban sections. The majority of urban dwellers are tenants who live in garden apartments and bungalows. Typically, the extended family (husband, wife, children, and close relatives) shares one house. Unless they are wealthy and can afford large homes, conditions are often crowded.

In the rural areas each extended family builds its own set of dwellings within a square or rectangular compound composed of as

Young Ashanti dancer. *Photo by Shiva Rea Bailey.*

many huts as necessary to accommodate its members. The huts are constructed of mud and wattle or adobe brick and are covered with thatch or corrugated metal roofs. Cooking usually takes place outdoors, and one room is commonly reserved for washing and bathing. While some of the larger and wealthier towns have piped drinking water from communal standpipes, most rural areas collect rainwater on roofs. Indoor plumbing and electricity are unknown in all but the most modern commercial areas of the major towns.

In the rural areas, men farm the land. Women tend the children and cook and sell produce in the village marketplace. Families maintain duo-locale residence; that is, the wife lives with her parents and her children, while the husband lives with his mother's sisters and his uncles. The wife moves in with her husband when her oldest child begins to need a father's attention. The Ashanti believe that the child gains his spirit, *Ntoro*, from his father, and his clan membership from the *Mogya*, or the mother's blood.

The Ashanti diet typically consists of "mash and sauce," a starch base of cereals covered with a stew of vegetables, shea butter, and

Ashanti people at a meeting with the Asantehene. *Photo by Shiva Rea Bailey.*

groundnuts. The starch paste is generally made from millet, sorghum, rice, or maize. The stew, often called "sauce," sometimes contains yams with some dried fish added. The Ashanti are known to consume beer in enormous quantities, and it is sometimes used in the sauces. Tomatoes, peppers, and plantains, as well as a variety of shellfish are purchased in the markets.

Western-style clothes are favored in the commercial urban areas, but are often combined with the brightly patterned cloths referred to as "Ghanian national dress." In the rural areas men generally wear a sleeveless toga, and the women wrap lengths of patterned fabric around their torsos and hair. The Ashanti weave the intricately patterned cloth, *Kente,* from cotton or imported silk. The fabrics are

Ashanti ceremonial dancer. *Photo by Shiva Rea Bailey.*

Shrine house priestess. *Photo by Eliot Elisofon. Courtesy of National Museum of African Art.*

generally reserved for ceremonial wear on festive occasions. Women wear traditional jewelry, rings, bracelets, and neck pieces of gold fused with copper and silver. Sandals of woven leather are worn, especially by the chieftains, who are not allowed to walk barefoot because it is believed that this will cause a famine. Chieftains wear skullcaps or crowns richly adorned with gold, beads, and other precious metals.

Art and literature. The art of the Ashanti is contained in the richly adorned religious artifacts, decorated stools, pottery, weapons, fly whisks, and personal jewelry of gold, bronze, copper, and silver. The Ashanti are also known for their carving skills. The men generally create stools and wooden figurines. These are then carried by the women to insure fertility. The most notable of the wooden sculptures are the *Ntumpane*, or "talking drums," used to convey messages over long distances with a special drum language. The women are known for their pottery making and terra-cotta ceramics.

Ashanti music and dance convey stories of famous battles and heroic acts and are often of a patriotic or military nature. Sometimes the songs are performed by popular troubadors.

The development of Ashanti literature came with the introduction of the Latin alphabet by missionaries in the 19th century. Ashanti oral folktales became the basis of written literature. These folk stories deal with many everyday subjects and often explain particular be-

Ashanti molds.

haviors. For example, one story tells how divorce became legitimate. A husband learned the language of the animals and in talking with them inflamed his mother-in-law. The tensions were so great that finally the Sky-god rescued the husband by permitting a divorce.

The Ashanti publish fables, novels, and plays. Today proverbs, poetry, and literature are written in English to reach a wider audience.

Drumming for an Ashanti chief. *Photo by Shiva Rea Bailey.*

An Ashanti chief with symbols of his office. *Photo by Shiva Rea Bailey.*

Ashanti history is the subject of much writing. One well-known author, K. A. Busia, described the Ashanti chief in his book, *The Position of the Chief in the Modern Political System of Ashanti.* The Ashanti also have newspapers published in Ashanti.

For More Information

Addison, John. *Ancient Africa.* New York: John Day Co., 1970.

Boahen, Adu. *Topics in West African History.* London: Longman Group, Ltd., 1966.

Kyerematen, A. A. Y. *Panopoly of Ghana.* New York: Frederick A. Praeger Publishers, 1964.

Lystad, Robert A. *The Ashanti: A Proud People.* Greenwich, Connecticut: Greenwood Press, 1968.

The World and Its Peoples, Africa South and West. Vol. 2. New York: Greystone Press, 1967.

Ashanti drummer. *Photo by Shiva Rea Bailey.*

BAGANDA

(buh' gahn dah)

The largest of the African groups in Uganda.

Population: 1,000,000 (1985 est.).
Location: Uganda, along the northwest side of Lake Victoria.
Languages: Luganda, English.

Geographical Setting

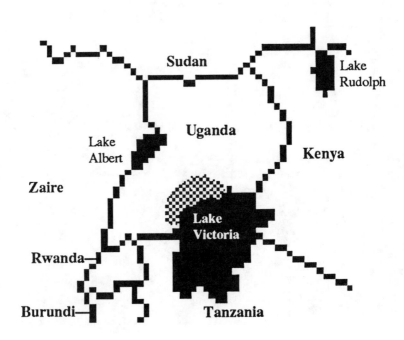

The country Uganda is shaped like a large bowl straddling the equator. A ring of mountains extends into Tanzania on the south. Lake Victoria lies in the middle of this bowl on the southern edge of Uganda. The altitude in the bowl of Uganda averages 4,000 feet, so the climate is mild even though the country is on the equator. An abundance of water, rich soil, and the moderate climate make the region of the Baganda excellent farm land. A number of cash crops can be successfully exported despite Uganda's being a landlocked country, far from shipping ports from which products leave Africa.

Historical Background

The influence of the Baganda in the area around Lake Victoria is reflected in the names of the area. The people live in the province of Buganda, located in the country of Uganda.

Origin. Baganda society traces its founding to a legendary leader of the Bito people named Kintu, who brought a group of immigrants from Mount Elgon to the east and settled them among the farmers and herders living along the northwest side of Lake Victoria. These developments date to about the 13th century. Gradually, a small kingdom of Buganda arose under a *kabaka*, or king.

Buganda Kingdom. The first kabaka to be a real ruler is thought to have reigned in the second half of the 15th century. The kingdom remained small until three strong kabakas in the 17th century succeeded in uniting many of the people around the lake and expanding Baganda territory. In the middle of the 18th century, another strong kabaka, Semakokiro, solidified power by destroying anyone who threatened his authority, including his own son. Succeeding kabakas followed this pattern and established Baganda dominance, ultimately ruling over the largest kingdom in East Africa. By the middle of the 19th century, the kabakaship had passed to Kabaka Mutesa, under whom the Baganda experienced great military and economic expansion between 1854 and 1884. His kingdom was divided into ten provinces, each with a governor, then subdivided into districts led by chiefs charged with collecting taxes. The Baganda gained a reputation as skillful administrators and exercised much legislative power during this period. Privileges were awarded to members of the landed class, and the king lived in splendor, surrounded by guards, slaves, a corps of secret police, and a harem of wives.

British rule. European missionaries made contact with the Baganda in 1877, establishing schools that were to make the Baganda the most educated people in the region. Less beneficial were the violent struggles that erupted between Christian and Muslim factions of the people. In 1894, the British made the kingdom of Buganda a protectorate. Under this rule, the "Uganda Agreement" (1900), a land distribution act, affirmed Baganda rights to much valued territory. In addition, the British encouraged a cash-crop economy, which placed the Baganda, already farmers, ahead of other groups economically. Initially the kabaka was allowed to remain king under the stipulation that he obey the British governor. Cooperation was short-lived, however. The Baganda ruler was deported in 1953. The act unified the Baganda into defiance of the British. Finally, the British accepted a peaceful agreement providing independence for Uganda in 1962 with the old kabaka elected to be Uganda's first president. The Baganda again became the ruling force among the people of Uganda. In 1966, however, their dominance was upset by armed force, and Uganda became a presidential dictatorship under Milton Obote, himself a Bagandan. The unification of Uganda was made possible by naming the Baganda kabaka Frederick Mutesa III president with Obote as prime minister. A year later, the kingdom of the Baganda was disbanded. Obote was deposed in 1969 by a military coup led by Idi Amin, another Bagandan. Amin set in motion a government of brutal and murderous terror. He also expelled many Asians who were living in Uganda and were managers and owners of businesses in the country. The result of Amin's policies was a disastrous decline in the economy of the country. Before these difficulties in the 1970s, the Bagandans were prosperous farmers, many of them having grown wealthy through their harvests of cotton and coffee. Partly to turn the attention of these people, who were the majority, from the problems of Ugandan economy, in 1979 Amin's army attacked Tanzania. This proved to be an error in judgment as the Tanzanian army then invaded Uganda and drove Amin from power. After a period of different, short-lived governments, Lieutenant General Yoweri Kaguta Museveni finally came to power and has tried to rebuild the Ugandan economy. Continuing unrest in northern Uganda and the instability of the price of coffee, one of Uganda's chief exports, have continued to make Uganda one of the poorest countries in the world.

Culture Today

Organization. The land of the Baganda lies across the equator in East Africa. It is a rich agricultural region, with most of the people living in small towns or villages. People in this country have not often experienced a lack of food. Without pressure to supply enough to eat, the Baganda lifestyle has developed very differently from other African groups. Not bound by the need to find food and water, the people have been free to move about. Men, who were the heads of the families, would frequently move from one village to another. Baganda territory is sparsely populated, so even frequent moves did not disrupt people's farming lives. Land has usually been readily available wherever a family moved.

Farming. The Baganda are not much dependent on relatives other than the immediate family, and each family is nearly self-sufficient. Today the villages reflect this independence. Houses are spread 50 yards or more apart with tropical plants such as bananas between houses and the farmlands stretching for 5 to 10 acres around each shelter. A principal crop is the banana, which grows easily in the tropical climate of the region. Cotton and coffee are grown for export. The Baganda raise some cattle, and in areas where grasses are fa-

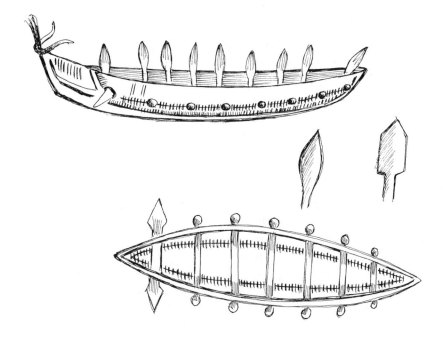

Ugandan sewn-wood canoe.

vorable, this is a major occupation. Until recently, however, the tsetse fly has been a danger in the cattle-raising areas. Efforts throughout many countries of Africa have now nearly eliminated this pest. Near Lake Victoria, Baganda men build canoes and fish to supplement their income.

Food, clothing, and shelter. The traditional Baganda family lives in a thatched house in the shape of a large beehive. Poles are arranged and anchored, and over them thick-bladed grass is spread to make thatch walls that reach from a point at the top and center to the ground. Some Baganda are excellent craftsmen, so these houses are carefully and neatly built. Often the homes are divided into several rooms, sometimes by hanging bark-cloth drapes. Cooking is done outside the main house, usually in a separate structure. This freestanding "kitchen" is equipped with large earthen pots that the women use for cooking plantain (green cooking bananas), potatoes, spinach-like greens, and beans. The home includes a pen for sheep or cattle in some areas, and additional houses should the man have more than one wife. It is common for an adult to have several spouses in sequence and children are often raised by kinfolk rather than parents.

Plantain is the principal item in the Baganda's diet. Planted around the house, plantains provide food year-round. Some are eaten as fruit, some are made into a kind of beer; but bananas are used primarily as a main course, much as potatoes are used in European countries. Cut unripe, they are cooked to make a meal with vegetables such as sweet potatoes or cowpeas and perhaps some fish or chicken.

During the day, both men and women farm and some men practice their skills as craftsmen. Dressed in wraparound cloth hung from the waist or draped over one shoulder, they construct roads and bridges as well as ornate buildings (sometimes used as temples) of reeds and grasses. Canoe building, ironwork, pottery, basketry, and the making of bark cloth are common activities.

Conditions are gradually changing as the Baganda are encouraged to grow cash crops and to market them to other people. As recently as the 1950s, women were considered property of the men. They knelt when greeting a man of equal or higher status. They did not go out of the living area alone, and they served as virtual slaves of the king and chiefs. Some women were chosen at birth to perform religious rituals such as tending the ritual fires.

Arts. The Baganda had no written language until English missionaries began to translate the Bible into their language. A rich oral literature of song and story, however, carries the history of the people. Music has been a favored art. Baganda people sing frequently. Accompanying the songs are sounds from drums, harps, and fifes. A typical Baganda village might have some sort of dance nightly.

Religion. Religion has long been important to the Baganda. The traditional religion is complex, with veneration of many objects. The Baganda worship gods who are universal (gods of the king), gods involved with their own clans, ritual objects that are manufactured but believed to have mystical powers for good and evil, amulets with similar powers, and spirits of the ancestors. This religion is being replaced. Today few Baganda venerate the ancient local spirits and those of powerful men. About 85 percent of all Baganda are Christian and 15 percent Moslem.

Changing lifestyles. Change is evident in many aspects of Baganda life. Once the Baganda dressed in bark cloth and the skins of animals,

Baganda drum, pot, and beer containers.

but now cotton dresses and pants are typical. Cooks use aluminum pots, many people ride bicycles, and there are some automobiles among the wealthy. Radios and phonographs provide contemporary music while the sophisticated drum language of beats and rhythms, which at one time was used to communicate throughout the kingdom, are still prevalent. The traditional six-month year of the Baganda is changing to coincide with the calendars used in other places, and more accurate measures are replacing traditional Baganda measures such as the handful. Now, some Bagandans prefer jobs in government or the service industries to the traditional occupations.

Traditionally the Baganda king, the kabaka, has been highly honored. Special houses were built for him. His chief queen owned land

Baganda dress.

and directed her own set of chiefs. The kabaka had his own special temple and, in theory, owned all the property of the Baganda. Today many Baganda still look to the kabaka for direction. They are divided into 36 clans, each named for a particular animal or plant symbolized by a totem. In the past, the kabaka was absolute monarch and also high priest and supreme judge, ruling alike over the contending Christians and Moslems among the Baganda.

For More Information

Africa South of the Sahara, 20th ed. London: Europa Publications, 1990.

Oliver, Ronald and Michael Crowder, editors. *The Cambridge Encyclopedia of Africa.* Cambridge, England: Cambridge University Press, 1981.

Roscoe, The Reverend John. *The Baganda.* London: Frank Cass and Company, Ltd., 1965.

BAGGARA
(ba ga'ra)

Nomads in the Sudan who are of Arab descent.

Population: 5,000,000 (est. 1980).
Location: The Republic of Sudan and the Republic of Chad between the Nile River and Lake Chad.
Language: Arabic.

Geographical Setting

From east to west, the southern Kordofan and Darfur provinces of Sudan change from semiarid savanna to moist grasslands and then to open forest. The region is dominated by the White Nile River and its tributaries—the Bahr al-Ghazar River to the southeast and the Bahr al-Arab River to the west. Dry air masses blowing from the northerly deserts bring dust storms that precede rain storms brought on by the humid air masses pushing up from the equatorial south. The westernmost part of the central belt in Darfur, below the gentle slopes of the Jabal Marrah range, receives adequate rain for agriculture and cattle herding. In the savanna area, rain and sandy soil permit the growth of acacia bush and short grasses. The central and northern areas are subject to long dry seasons, while the south typically has a six to nine month wet season. Overall the climate is hot and humid and the average annual rainfall exceeds 60 inches in the south.

Historical Background

Origin. Baggara, the Arabic term for "cow," is a name that identifies the occupation of cattle-owning Arabs as opposed to the camel-owning nomads of the region. The people referred to as Baggara are descendants of the camel-herding Arab nomads who migrated from Upper Egypt in the 14th century and the black inhabitants in the area that is now Sudan and Chad.

As the Arab migrants pressed southward, they invaded existing African kingdoms in their path, intermarried with Nubians and other peoples, took slaves, women, and cattle, and slowly spread westward. Before the 18th century, the intermix had resulted in a dark complexioned people with Arabic facial features and slender builds—the Baggara. These people clung to their nomadic traditions—living in tents, traveling by camel, and raiding other peoples for slaves to provide their manual labor. They also borrowed agriculture from the Sudanic farmers and incorporated the kin-related tribal systems of the earlier Africans.

The region from Kordofan to Darfur in present-day Chad was the home of several Arabic-speaking tribes that practiced semi-nomadic cattle herding along with some farming. A non-Arabic sultanate, the Fur people, raised cattle in the region between the Jabal Marrah Mountains and the Bahr al-Arab River. In the same region, Fertits, descendants of escaped slaves, lived as farmers. The Baggara settled in the territory between the Fur and the Fertit, a region that had long been used for capturing and holding slaves. As they spread westward, the Baggara found the wet grasslands less suitable for their camel herds and turned to cattle raising and a hoe agriculture. Invading the slaving grounds, they captured slaves to grow their food for them, and absorbed other peoples into their military service.

The Baggara relied on slaves for manual labor and fighting. Seizing territory along the routes of the Arab slavers, they competed for the same people. By the 19th century the slave trade was booming. Great profits were to be made by exporting slaves to Egypt for sale to the Middle East. The Baggara became employees of the sultans in the slaving business and developed the reputation of being the primary suppliers of slaves.

British and Turks. This trade grew more explosively when the British and Turks expelled the Mamluk governors from Egypt and installed Pasha Mohammed Ali as ruler. He immediately began to build the Egyptian army with slaves gathered from the Sudan. Then in 1835, a Turco-Egyptian force founded a capital at Khartoum and established a state monopoly in the slave trade. In 1843 this government issued licenses to the Baggara for slave hunting, issued them guns, gave them access to steamboats, and employed them as private slave raiders. Competition among the private slavers and government forces threw the region into a state of chaos.

To end the chaos, the British sent Charles Gordon and a military task force from Egypt to the Sudan. Gordon set up command at Khartoum, disbanded the army of the governor, Zubayr Pasha, and removed Zubayr to Cairo. This act virtually put the Baggara slave traders out of business. The slave trade was only partially resumed when Gordon resigned his commission in 1880.

In 1884, a self-proclaimed prophet, the Madhi, emerged at Darfur and promised to wage a holy war to restore Islamic purity. He enlisted a Baggara, Abdallahi, as a military strategist. Large numbers of Baggara were recruited for the Madhi's army. Hearing of this action and of preparation to besiege Khartoum, Gordon returned with Zubayr Pasha to battle the Madhists. Gordon was killed and Khartoum fell.

The Khalifah. Shortly thereafter, the Madhi died (1885) and Abdallahi rallied support of the Baggara tribes as he took charge of the Muslim movement, naming himself the Khalifah, the successor. A Baggara leader was named emir (prince) to rule over each province as Abdallahi assumed absolute rule of the Sudan. British forces again invaded the territory (1898) and forced the Khalifah to retreat to Kordofan. An Anglo-Egyptian Condominium to rule the region was agreed upon in 1899. Missionaries and British civil administrators set out to relieve the people in the southern provinces who had been chief Baggara slave targets. At the start of the 20th century sweeping changes initiated land reform and established land tenure rules to protect southern tribal boundaries. The Baggara were confined to their own areas and tax rates were fixed by the size of the Baggara herds. By 1920, Baggara slave merchants had been expelled, and provincial courts had been set up.

The nomadic Baggara were confined to their cattle-herding territory, which extended from the open forest on the west bank of the Nile River to the inland of Darfur. The once feared slavers were stripped of their power. They have earned a reputation as wild horsemen and still from time to time engage in intergroup warfare and banditry.

Culture Today

Social organization. Although they are of Arab descent, the Baggara are distinct from the urbanized Arabs of the north who represent the educated citizens of Sudan. The Baggara are divided into a number of tribes that may or may not be related. They are a nomadic society with no political organization higher than the tribe. Each tribe is divided into smaller units, usually a lineage headed by a sheik chosen on the basis of patrilineal descent (inheritance through the father's line). A large tribe, a *nazirate*, forms an administrative unit and a local court under the direction of a *nazir*. The nazirate is divided into smaller tribal units, *omodiya*, and finally into the *surra,* which consists of an extended family—a man, his sons, their sons, and the sons of unmarried daughters. To preserve the lineage, children of brothers are the preferred marriage partners among the Baggara.

Economy. Baggara tribesmen combine cattle herding and land cultivation. They are highly mobile; climatic changes force them to move constantly in search of grazing land. Migration takes many Baggara from the southern Sudan in the dry season to the north during the wet season. Men move with their herds while the women and children stay behind to plant gardens before rejoining the herds. Some tribal sections have acquired the right to return to the same land from year to year.

The herders raise cattle, sheep, and goats, along with some camels, horses, and donkeys. Among these livestock, cattle is the most prized; the ownership of cattle is the mark of prestige and wealth. Harvested crops include millet, sorghum, and sesame. In the southern savanna, sandy soil allows for the cultivation of the acacia, sometimes called hasab trees, from which Arabic gum is obtained by tapping. Government assistance in irrigation and mechanization has allowed the cultivation of cash crops such as cotton, oilseed, and sometimes sugarcane.

Religion. The Baggara live much like their ancestors did for centuries before them. Religious life governs family and personal matters. The religion is Islam, but among the nomads Islamic faith is influenced by local customs in events such as marriage, birth, inheritance, death, and harvest rights. Each religious unit is overseen by a *faqih*. The faqih is not a priest, but possesses a religious authority based on knowledge and interpretation of the laws of the Koran—the text of sayings, codes of behavior, and traditions of Mohammad.

Shelter. The Baggara home is the Bedouin tent, which can be dismantled and moved from place to place. The shape of the tent varies according to the tribe, but it is often constructed of a wooden frame covered by cloth and animal hides. Those Baggara who are less nomadic live in villages where houses are constructed of earth reinforced with camel or goat hair. Nomadic settlements consist of a series of tents of palm matting or woven wool or cotton stretched over wooden poles. Each camp has a small wooden shack called the *tukul,* which serves as a kitchen. This shack is abandoned when the villagers move. Inside the typical tent there are a bed made of palm ribs tied together by strips of leather, saddlebags for storing and carrying grain, goatskin bags for water and milk, and decorated animals skins that serve a variety of purposes.

Family life. The tent belongs to the women. If a man can afford to he may have up to four wives, each of whom he must provide with her own tent. Children are property of the mother, but their education is the responsibility of both parents. Mothers teach their daughters cooking and household duties. Fathers instruct their sons the responsibilities of herding and caring for livestock. In the traditional Baggara family, the women milk the cattle and goats, prepare meals for their family, plant and harvest crops, clean their homes, and raise the children. Men tend the cattle, which are kept in a *zeriba*, a pen made of thornbush. They are assisted by their sons during the annual migrations. The nomads travel from their settlements to markets in the south where they trade milk and butter for grain and household goods such as tea and cooking utensils.

Most tribal groupings include Arabized slave or serf families, descendants of the former slave women and children who are used to herd cattle and produce food crops. Many former slaves have been absorbed into Baggara families. Others function as servants, sleeping in their own tents and performing all the manual labor while attending to the needs of their cattle-wealthy masters.

Food. Baggara diets consist mainly of milk and milk products, flat unleavened bread called *umm duffan*, and a millet porridge called *kisri*. To prepare the bread, grain is ground into flour using a flat stone. The flour is then mixed with water, kneaded into dough, flattened on a stone, and buried in the sand under a camp fire. When the bread is baked, it is dug up. The ashes are dusted off, and the bread is broken up, covered with liquid butter or a sauce made of onions and spices, and served in a pan. Occasionally meat is eaten, usually roasted goat. A portion of mutton may be part of a stew, or the animal's head may be buried in hot ashes and baked overnight.

Women make butter by shaking milk in a goatskin pouch for hours until it solidifies. The butter is often liquified for use by boiling. Since cattle represent cash and wealth, these animals are rarely slaughtered for food. Rather, the Baggara milk the cows twice daily and live on the milk. Milk is stored in a goatskin, and must be drunk while squatting in accordance with Arabic etiquette.

Women also haul water from the wells and store it in skins or bottles. A tea is brewed all day long in a black metal kettle. It is mixed with a great deal of sugar and drunk from enamel mugs. Foods such as salt, dates, spices, and sugar are taken in trade for goats and sheep at local markets.

Muslims do not drink alcoholic beverages or smoke tobacco. However, since the Baggara are not very religious, the men often relax by smoking and talking with each other. Women socialize with other women but are forbidden to drink and smoke and may associate with men who are not their husbands only during courtship or while serving meals to guests.

Clothing. During the wet season there is a high risk of malaria. Mosquitos breed in pools of water and infect both people and livestock.

Clothing and tents are designed to protect the Baggara from insects. Fabric for the tents, lengths of material called *shuggas*, is woven from wool sheared from sheep or camels. Men wear *jibbas*, a long white cotton robe to the knees, and pantaloons. They often shave their heads and cover them with headdresses of cotton strips. The men usually have beards, wear cowskin sandals, keep wooden beads around their necks, and carry rifles and daggers. The women cover themselves with a length of coarse blue cloth. One end is wrapped around the waist like an underskirt that reaches to the ankles. The bodice is covered with a flowery cotton dress, and the other end of the blue cloth is draped around the shoulders and sometimes pulled onto the head. Women wear their hair shoulder length, fix it in many fine braids, and treat their hair with butter to give it luster. They also adorn themselves with thick gold and ivory bracelets, amber necklaces, nose jewelry, rings, and silver anklet chains.

Arts and literature. Many Baggara are illiterate. The few who can read or write are usually religious men who memorize and quote the Koran. The nomads believe that the written word holds magical power and they buy charms made by the faqihs and inscribed with verses from the Koran. These charms are believed to protect men against gunshot and knife wounds. They are worn in leather pouches attached to their wrists.

Because of their mobility and the isolated existence of nomadic life, the Baggara value the gift of conversation and story telling. To break the monotony of everyday life, the men gather in groups and tell stories to each other. Most of them are about raids and fights with other tribes. The stories are embellished with each retelling until they reach epic proportions.

In the mornings young boys sing a four-line verse called *dobbayt*, repeating it over and over as they graze the cattle. The songs are rhymes about beautiful maidens, hunting, races to watering holes, and men who have fallen in raids or treks.

Baggara crafts include weaving or decorating leather saddles, bags, hassocks, sandals, and other practical objects. Songs are created in a style borrowed from the Arabs of the north, and are accompanied on simple, stringed instruments. The poetic verses are often sung to the soft thumping of an animal skin stretched across a metal tin or a wooden cylinder.

Values. The Baggara are a proud and independent people. Their cultural tradition involves vengeance and blood money paid to the family of a murder victim. They remain a comparatively fierce society today. The warriors hunt big game, elephants and hippopotamuses, by riding them down and killing them with long spears called *kibis*. They also hunt gazelles and small animals with quivers of arrows carried in a *turkash* that is slung over the left side of the saddle.

For More Information

Asher, Michael. *A Desert Dies*. New York: St. Martin's Press, 1986.

Herskovits, Melville J. *The Human Factor in Changing Africa*. New York: Vintage Books/Random House, 1967.

Jackson, H. C. *Sudan Days and Ways*. London: MacMillan and Co., 1954.

Murdock, G. P. *Africa, Its Peoples and Their Cultural History*. New York: McGraw-Hill, 1959.

Sudan, A Country Study; Area Handbook Series. Washington, D.C.: American University, 1982.

BEMBA
(behm' ba)

Called AbaBemba by the people themselves; a Bantu-speaking people who farm the plateau region of northeastern Zambia.

Population: 150,000 (1985 est.).
Location: Zambia, parts of Zaire, Zimbabwe.
Languages: Bemba, English.

Geographical Setting

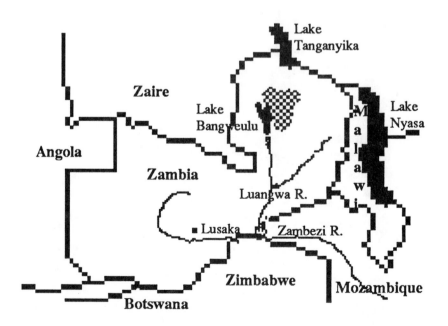

The lake country of the Great Rift Valley lies along the northeastern section of the modern country of Zambia. Here mountain ranges give way toward the west to savanna woodland and then grasslands. Just east of the mountain ranges on the northern edge of Zambia lies the Copperbelt, an area of great mineral wealth with two large cities, Ndola (population 440,000) and Kitwe (470,000). The average rainfall in the region is 20–40 inches a year and the altitude varies from 1,500 to 5,000 feet. The historic Bemba land lies on a plateau in the mountain areas of the far northeast in Zambia. Here the average altitude is 4,000 feet, and rainfall, although not always predictable, averages 35–40 inches a year.

Temperatures are mild in Zambia, averaging between 68 and 88 degrees Fahrenheit. Much of the wealth of the country comes from copper mines in the northeast. In southern Zambia, the Zambezi River flows south then east and northeast toward the Indian Ocean. Many tributaries to this river course through the land of the Bemba.

Historical Background

Origin. It is believed that the founders of the first Bemba kingdom, Chitimukulu, came to the territory they now hold in Zambia from the Congo (Zaire) region in the late 17th century A.D. or earlier. By the late 17th century, the Bemba were fully settled in a section of the area they now inhabit in northeastern Zambia. There the men became known as excellent hunters, while the women were the settled farmers. Bemba chiefs established village-states in the area and came together in a complexly organized kingdom under the sacred monarch Chitimukulu. Powerful, warlike, and active raiders for slaves in the 18th and 19th centuries, they instilled fear among their neighbors.

During the 18th and 19th centuries the Bemba territory expanded through a large part of what is today northeastern Zambia. As they expanded, they also became traders, dealing in ivory, copper, and slaves. Slave trading was not unusual for the Bemba, who had often taken slaves as payment for debts or as compensation for serious crimes.

Bemba and the British. In 1890, the British South Africa Company, in charge of the land south of the Zambezi River, made treaties with and obtained concessions from the Bemba and other chiefs in the north in order to be able to conduct business in the area. Then in the late 19th century the slave trade was abruptly halted by the Company. Its representatives also defeated the Bemba chiefs, destroying their political system. At the same time, the company monopolized the ivory trade so that many Bemba were forced to become migrant laborers in the copper mines of Zambia and in neighboring countries such as South Africa.

In 1924 the British South Africa Company withdrew from the area and rule fell to the British colonial office. Under this management, copper mining was greatly expanded. Much of the agricultural activity and hunting gave way to city life and to work in the mines.

During World War II, Bemba soldiers served with the British King's African Rifles. This war changed the pattern of economic life for the Bemba people. Before the war, most young Bemba men left their family village to find migrant work elsewhere, leaving their wives and children for long periods of time. After the war, women joined their husbands in the migrant labor force and Bemba were, therefore, often financially able to return to their villages at an earlier age. By the 1950s, the Bemba had become the largest labor force living in Zambia. Contact with cities had shown them that independence from the British was possible. In 1961 they became the major liberation leaders in a nonviolent rebellion that led to African majority rule in Zambia. Zambia became an independent republic, which flourished in the 1960s and 1970s as the economy grew and as the people became thoroughly Westernized and urbanized. Fortunes changed in the 1980s. Due to a decline in the value of copper, Zambians have struggled economically. The Bemba, who formed a large part of the copper mining labor force have been greatly affected by this economic downturn.

Culture Today

Economy. Once, the Bemba hunted, fished, and raided for a living. As they became more settled, Bemba farmers grew their staple crops millet and sorghum along with manioc and maize. But the soil was too poor to sustain the growing population. Employment in the copper belt of Zambia became and remains a main source of cash with which to supplement the meager crops. Today, those Bemba who continue to farm raise the traditional crops as well as tobacco, wheat, rice, cotton, and soybeans. Farming practices are gradually becoming updated with the use of fertilizer and the development of cash crops.

But change is slow in Bemba territory, which is large and sparsely populated. Bemba villages are scattered in woodland and brush clearings near streams, and may lie as far from one another as 20 miles. The traditional Bemba form of agriculture is still practiced in many places on the plateau. Known as *chitimene*, this system begins with burning brush to form an ash bed on which the seeds are sown. The land is prepared by cutting trees and brush in May and June. The cut brush is burned in September or later. The farmers then wait for the first rain to plant a crop that will hold the soil—sorghum or maize. Around December, the main crop, usually finger millet, is sown to be harvested in May. In this manner the same farmland is planted for three or more years before it is exhausted.

Because of the low soil fertility, Bemba must frequently clear new fields, leaving the old fields fallow for many years. Thus an average Bemba family needs a great deal of land for long-term survival. As the population increases, the amount of land cleared of trees and brush grows at a rapid rate, and the soil begins to erode. For this reason, many Bemba have found it necessary to become migrant workers in the Copperbelt to the south and west of their plateau. Young men and women move to the Copperbelt cities to earn money and return to their native villages when they have saved enough or have grown too old for the mines.

Shelter. In the past, men were encouraged by the culture to have many wives, providing each with her own separate dwelling. Traditional homes have a cone-shaped roof and cylindrical walls made of plant poles, wattle, and earth. This type of house is still used in the more rural areas of the Bemba. But today most have become city dwellers, living in communities of more than 5,000 inhabitants. In these cities, the European influence is reflected in Western-style houses.

Religion. Bemba religious tradition centers around the worship of spirits, with the role of the chief being the performance of ritual. Converted by Roman Catholic missionaries in the 19th century, many Bemba have become Christian.

In the past, women wore blue and black. Along with liberation in Zambia came a change from these darker shades to colors like red, yellow, and orange, which the Bemba associate with victory and life.

Recent change. Rather than having distinct economic, political, and social characteristics (and perhaps largely because of their role as migrant laborers), the Bemba have now become thoroughly modernized. Possibly the most notable trait of the culture today is the definition of the people as citizens of Zambia. So well have the Bemba people participated in the struggle for independence and in the economic development of Zambia, that in that country, their culture has been nearly lost. Today, even the term *Bemba* is given several meanings. It may identify the people of Zambia's northern province, any person who is related in any way to some Bemba ancestry, or any people with similar language. In large measure, the identification of the Bemba has become national rather than cultural.

For More Information

Africa South of the Sahara, 15th ed. London: Europa Publications, 1985.

Cambridge History of Africa, 8 vols. London: George G. Harrap and Co., 1927.

Mountjoy, Alan B. and Clifford Embleton. *Africa, A New Geographical Survey.* New York: Frederick A. Praeger Publishers, 1967.

Peoples of the Earth. Vol. 2: *Africa from the Sahara to the Zambezi.* Danbury, Conn.: Danbury Press, 1972.

Richards, Audrey. *Chisungh, A Girl's Initiation Ceremony Among the Bemba.* New York: Routledge, Chapman and Tall, 1982.

BETSILEO
(beh tsih' leo)

Malayo-Polynesian people of the Central highland
plateau of Madagascar.

Population: 1,200,000 (1985).
Location: The central highlands of Madagascar.
Language: Malagasy, a Malayo-Polynesian language.

Geographical Setting

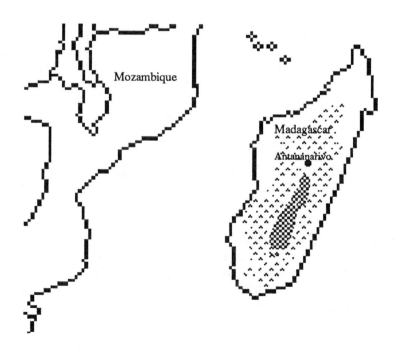

Madagascar, the "Great Red Island," lies in the western Indian Ocean off the coast of East Africa. The island, more than 900 miles long and 360 miles wide, is dominated by a central mountain range. East of this range, the land descends abruptly to the Indian Ocean. Westward, the mountains slope gently to a dry plain and the Mozambique Channel.

Elevations of 4,000 to 8,000 feet in the mountains include steep slopes, grassy valleys, high plateaus, and rounded barren peaks. The altitude tempers the tropical heat that warms the coastal areas. Slash-and-burn land clearing for rice cultivation has destroyed the forest growth that once covered most of the island, leaving it with a cover of thorny savanna scrub. The high plateaus are in spots barren because of soil erosion, but small farming villages dot the landscape and rice terraces appear. Irrigating them are mountain streams and basins fed by the Mananara, Mongoro, and Maningory rivers flowing from the central highlands and Lake Alaotra. These central highlands are subject to heavy rains carried by monsoon winds. Annual rainfall averages 40 to 60 inches.

Historical Background

Origin. The cultures of Madagascar are varied. Some are believed to be of Indonesian origin, descendants of Malayan seafarers from Borneo. Others reflect the influence of Arab visitors and settlers, and some are of wholly African ancestry. The mixture of Bantus (see BANTU) with immigrants from Indonesia resulted in a new culture, the Malagasy, of which the Betsileo are a subgroup. These people of Madagascar lived in independent small kingdoms and other groupings until they were united by the great king of Madagascar Radama I in 1810. Following his death, the kingdom again disintegrated into units ruled by local chiefs.

The precise origin of the Betsileo, like most Malagasy societies, remains unclear. Like the Merina people, they are of Indonesian descent and are excellent rice cultivators. Some believe that the Betsileo are related to the coastal Antiamoro and that they migrated from the east to the highlands of Madagascar sometime before the 16th century. Oral tradition tells of some skilled Betsileo craftsmen who remained on the east coast, but the majority settled the Central Highlands and established small villages on the steep slopes. These villages flourished, the people terracing the slopes to cultivate rice and raising Zebu cattle for subsistence. This society lived peacefully until the arrival of the Merina people who settled in nearby Imerina. These people, the most Asian-like of the Malagasy, frowned upon intermarriage. They maintained their own culture even while absorbing the Betsileo.

The French. French settlers arrived on the island in 1642 and set up a fort in the hopes of colonizing the region to take advantage of the rich resources and the trade possibilities. Interclan disputes and slave trading between various groups of the Malagasy had become firmly established by this time. Moreover, the island had become a calling station for the Portuguese, Dutch, British, and French merchant ships engaged in the slave trade. The brisk trade for slaves brought guns to groups such as the Sakalava and made it possible for them to demand tribute from other groups such as the Merina and Betsileo.

The French attempted to establish friendly relations with most of the Malagasy groups of the southeast coast, but, with arms from the slave trade, the Malagasy rebelled and forced French withdrawal from the island. Not until 1750 did the French return to build several bases from which to colonize the island. By this time, the Merina had developed internal frictions that deeply divided them. In 1787, Prince Andriananimpoina set out to unify the Merina. Under his strong leadership, internal fighting ceased, irrigation dykes and roads were constructed, and Antanonarivo, the capital city, was fortified. Then the prince armed his soldiers with guns and spears and began a war of expansion. One of the first neighboring groups to submit were the Betsileo.

Independence. In the late 18th century, four princedoms of Betsileo were united under one ruler, Andriamanalimbetany of Isandra. But the peaceful Betsileo exerted little resistance to Merina rule. As part of the Merina kingdom, they were permitted to keep their own local chieftains and to cultivate their own lands as before. In fact, the Merina ruler encouraged their dependence on him by providing help with new irrigation systems. Soon the Betsileo became respected as the best of the rice producers and gained a share of the Merina's privileged position on the island. With military assistance from the Europeans, the Merina conquered other peoples and established a chief and fief relationship. Merina nobles formed village councils, the *fokonola*. The conquered citizens were required to pay rent, serve in the military, perform public works, and pay tribute.

Radama I succeeded his father to the throne in 1810. He welcomed French and British help in conquering the rest of the island, and in return allowed missionaries to open schools and churches. Many Betsileo are said to have converted to Christianity during the rule of Radama I. Until his death, the education-loving Betsileo enjoyed a privileged status. In 1830, however, the king's wife succeeded him on the throne. With her sorcerer advisers, the queen began a purge of her subjects. She closed all schools, expelled the European traders and missionaries, and began a persecution of the Christian converts. The Betsileo principalities lost their partial independence and were drawn fully into the Merina kingdom.

The movement was reversed in 1861, when Radama II took the throne. Beginning with his reign, the French became allies, British trade was encouraged, and both Protestant and Roman Catholic missionaries were permitted to convert and educate the Merina people. The London Missionary Society advanced the cause of education by creating a Malagasy alphabet and written text. The queen, Ranavalona II, and her husband were converted to the British Protestant faith, and French missionaries took charge of education among the Betsileo.

French rule. In 1896, Madagascar was declared a French colony and was ruled by Governor Gallieni. Gallieni encouraged the opening of provincial schools. French officials were advised to speak Malagasy, and schools were instructed to teach French in an effort to instill a sense of equality among the Malagasy and colonists. All Malagasy groups were given equal voice in the government councils. These reforms eroded Merina power over the island. By 1903 local self-government had replaced Merina rule, and the Betsileo were allowed to own and cultivate their own land.

The situation reversed once again after 1905 when Gallieni left his post. Schools were closed, Betsileo and Merina government positions were ended, and the Betsileo were forced to labor without pay. The object was to increase the French government's store of materials for export. Betsileo farmers were given production quotas and were fined heavily for failing to raise the demanded amounts of rice.

The forced labor and higher taxation grew to finance World War I. Although they were denied participation in the government, many Betsileo served in the armed forces. Those who remained behind toiled to produce massive quantities of foods and graphite for the French in the face of personal food shortages and other hardships.

When Betsileo veterans returned home after the war, they brought back liberal ideas of self-rule and began an anti-French action called V.V.S. Jean Ralaimongo, a former teacher who started a Malagasy organization in France, was an influential leader in this movement.

World War II temporarily slowed progress toward Malagasy nationalism as troops and laborers were sent to France. However, French surrender to the Nazis caused the British to capture Diego-Saurez, Madagascar's largest harbor, and later the entire island in order to prevent Japanese deployment there. After a few months of British control, the island was returned to Free French rule. Now both the Betsileo and Merina pushed for Malagasy independence. Action was begun through the United Nations to form a Malagasy government. However, before that action could be effective the citizens began a rebellion against the French. In 1947, this revolution was crushed, with great loss of lives.

Independence. In 1960, the Malagasy Republic became independent and gained United Nations recognition. Many Betsileo then entered the civil service of the new country. Civil government gave way to military rule in 1972, then civil government again in 1975. Meanwhile, peoples living in rural areas suffered an outbreak of robberies in the 1970s and early 1980s, the thieves stealing cattle, crops, and other goods. As a result, some of the rural families are seeking safety by moving to towns.

Culture Today

The Betsileo are mainly concentrated in the villages and towns of Fianarantsoa Province in the central highlands. Here they live as hardworking rice farmers and cattlemen. Nearly half of the people are bilingual, speaking Malagasy and French.

Trucks, buses, taxis, and cars drive carefully along the black-tarred roads that wind through the dangerous inclines and dips of the mountains. The capital of Finanarantsoa, once a popular French administrative post and Catholic missionary center, is no more than a small town. It is a gathering place for intellectuals, and includes government buildings, markets, stores, bookshops, and a modern hotel. The roads leading in and out of town are lined with old colonial villas built in the Victorian style, some handsome church buildings, and scores of rice paddies set into the sides of steep mountain slopes.

Village life. The tempo of village life is subject to seasonal conditions—the wet and dry months—that govern work and leisure, the
amount of food available, and meal patterns. Most villages appear
deserted during the day. Villagers spend their days working, rising at
dawn to cultivate their rice field and to attend to domestic duties.
Each household is expected to help in the production of crops for
their own use and commercial trade. Very few Betsileo stay home:
men attend to the cattle and prepare the rice fields for planting;
women plant the rice shoots, raise other food crops, cook and clean
their houses, and look after their children. The families return home
in the cool afternoon to eat their midday meal, socialize, and discuss
local affairs with neighbors.

Many Betsileo are prosperous landholders. Others work in provincial government posts, schools, and local private enterprises. The
cash economy has encouraged Western-style habits. People tend to
own bicycles, sewing machines, record players, and transistor radios.
A portion of their income is spent on the building and upkeep of
family tombs and on funeral ceremonies, which they believe links
them to their ancestral spirit world.

Betsileo village roads are paved, but lined with homes that are
without electricity. A small railroad system is used to transport rice,
coffee, sugarcane, cloves, and vanilla as well as graphite, uranium,
and chromite to commercial markets in Tananarive, the capital city.

The influence of the returning war veterans from overseas military
duty has affected the quality of housing in the Betsileo provinces.
Home construction in the well-to-do rural areas is solid and profes-
sionally done. Most homes are furnished with simple, Western-style
household effects.

City life. Because of their high educational standards, the urban Betsileo are often employed in administrative positions, making up a
large percentage of the professional class. In the cities these workers
dress in Western-style clothing, drive cars, live in modern apartments
and homes, and spend their incomes on consumer goods, food, clothing, and vacations. Betsileo frequently save part of their earnings and
contribute the savings to their *tanindrazana*, the ancestral village, for
community projects.

Middle class urban dwellers live more modestly, and are found
in the lower echelons of government and private industry. Many own
rice fields, which they rent to tenant farmers. Like their more affluent

counterparts, they have adopted European ways in clothing, food, housing, and social and leisure activities.

Family life. Betsileo farmland is inherited through the father's lineage, but rice fields can be owned by either sex and inherited from either parent. The head of the household is usually the oldest male and presides over a family unit that includes grandparents and relatives. Several related families may join together to farm the land. Larger groups sharing a common ancestor are called *foko*. They are bound by the belief that their ancestors influence the welfare and daily affairs of the living. Often relatives are buried in a common burial tomb. Family tombs, tall narrow structures of wood or stone, are erected in many places in the highlands of Madagascar. The importance of the dead demands a special funeral rite, *famadihana*, a ceremony that includes music and dance, and in which long-dead kinsmen are exhumed, rewrapped in colorful silk shrouds and paraded through the streets to the tune of happy singing and the offering of gifts.

Religion. Both the Betsileo and Merina have combined their traditional religion with the newer Christian faith. Ancestors rank as minor intermediaries between the living and the one supreme God, Zanahary, creator of the universe. Churches and tombs are often impressive structures, built and maintained by wealthier members of the foko who may have, themselves, moved away from the ancestral home.

Social structure. The Betsileo inherited castes, or social classes, from the Merina social structure. Making up the major castes are nobles (*Adrian*), freemen, or commoners (*Hova*), and slaves. In modern times much of this classification has given way to a hierarchy based on wealth. Regardless of their positions, however, most people still consult the *ombiasi*, or diviner, concerning a major decision such as marriage or the building of a new house. Also, they still observe the rites and rituals associated with dead ancestors who are the guardians of social rules and customs, or *fombe*.

Food. The main staple of the Betsileo diet is rice. It is almost always prepared by boiling without using salt or fat, and eaten plain without sauces or green vegetables. Sometimes a little meat or fish, occasionally spiced with chili, is eaten with the rice. The Betsileo observe a great many food taboos that include eggs, some fish, and certain fruits.

Meat is eaten only when an animal is slaughtered for sacrifice. Then it is cooked and eaten immediately or smoked and cut into strips for later use. A wide variety of tropical fruits grow in abundance on the high plateau and are eaten in large quantities. Bananas are generally boiled, mashed, and mixed with rice. Coffee, sugar, corn, and flour are bought in food stores to supplement the diet. In addition, the Fiananratsoa Province is known for its fruit wines marketed under the name of Lairavo. The national beverage, however, is *ranopange*, made from boiled rice water and consumed after meals. Green coffee beans are roasted and ground at home and the coffee drunk between meals.

Cooking is done indoors over a wood or charcoal fire in a separate kitchen that contains pots, bowls, spoons, and other utensils. The entire family gathers around the dining table, but meals are eaten according to age. Children may not eat before their elders; grandfathers and fathers are served first, then mothers, and finally the youngsters.

In urban areas Betsileo diets are more varied since people have access to bread, fruits, meat, fish, condensed milk, and imported products found in modern food markets. The style of food preparation at home and in restaurants tends to be French-influenced, although food taboos are sometimes still observed among the middle class.

Clothing. European-style clothes prevail throughout the island, but regardless of wealth and social status, nearly everyone wears the traditional shawl, the *lamba*, over the shoulder. The lamba is used to carry infants and to bury the dead. Wealthy women wear a lamba made of fine silk to church services. Men wear a light flannel costume, a long shirt called a *malabar* worn over loose trousers, and the lamba. Women wear colorful print dresses imported from America and sold in secondhand shops. They frequently make clothes for the entire family on the home sewing machine. In the cities women wear fashionable dresses and shoes imported from France and Japan. Men wear shirts, trousers, and suits with leather shoes or sandals. In the highlands, people favor hats, particularly those that have a wide brim. Women usually style their long hair in tight little braids and use cocoa oil to give the hair a shine.

Arts. The Betsileo are known for their pottery-making skills and for weaving fine silks. Betsileo furniture makers craft intricate inlaid and mosaic cabinetry work. Beds, sofas, tables, and chests combine original styles with those of the French or English. In decorating tombs, clothes, churches, and everyday objects, the people use geometric designs.

Oral literature is the most common form of literature among the Betsileo and includes moral and comic stories, poetry, folk-tales, legends, riddles, and children's stories. These works are accompanied by rhythmic chanting. After World War II, plays, essays, poems, and other works written by educated Malagasy were published in French. They have a strong lyrical quality.

The most common Malagasy instruments are drums and a harp called a *valiha*. Dances, characterized by graceful hand and leg movements, are always performed by a group, not by one individual.

For More Information

Area Handbook for the Malagasy Republic. Washington, D.C.: American University, 1973.

Bunge, Federica M., editor. *Indian Ocean, Five Island Countries: Area Handbook.* Washington, D.C.: American University, 1983.

Carpenter, Alan and Matthew McGinnis. *Malagasy Republic (Madagascar).* Chicago, Ill.: Regensteiner Publishing Enterprises, 1972.

Murphy, Dervla. *Muddling Through Madagascar.* London: John Murray Publishers, 1985.

Tompson, Virginia and Richard Adloff. *The Malagasy Republic; Madagascar; Today.* Stanford: Stanford University, 1965.

CAPE COLOURED
(Cape Colored)

People of mixed ancestry from unions between South Africa's
early European settlers, native Africans, and slaves
imported from the Dutch East Indies.

Population: 2,500,000 (1980 est.).
Location: South Africa: mainly in Western Cape Province, Natal
Province, and Transvaal Province.
Languages: Afrikaans, a Dutch dialect influenced by French and
Malayan; English.

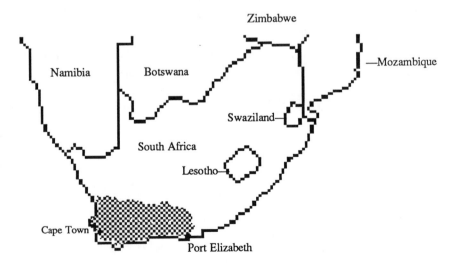

Geographical Setting

The southern tip of South Africa, bounded by the Atlantic and Indian oceans, features a narrow coastal plain separated from the semiarid interior by a crescent of mountain ridges. The inland terrain includes broad plateaus, undulating grasslands, and a plain of scrub brush that reaches to the southern Kalahari desert in the northern Transvaal Province. The coastal lowlands are green and fertile with a Mediterranean climate. The northeastern Transvaal is semiarid, and the eastern coast of Natal features subtropical farmlands and a forest belt. The central plateau, called the Veld, is dry and dusty, marked by the mineral-rich Witwatersrand ridge where the Orange and Vaal rivers converge. Most of the interior country is arid and mountainous, and less than 15 percent of the land can be cultivated. Overall temperatures range from 62 to 70 degrees Fahrenheit, and rainfall averages from 25 to 45 inches annually.

Historical Background

Beginnings. The Cape Coloureds of South Africa emerged as a distinct cultural group in the 17th and 18th centuries. They resulted from marriages between the Dutch Boers (see AFRIKANERS) and the Khoikhoi and San peoples (see KHOISAN) who inhabited the Cape, and later the slaves imported from West Africa, the Dutch East Indies, Ceylon, and India.

The mixed group had its origins when the Dutch East India Company built a supply station for its ships at the Cape of Good Hope in 1652. It was not the company's intention to colonize the area but to establish a farming community that would grow fresh foodstuffs and provision Dutch ships that stopped midway on their long voyages between Europe and India.

Boers, Khoikhoi, and San. As the white settlers, the Boers, developed their farms on the fertile land, they encountered the local inhabitants: the Khoikhoi, herdsmen who pastured their livestock on the greenbelt, and the San, nomads whose hunting and foraging way of life was unlike that of the Khoikhoi herders. The Boers found the Khoikhoi easy to deal with since they had already been in contact with the Portuguese discoverers of the Cape and with early English and Dutch merchant ships.

Desperate for livestock, the Dutch Company established trade relations with the Khoikhoi in 1652. The Dutch exchanged glass beads, tobacco, and alcohol for cattle and sheep. At first the arrangement proved ideal, but the Khoikhoi's generosity diminished as the Dutch encroached on their pastureland. Two Dutch-Khoikhoi wars, in 1659 and in the mid-1670s undermined Khoikhoi independence and led to the decline of their economic freedom and their conversion into a servant class of the Dutch colony.

Relations between the all-male Boer settlers and Khoikhoi women was discouraged by both the Christian Dutch and the Khoikhoi societies, yet many "irregular" unions took place. The offspring of these Boer and native unions, the ancestors of the Cape Coloureds, were classified as European and were absorbed by the farming community. The disgrace of mixed marriages waned after the first such wedding was approved and recognized in 1664, when the black translator Eva married the Dutch explorer van Meerhoff.

The blending of peoples quickened when the Dutch Company found itself unable to meet increasing demands for provisions because of the growing number of ships that came calling at the supply station. The output of the farming community was meager, so it was decided to import slave labor to increase production.

Slaves. An influx of slaves from West Africa, and later Malayan-Polynesian natives from the Dutch East Indies, added a new dimension to the Coloured population on the Cape. In the first 20 years following the Dutch settlement, some 75 percent of the children born on the Cape were a result of unions between Khoikhoi slaves and their Boer masters, and between Khoikhoi and other slaves and sailors who stopped at the port.

While marriages between Hottentot women and Europeans were not outwardly approved by the State and the Church, many Boers preferred to take Khoikhoi women as wives because they did not belong to the lowly caste of slaves. These marriages produced children with Dutch names, many of whom looked like their white fathers. Over the years, these children came to consider themselves superior to the European-slave and slave-Khoikhoi unions.

European landholders. In 1688, the Dutch Company began to attract European immigration with free passage and free land in exchange for farm labor. The offers brought 600 farmers of Dutch, German, and French extraction to the Cape. Among the Dutch immigrants were a large contingent of French Huguenots, displaced farmers and winegrowers who had fled religious persecution in France and were given refuge in Holland. The French quickly adopted the Dutch language and customs. Many took Dutch wives and Khoikhoi or San servants into their homes and introduced new agricultural techniques that improved production of the farming.

By the early 1700s, with the growth of the European and Coloured society, the tightly woven fabric of the Dutch settlement began to fray. Immigration was halted because the Dutch feared becoming a minority among a population that had tripled since the settlement began. Every aspect of life became monitored by the state; a hedge was built to keep the San away, and trade restrictions and land controls were instituted. The second and third generations of French and Boers, growing in population and facing poorer prospects in the colony, began to seek land in the unpopulated hinterlands. Gradually they spread eastward from the Cape throughout the 18th century.

These early *Trekboers*, ancestors of the White Afrikaner nation, settled on pasturelands and became cattle ranchers. Away from the influence of the European community, they were content to live in isolation, and they followed a strict religious ethic based on the Old Testament. Living in close association with their Coloured families, servants, and slaves, they slowly developed their own language, a pidgin Dutch dialect influenced by French, Malayan, and Khoi. The Trekboers settled along the Orange River, and in Transvaal and Natal, which would later become the Union of South Africa. Coloured subgroups emerged in the process. The Cape-Malays, children of slave-Khoikhoi unions who adhered to the Islamic faith of their forebearers, remained at Cape Town and isolated themselves from White domination. Another Coloured group, the offspring of Boer-Khoikhoi unions, many of whom took Dutch names, identified with the European city culture and not with the Afrikaner peasant of the countryside. A third group, the Griqua, who claimed White-Khoikhoi ancestry, were pushed north and east until they found themselves at odds with the Boers in the Orange River colony. Still other Coloureds lived in the Boer frontier society.

British control. In 1795 the British assumed control of the Cape in order to secure it from the French who had occupied Holland. British rule brought missionary education and reforms to the Cape Colony. In 1807 the trade in slaves was banned, and by 1820 some 4,000 British colonists were settled to the west of the Great Fish River in order to establish a neutral frontier zone and effect peace between the Dutch and African societies.

British occupation affected the Coloured community. Unions between English colonists and Khoikhoi occurred along the eastern frontier, and their descendants adopted European habits and dress and spoke a Cockney-sounding English dialect. British rule also liberalized the laws and improved the positions of the slave and Coloured populations. Before the British period, mixed-breed children could attain the status of a free person only upon reaching a certain age fixed by law. But in 1828 a British ordinance placed the free-Coloured and Europeans on an equal standing before the law.

With the abolition of slavery throughout the British empire in 1833, Cape Colony slaves were emancipated. Newly freed slaves and Coloureds began to achieve a degree of economic independence. Afrikaans-speaking Coloureds with Dutch names, now with access to law and education, copied European culture and sought to distance themselves from African natives. Before the mid-19th century the descendants of Boer-Khoikhoi unions established new settlements in the northwestern Cape Province and in Southern Namibia and long maintained their independence. Further, since they considered themselves superior to the Africans and slave-Khoikhoi mixed-breeds, they isolated themselves by marrying their own kind.

By 1865 policies of racial segregation had begun to isolate blacks from whites, but the majority of the Coloureds retained their privileges. The discovery of diamonds in 1867 created the city of Kimberley near the Orange and Vaal Rivers and displaced the Griqua. They returned to the Cape Province to be absorbed by the Coloured population. In 1886 the discovery of gold in the southern Transvaal created new cities and brought prosperity. The Coloureds grew in population, became urbanized, and later emerged as traders, skilled workers, and craftsmen.

Education and new employment opportunities raised the economic status of the Coloureds who stayed in Cape Town. Those who were born on the frontier, or those who with the help of English missionaries moved into new areas, developed different cultural groups. Although the Coloured community in all the states constituted 55 percent of the population and had enough property to vote, they had no influence on electoral politics. Most were socially and politically oriented to the European community and sought to emulate its culture as closely as possible.

The election bills of 1887 and 1892 in the Cape area introduced voter qualifications that were more strict, making it impossible for the growing native population to vote. Only those who could afford the cost were able to vote and were outvoted by the Cape Coloureds, who voted with the White minority.

The South African Union. The bitter Anglo-Boer War of 1899 led to the creation of the South African Union that now included the Cape Province, Natal, and the Transvaal and Orange River colonies, By 1910, this new country included mainly native Africans with a White minority and a small percentage of Coloureds and Asians.

In the first half of the 20th century, the Coloured society experienced personal and political hardships. Many Coloureds who were unskilled farm workers struggled to earn a living in the cities. In order to vote, they had to submit to reading and writing tests that some found difficult.

The 1948 elections brought about the policy of *apartheid*, the classification of the population along racial lines. These "separate development" laws assigned each racial group to a specific residential area. Coloureds were restricted to small townships set apart from the White suburbs and cities and the native African towns.

The Coloured elite, who once thought of themselves as part of the European society, were suddenly outcasts. Regardless of their wealth, even businessmen and professionals found themselves living next door to their poorer relations. Accordingly, they had to attend inferior schools and obey pass laws (laws governing movement from place to place), and although they voted, they did not have the choice of electing their own representatives. New laws relegated many to low-paying jobs, and the ban on intermarriage prevented the Coloured from entering Afrikaner society.

In 1956 the Coloureds lost their voting rights and joined the legions of native Africans who were denied the vote. In 1961 South Africa became a republic and chose to withdraw from the British Commonwealth.

A government policy of resettlement resulted in bulldozing Coloured townships and replacing them with White neighborhoods. Racial laws began to split families and communities and the Coloured community found itself shunned by both the white minority and the native African majority.

Stripped of their political rights and cultural heritage, the Coloureds became a powerless minority and joined the ranks of the low-paid migrant workers who were forced to toil in racially segregated occupations. Despite low salaries, racial injustice, prohibition against intermarriage, police brutality, substandard education and health care, and the enforcement of separate residence and public facilities, the Coloureds did not ally themselves politically with the native Africans.

It was not until the 1980s, when Coloured students staged boycotts and protests demanding an end to their "gutter education" and the right to study at White universities, that public attention was focused on the substandard educational system of the nation's non-white population. The Coloured students' activism signaled what many thought to be a new awareness among the once politically disinterested cultural group.

Culture Today

South Africa's Coloured minority, which represents less than ten percent of the nation's population, is concentrated in the cities of Cape Province. The loss of the vote and the enforcement of racial barriers have broken families and uprooted Coloured society. Those people who have historically identified with the Whites now find themselves placed alongside the suppressed native majority. Those Coloureds who resemble Europeans, and have had their "whiteness" officially recognized by the authorities, form a privileged class of merchants and professionals.

Business. Regardless of their economic or educational status, the majority of those officially declared as "Coloured" have been isolated as a cultural group and forced to relocate from safer, mixed communities to crime-infested ghettos designated for them by law. Unskilled Coloureds survive as low-paid migrant laborers and domestic workers and are confined to living in poverty conditions. The semi-skilled commute to work as day laborers in nearby white areas, notably in the mining industry. The educated but less prosperous Coloureds are employed as teachers, craftsmen, postal workers, and police officers.

Deprived of their national heritage and identity, the Coloureds remain a vibrant cultural group whose strength is derived from close association with its Christian churches. Their social groupings are confused by a high incidence of teenage pregnancy and illegitimate births. Nonetheless, kinship ties are very strong among the less prosperous and they lean toward descent groupings based on the father's lineage.

Clothing. South Africa's Cape Coloureds represent a wide economic cross section and, as such, their European-style clothes vary according to their financial status. In the middle class, businessmen and upper-income women wear stylish suits and the latest European and American fashions. This middle class, although segregated from the Whites, lives in relative luxury in homes with modern conveniences and spacious landscaped gardens.

The majority of Coloureds, however, live in poverty. Most wear secondhand European style clothing and often go barefoot. Those who make up the unskilled and semiskilled labor force fare somewhat better than the poorest, but their lives are a constant reminder of their lower social position. In the 1980s they rode to work on segregated public transportation—buses and railway lines that link the racially separated Coloured communities to the White neighborhoods that surround the cities.

In Cape Town, some Coloured women eke out a living by selling fresh flowers. They can be found wearing bright cotton house dresses and wide-brimmed hats as they sit behind the same flower stands they have tended for decades. Women who work as domestics wear simple cotton dresses and shoes. Male laborers wear T-shirts and trousers or protective work clothes. Elderly Coloured pensioners can be seen on the streets wearing old suits and straw hats.

Shelter. Living conditions within the Coloured reserves vary according to economic status. Homes of the poverty-stricken coexist with those of the low- and upper-income wage earner. They range from two-room metal shacks with no electricity or running water and with communal outhouses for the poor; to neat cottages with gardens for the lower and middle-class; to the modern brick homes with security gates for the wealthy. However, overcrowded housing conditions, inadequate water and sewage systems, and bad dietary habits contribute to a high death rate among the poor.

In the poorer shantytown sections crime is high and the standard of living is low. There is a high incidence of teenage pregnancy, as well as dietary deficiency, disease, and poor health among infants and young children. Children often are absent from school in order to earn a bit of money by watching a store for a shop owner. It is not unusual for fathers to be absent from the family and for an entire extended family of parents, children, and relatives to share one small cottage.

Food. With the exception of outdoor barbecues, cooking is done indoors on gas stoves in low-income households. Generally, Coloured diet is representative of Cape Dutch cuisine introduced by Malayan and native slaves in the pioneer kitchens. Their skills and imagination influenced virtually all food preparation in South Africa: from cured meats to pickled fish, preserved fruits, vegetables, and condiments, and from millet and corn porridges called *mealies* to pumpkins, potatoes, rice and pastas, pancakes, and roasted breads. Mutton, game, and fish are specialties served on holidays, as are sweet cakes and homemade candies. Among the national Cape Dutch favorites are *ingelegde*, deep-fried fish slices served with a vinegar sauce of onions, chillies, turmeric, ginger, and curry powder, and *smoor-vis*, a cured sea-pike called *snoek* that is braised with onions and cubed potatoes. For beverages, the people drink coffee, tea, soda and beer.

Arts and culture. The Coloured minority is known for its traditional music played on the concertina, mouth organ, and guitar. Their songs are often sad and evoke memories of racial harmony. On January 2, the Coloureds of Cape Town dress up in lively costumes and celebrate a carnival day, which is attended by many White South Africans.

Coloured writers who publish in Afrikaans include S.V. Petersen and P. J. Philander: however, most literature, such as the works of poet and writer Don Mattera, is written in English.

For those who can afford it, there are restaurants, cafes, jazz clubs, speakeasies, discos, and movie theaters. There are radio and television stations that appeal to the upwardly mobile Coloured population. However, the Christian and Anglican churches provide for the general social needs of the community.

Language. The struggles of the Coloureds can perhaps be best illustrated by the scorn attached to their language by the Boers. Their own dialect of Afrikaans is called a "kitchen language," another means by which the White minority has attempted to erase its relationship to the culture it spawned.

The Coloureds make up a large percentage of both Afrikaans- and English-language newspaper readers. Publications such as *Die Burger* and *Rapport* reach the Coloured population with reports of social and sports events. A large Coloured readership is also claimed by *Vrye Weekblad*, a politically radical Afrikaans-language weekly.

Holidays. During the carnivals, competing Coloured groups dress up in gay costumes and sing and dance in the streets. They are renowned for the spectacular sword dance called the *chalifah*, in which the dancers seemingly become entranced and often wound themselves without show of emotion. Many choral societies and string bands participate in the New Year celebration. Singing is a large part of daily life as well and is performed at weddings, feasts, funerals, and other communal gatherings. Folk songs, known as *ghommaliedjies*, handed down from generation to generation, are sung at family gatherings, picnics, and sports events.

Recreation. Many Coloureds value sports activities. Local athletic facilities provided by government agencies have spawned nationally known Coloured athletes—such as fencer Len Davis—who take part in national and international games, particularly in rugby, tennis, soccer, and gymnastic contests.

Religion. The majority of Coloureds are Christian and 90 percent of them are members of the Dutch Reformed Church or the Protestant Church of England. The Cape Malays, representing seven percent of the Coloured population, are Muslim, and their family and home life has remained strongly centered around the religious activities of Islam. Malaysian Coloured men wear the traditional Muslim head covering, the *fez*.

For More Information

Frederikse, Julie. *South Africa: A Different Kind of War.* Boston: Beacon Press, 1986.

Mattera, Don. *Sophiatown: Coming of Age in South Africa.* Boston: Beacon Press, 1987.

The World and Its Peoples: Africa South and West. New York: Greystone Press, 1967.

CHOKWE
(choh' kway)

A central African people who separated from a larger group in the 17th century and grew to become a major trading empire.

Population: 1,300,000 (1987 est.).
Location: Angola, Zambia, Zaire.
Languages: Chokwe (a Bantu language), Portuguese.

Geographical Setting

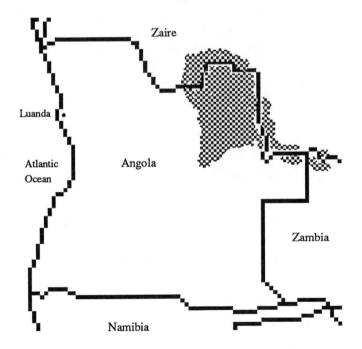

Lying just south of the equator, the country of Angola is tropical and subtropical. Much of the land is a high plateau more than 3,000 feet above sea level. The country is covered by forests and savanna grasslands. Toward the northeast, the plateau is crossed south to north by rivers that feed into the Zaire (Congo) River system. Here many streams have cut the land into rolling hills. This northeastern section of Angola, which stretches into Zambia and Zaire, is the land of the Chokwe people. It is a land of distinct weather seasons: cool and dry from May to October, and warm and rainy from November to April. Joining the mines of Zaire and Zambia with the coastal ports of Angola, a railroad crosses the southern edge of the Chokwe territory. Some of the land is suitable for agriculture and has adequate rainfall. Here the Chokwe have settled as farmers and cattle herders.

Historical Background

Origin. According to Chokwe accounts, their people began as part of the Lunda kingdom. The sons of the principle chief of the Lunda were disinherited and moved out. One moved west of the main group, conquered the people on his path and founded the Chokwe people about 1600 A.D. Although they had been cut off from the Lunda kingdom, the Chokwe still paid tribute to the Lunda chiefs until 1885. In that year, the Chokwe invaded the land of the Lunda and conquered them.

Trade with Europeans. As the Chokwe people expanded west, they met the powerful Ovimbundu people on the central plateau of what is now Angola. The Ovimbundu were a prosperous society who acted as middle merchants between the Portuguese on the coast and the people of central Africa. Joining the Ovimbundu, the Chokwe first provided slaves for sale to the Portuguese. The plateau of what is now Angola was one of the principle targets for slave traders. In the early 1800s slaves were captured here and shipped mostly to Brazil. One result has been that the land of the Chokwe is among the most sparsely populated regions of tropical Africa.

The trading business later expanded to include ivory, food, and finally wax, which had become economically important by 1840. All these products were sold to the Portuguese and to Ovimbundu middlemen. In the 1860s, production of rubber from forest vines became popular. In exchange for these materials, the Chokwe received goods such as guns and built an arsenal of firearms. Expanding their territory through violence and disorder, the Chokwe attained their greatest power by the early 1890s. Although Belgian King Leopold attempted to quell them, the Chokwe resisted. In the 1900s they spread to the areas they now inhabit, retaining their established lifestyle.

Portuguese rule. Chokwe land fell under Portuguese rule for nearly two centuries. It was largely neglected until the Berlin Conference of 1884–85 established the Angola boundaries. By that time, the various African peoples had established their own communities. There followed a period of struggle between Portuguese rulers and their supposed African subjects that lasted until a United Nations act in 1962 condemned the "repressive measures" of the Portuguese.

Independence. From 1962 to 1975, the Portuguese government faced growing rebellions in its Angolan territories and made increasing efforts to improve the lot of the Angolan people. But these efforts were too late to avert the country's move to independence, which the people won in 1975. The years of neglect following years of active slave trade served to hold down the general population of the land and to make the people of the Chokwe region among those Africans least effected by Europeans.

Culture Today

Food, clothing, and, shelter. Once the Chokwe were hunters, specializing in capturing elephants for ivory. Many still prefer a steady diet of game and manioc mush. However, today most Chokwe are subsistence farmers raising manioc (a starchy tuber, cassava), peanuts, yams, millet, beans, and maize, and some cattle. They live in small villages on the Angola highlands and extend into Zaire and Zambia. Fewer than half the Chokwe people live in villages and towns of more than 2,000 people. Each village contains houses made of branch frames covered with leaves and sod. As the harvest is reaped, villagers often build log frames on which large baskets are placed for storing grain. Another storage method is to place large baskets on tree-trunk poles to raise them above danger from pilferage by animals.

The Chokwe people are very scattered and have not much accepted European ways. Women still dress in long wraparound skirts and blouses. A shawl or blanket is worn over the blouse and another cloth wrapped around the head to serve as a carrying platform. The women wear their hair in braids fastened with ivory or bone hairpieces. In addition, massive necklaces of wood, stone, and metal are common. Chokwe people frequently wear copper or tin bracelets stacked in numbers on the forearm. Men wear either a single piece of cloth wrapped around the waist and reaching to the mid-calf or European-style pants and shirts. In cooler weather a blanket wrapped around the shoulders is added to this costume.

Family life. Women are the main farmers among the Chokwe. They tend cassava, corn, and vegetable fields, and spend a great deal of their time preparing meals from this produce. Men hunt during the dry season and work as traders and merchants. One typical small town (Kahemba) has shops in which the men sell salt, sugar, coffee, sardines, clothes, batteries, bicycle tires, and lanterns. The men are responsible for earning the cash for household needs such as school tuition, salt, cloth, and kerosene.

At the time of a marriage, the young man and his wife go to live in his mother's brother's village. There, the new bride has little relationship with the community until she has her first child. Uncles and aunts are so much a part of the family life that the same term of address is given to fathers and uncles, and to aunts and mothers.

Chokwe social life with relatives is carefully structured. Relations with familiar kin (*alelu*) are less formal and include joking relationships—people with whom it is acceptable to joke. Less familiar, or avoided kin (*ajiya*), require more formality. For example, a woman must greet her in-laws, who are ajiya, very formally with light hand clapping and greetings in plural form. She must never eat from the same dish as her in-laws, or even in the same room.

It is the responsibility of the grandparents to counsel young people about romance and to instruct them about proper adult relationships between men and women.

Organization. Villages consist of compounds that include square or round grass houses. The homes are grouped in circles around a central meetinghouse. The traditional political structure of Chokwe villages varies. Some villages are self-ruling. Others are parts of chiefdoms that collect tribute from villagers. Political life in the 19th century was turbulent, with histories of political assassination, the dethroning of chiefs, and battles between rival families. Today, most village chiefs hold their power by demonstrating personal qualities of wisdom and leadership, a change from the earlier days when lesser chiefs held rank because they were relatives of the paramount chief. In keeping with their history of never having been united under a single ruler, the Chokwe villages of today operate so independently that the extent of the chief's powers varies from area to area.

Religion. The Chokwe believe in an all-powerful being who created the earth. However, according to their belief, this god has no concern for what people do on earth. Instead, nature spirits and spirits of Chokwe ancestors, which derive their power from the supreme being, watch over earthly affairs. A central sacred ground in Chokwe villages is reserved for ancestor worship and reverence to these nature spirits. Individuals are responsible for honoring their maternal ancestors. In times of misfortune or illness, ceremonies call for help from these ancestors.

Their religion also includes belief in the evil powers of the sorcerer, which can only be counteracted by a defiant chief's magical powers or the healing power of the traditional doctor. The Chokwe believe that death is caused by sorcery, often prompted by the individual's overattention to personal gain. However, shrines of miniature houses and carved or clay figures are constructed to promote prosperity and food is left nearby for ancestors.

Arts. Chokwe craftspeople are well known for many kinds of artistry. Over a period of more than 220 years, they have carved masks, shaped statues, created pots, and made baskets. Some of the best work was produced before 1860, while the Chokwe were still subjects under the control of more powerful Lunda rulers. Today typical creations are realistic sculptures of ancestors as well as abstract human and animal forms. Large wooden figures represent culture heros. Chokwe artists are skilled carvers of wood, ivory, and bone. They create necklaces, hair ornaments, belts and other jewelry from these materials as well as from copper, bronze, and iron.

Even though there are no professional storytellers, the art of storytelling is popular among the Chokwe and serves both entertainment and educational functions. Called *yishima*, stories of experiences of the past that give insights into the Chokwe way of life, and may even be used in settling disputes in court. They are among the stories of morality and fun told by storytellers in evening gatherings. The people place great stress on the artistry of storytelling. Good storytellers can draw their audiences into conversing with the story's characters. Their stories often include singing.

Change. Chokwe, Ovimbundu, and other African peoples of Angola are scattered over the highlands in a country that has been much abandoned by the European settlers. Their lives have been slow to change. More than 40 percent of the people are under 15 years old, and the expected life span is still a low 41 years. Because of war and government policies, the people of this area do not grow all the food needed for the country. About half of the food must be imported from other countries. But if allowed peace, Angola is a country with strong potential for economic growth. Change is slowly overtaking the Chokwe. In 1955, oil was discovered near Luanda and production

A masked, traveling entertainer of the Chokwe. *Photo by Eliot Elisofon. Courtesy of National Museum of African Art.*

of iron began in the country, events that have begun to attract foreign investment needed in Angola. By 1988 a railroad ran through Chokwe land from Zaire to the coast. In these recent years, outside influences have begun to effect Chokwe ways. For example, those who become ill may visit a doctor at a clinic nowadays as well as seeking aid from their own native healer. Yet the population remains widely scattered and change is slow to take hold among the Chokwe.

For More Information

Hoover, Louis F. *African Art*. Bloomington: Illinois State University Press, 1974.

Martin, Phyllis M. *Historical Dictionary of Angola*. Metuchen, New Jersey: Scarecrow, 1980.

Mountjoy, Alan B. and Clifford Embleton. *Africa, a New Geographical Survey*. New York: Frederick A. Praeger Publishers, 1967.

DINKA
(deen' kuh)

More than 20 seasonally migrating, cattle herding, tribal clusters
of tall, slender people of the upper Nile basin.

Population: 1,000,000 (1980 est.).
Location: South central Sudan and southwest Ethiopia.
Language: Dinka, a branch of the Eastern Sudanic languages.

Geographical Setting

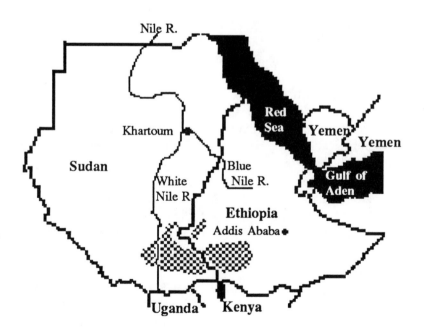

The vast plain of the southern Sudan features a severe subtropical climate and a dry sandy soil covered with bushgrass. As the plain approaches the fringes of the Sudd, the enormous basin said to be the largest swamp on earth, it is met by thick tropical forest growth broken up by lagoons and marsh pools filled with reed grasses and other water plants. The vast tangle of jungle vegetation plugs the flow of the White Nile River and causes it to drain into the Sudd basin for thousands of square miles. This backwater is further fed by the Renk River to the north, the Bor River to the south, and the Aweil River to the west. During the dry season, the embankments along the White Nile provide well-drained grazing land for the cattle herders. But during the six-month rainy season, the rivers overflow and flood, turning the Sudd into a vast marshland. Humid southerly winds from the equator sweep across the Sudan, bearing massive rainstorms that force cattle herders to retreat to higher ground. While the tropical climate is generally very hot and humid throughout the year, rainfall, which averages from 30–60 inches a year, brings some relief from the blistering heat.

Historical Background

Origin. The precise origin of the Dinka is uncertain, but it is probable that some time around 3000 B.C. their ancestors, early people of the region between the White and Blue Niles just north of the Sudd zone, began to settle the plains of the Sudd region. These ancestors of the Dinka were cattle raisers who milked their cattle, fished, and grew some crops, such as sorghum. Over the period from 1000 B.C. to 1000 A.D., the early immigrants from the Nile region separated into three major societies, the Luo, Nuer, and Dinka, all living in neighboring parts of the plains of southern Sudan.

At first a small society, the Dinka spread out widely across this region between 1500 and 1800. In the decades from 1820 to 1890, they faced two severe challenges to their dominant position. One was the gradual expansion of the Nuer into the middle of their territories, and the second was the spread of slave-raiding and, later, slave traders in the region.

The Dinka fighters, armed with spears, collided head-on with the Ottoman Turks who possessed modern firearms. When slave merchants began to frequent the area after the 1850s, the Dinka sometimes joined the traders against the Nuer, but on the whole they successfully resisted incursions and attempts at conversion to the Muslim faith.

British control. The British took control of Egypt in 1879, and from there controlled the Sudan. But in 1884, the British abandoned the Sudan, leaving a Muslim ruler, a caliph, in control. The Muslim religion began to reach the Dinka. European colonial rivalries led to British reconquest of the Sudan and the forming of the Anglo-Egyptian Condominium from 1899 to 1955. However, even though the British recaptured the country in 1899, the British governors ignored Dinka territory. The result was that by 1920 the British felt it necessary to purge the southern provinces of the Sudan, where the Dinka lived, of all Arab influence. The Dinka now came under the administration of local district officials drawn largely from the British military officers. These officers were generally sympathetic to the Dinka and other African tribes and antagonistic toward the Arabs, who under their Khalif dominated the northern Sudan.

North vs. south. Dinka territory came under the administration of local district officials—for the most part British military officers. After World War II, the British attempted to unify the Sudan by placing the southern peoples under the control of the Arab-dominated north. The result was that when the Sudan gained independence in 1956, the Dinka and other southern peoples were nearly without representation in the government. A civil war between the southern peoples and the central government continued until a settlement in 1972 gave southern provinces more self-government. Late in 1982, however, the ruler Nimeri reversed his agreement with the south and extended Islamic rule throughout the country. Another civil war resulted, and Nimeri was ousted in 1985. His successors have not succeeded in achieving harmony between the south and north.

In 1988, the Dinka homeland was further ravaged by a famine that forced thousands of refugees to flee north. Again the dominating northern military government was uncooperative, blocking relief efforts by the United Nations and the Red Cross and forcing many of the sufferers to return to their strife-torn and famine-stricken homeland. Other more fortunate Dinka such as National Basketball Association center Manute Bol, have left their homelands to earn money for both themselves and their families.

Culture Today

Today the Dinka make up 40 percent of the population of the southern province, and the majority live in the rural villages of their traditional homeland. Because of their large numbers, they are the main political group of the southern region and make up the backbone of the rebel forces known as the Sudanese Liberation Front.

Despite the encroachment of the Western world in the northern cities of the Sudan, the Dinka of today continue to exist much as they have for centuries in their harsh environment, moving their cattle herds and camps when the rainy season turns the savanna into swampland. The Dinka have remained partially self-governing because few outsiders care to venture into the hazardous backwater areas of the Sudd to which these cattle herders are so well adapted.

Economy. The focal point of the Dinka economy is their cattle, and Dinka life revolves around the protection and maintenance of the herds. At the time of adolescence, a boy receives an ox of his own, for which he develops a personal attachment. He spends all his time grooming and caring for this ox, and his affection grows so deep that he sings songs of praise to it. The "song ox" is a man's most valuable possession. A young Dinka man twists his ox's horns into elaborate shapes to beautify them and looks after its health constantly. The Dinka do not kill their cattle for food, nor do they use them as beasts of burden or for trade. The men sleep with their herds to protect them against night attack by lions or other wild animals. Only after an ox is sacrificed or a cow dies of old age or accident will the Dinka eat its meat.

Family life. Their world is governed by a closely knit clan structure based on blood relationships. The family is fundamental to the Dinka, who believe that without a family a man is nothing. Every Dinka is expected to marry. However, the people are protected by taboos forbidding members of the same clan and, therefore, near relatives to marry. Marriage is the principal means of acquiring cattle, the symbol of Dinka wealth. Brides are obtained with cattle paid to the bride's family by relatives of the groom in a practice called bridewealth. Therefore, women are of economic value to their families. A family with many daughters is assured of riches through bridewealth. On the other hand, a wealthy man may have as many wives as he can afford with his cattle.

It is essential that the marriage produce a male child to continue the lineage of the father's clan. Every Dinka child must know how to trace his ancestry and must learn to be proud of his clan. Knowing one's ancestors and relatives is central to preventing intermarriage between clan members. The obligations of kinship demand that all blood relatives support each other in time of need.

Social organization. A Dinka village consists of one or more clan-families, each identified by a symbolic animal or plant. The animal or plant chosen for the clan is believed to represent the clan's ancestors. In respect for these ancestors, members of the clan do not harm or kill the plant or animal.

Dinka society is egalitarian; except for distinctions of wealth, there is no hereditary elite class. Wary of established authority, the Dinka have traditionally had no complex political organization. An important element of organization in the Dinka society is the age set. Groups of Dinka of similar ages pass through stages in which they have distinct roles within the society. To outsiders, the lack of recognizable political organization is often taken to mean that Dinka society has no laws or rulers. However, their society is tightly governed by rules and taboos of a spiritual nature such as the taboo on harming one's clan plant or animal. The Dinka are acutely aware of their violent past as a warrior nation and the tragic consequences of the slave trade and of outside rule. Therefore, their rules and taboos are designed to avoid centralized power and tyrannical rule and they do not accept worldly authority. They are also skeptical of sorcery practiced by the diviners and the traveling medicine men who are common sights among the other peoples that inhabit the southern Sudan.

The Dinka prefer to govern themselves through a system of justice that relies on the powers of truth and persuasion rather than violence. Each camp has a chief, but his authority is limited to keeping the peace and he cannot make decrees for the entire group. The chief's main role is to work for the good of his camp through reason and persuasion, and he may not indulge in religious authority. The most influential leaders are the Chiefs of the Fishing Spear, who are the spiritual leaders. The fishing spear is the symbol of the chief's office and responsibilities.

Gradually, the tightly knit world of Dinka tribes has been affected by modern education and national law. Some Dinka have been educated among the English-speaking people and have tasted change.

Nevertheless, these people are expected to remain faithful to the old way of life while playing important roles in the vanguard of political action seeking to separate the south from northern influences. So it is not uncommon for Dinka men to wear shirts and trousers to work, then shed these clothes in the evening to paint their bodies with cattle dung and red ochre in order to attend a Dinka dance.

The Dinka and the Sudan. In modern times, the Sudanese government has introduced a legal system that grants official powers to chieftains in the southern provinces. These men administer both local and national laws. However, the Dinka have little use for this government, which they regard as an outside force, and prefer to retain their autonomy and the old village system of justice, which is administered by a group of elders. There is no punishment for offenses, and penalties for crimes take the form of compensation to the injured party. Since most disputes involve cattle, the village court of elders decrees the amount of payment for livestock. In the close life of the Dinka village everyone is privy to everyone else's business and there is no shame attached to airing private affairs and family disputes. The Dinka welcome the opportunity to discuss their problems and to have them resolved publicly. The Dinka resort to regional courts set up by the Sudan only in the instances of the worst criminal offenses.

During regional elections, Dinka politicians try to rally local support by visiting each village. Village elders welcome the candidate into the village to discuss their grievances, the health of their cattle herds, problems with government medical services, schools, tribal disputes, and even private matters such as bridewealth. If the candidate is favored, their speeches are followed by the ritual slaughter of an ox and a celebration that includes dancing, clapping, footstomping, and drumming.

Religion. The pride of the Dinka centers on living a life of honor and dignity, which is essential for maintaining a good name among family and community. The society does not permit social barriers. Regardless of wealth and status, every Dinka is expected to be kind and generous in order to win prestige.

Dinka religion centers on one God, the *Nhialic*. However, spiritual life tends to revolve around ancestor spirits, which are thought to influence everyday affairs. The Dinka believe in life after death. To gain immortality, a Dinka man must perpetuate his name by fathering a son. If he dies without having a son, the elders arrange to give his name to another man's boy.

Normally the Dinka do not observe any funeral ceremonies. However, when a highly respected man dies, it is cause for a festive tribute. After a bull is sacrificed and the body of the deceased is buried, all the young men and women of the village gather and dance to the sound of drums. The tribute lasts for several days with more dancing and the sacrifice of more animals.

Food. Dinka diet has traditionally consisted of sour milk and fresh blood collected from their herds. They obtain the blood by piercing the animal's vein with a spear and letting the blood drip into a gourd. Some Dinka tribes are fishermen. Once each year these communities begin a fishing festival with a sacrificial drowning of a hen. Then, while the men plunge into the river with their spears and nets, their families wait on the shore to collect the catch. Whatever fish are not eaten during the festival are dried in the sun and later sold at market.

The Dinka supplement their diet with wild fruits and nuts from the doleib and sheabutter trees. Lemon-flavored pods from the tamarind tree are used to make a drink, and the sweet yellow nuts from the *thou* tree as well as mangoes are eaten. Most Dinka meals consist of thick porridge made either from sorghum grain or beans which have been ground into a flour. This porridge is served with milk. Sometimes green beans are used with roasted groundnuts to make a vegetable stew. Women cook the meals in pots over outdoor hearths constructed from stones. The Dinka eat three meals a day, using wooden spoons and bowls made from gourds. A fermented beer is also brewed from the sorghum and the tender stalk is chewed to produce a sweet sap.

Clothing. Traditionally very little clothing is worn in the villages, especially by children. Young girls usually wear only a piece of fabric around their hips or wear a short skirt; women wear loose cotton wraps tied at one shoulder. Men often wear a loin cloth or a full-length Arabic tunic called a *jelleba*. In recent years, all manner of Western clothing has found its way into Dinka apparel. Men are seen in bathing trunks and T-shirts while women wear printed housedresses, skirts, tank tops, and slips.

The Dinka are known for their fastidious grooming. They rub their skins with oils made by boiling butter or seeds from the shea tree, wear dung ash to repel mosquitoes, and decorate their faces and bodies with ornamental painting. Women shave their eyebrows and hair, leaving only a small top-knot on their heads. Men use cow urine to turn their hair a bright red. Both sexes wear jewelry—bead necklaces and earrings, feather and buffalo hair tassels, and brass or ivory leg and arm bracelets and rings. The Dinka remove their lower front teeth to beautify themselves, and they etch flower patterns and abstract designs by scarring their skin with a sharp blade. On festive occasions an elaborate bodice or vest of multicolored beads is worn.

Shelter. During the rainy season, the Dinka retreat to their more permanent villages on the higher, dry ground of the savanna. Here homesteads are constructed of dried mud and wattle and have cone-shaped roofs. Each family house has a wooden platform built on stilts and covered with dried mud to provide protection from moisture. While women and children sleep indoors, men and young boys sleep outdoors with their cattle herds in pens covered with a dried mud canopy.

Temporary camps are built along the riverbanks during the dry season. These shelters consist of igloo-shaped huts made of dried grass placed over a sapling frame. The huts are built low to the ground, making it necessary to crawl indoors on hands and knees.

Music. An important element of Dinka culture is poetic language and song. The songs the Dinka man sings to his ox are creative compositions that serve as outlets for saying things one could not ordinarily say without offending someone else. The chants include love declarations, personal feelings, insults, accusations, and pleas, as well as poems dealing with battles, and the pride a young man feels for his clan and his ox. A good song, it is said, will move its audience to take action. If the song is about war, it should rouse a warlike spirit in its listener.

The Dinka also use song to transmit legends from generation to generation within the clan. Singing is used for courtship, and the women sing special songs to prepare the bride for marriage. During ritual ceremonies of initiation, the scarring of a young boy's forehead is followed by singing and dancing. Recently, however, the more educated Dinka have now begun to abandon this practice.

Art. The Dinka use their bodies as canvasses to display their artistic abilities. The skin painting is highly imaginative and employs designs taken from nature as well as stylized abstract ornamentation. Dinka women are skilled pottery makers and papyrus mat and basket weavers. The men make metal spears, and the blacksmiths forge hammers, farm implements, and cooking utensils.

For More Information

Deng, Francis Mading. *The Dinka and Their Songs.* London: Oxford University Press, 1973.

Nelson, Harold D. *Sudan: A Country Handbook.* Washington, D. C.: American University, 1982.

Ryle, John. *The Dinka: Warriors of the White Nile.* New York: Time-Life Books, 1982.

EWE

(ay' way)

African people who migrated from southwest Nigeria to the coastal
and inland areas of the Gold Coast and Benin.

Population: 3,200,000, (1989 est.).
Location: Togo, Ghana, and Benin.
Language: Evegbe, a language in which tone (pitch) is very important
in differentiating the meanings of words.

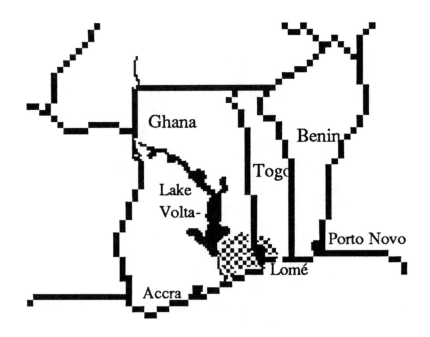

Geographical Setting

Togo is a thin strip of land no more than 80 miles wide and 400 miles long. Bounded by the Gulf of Guinea, the southern coastal border is a narrow and sandy beachfront with palm trees, skirted by a series of inland lagoons. This swamp zone contains reed grasses, mangrove trees, and salt-producing pools and creeks, the largest of which is Lake Togo. Beyond the lagoon zone is a 20-mile wide savanna-type plain of barren and sandy soil. This sandstone plateau rises gradually toward the interior and meets with rolling hills. This is Togo's mountain range. Its highest peaks are the 1,960-foot Adakluto, and the 3,350-foot Aguto. The mountain range cuts across the entire land and creates a central plain with forested uplands. Here the Mono River rises and flows southward along the eastern border of Benin. To the north, the Oti River, a tributary of the Volta, forms a part of the northwestern boundary of Ghana. The climate of the coast is relatively dry and hot, while the interior zones are hot and humid. Overall average temperature ranges between 72–95 degrees Fahrenheit. Annual rainfall is 25–30 inches in the southern lowlands, 44–55 inches in the central plains, and as much as 70 inches in the forested highlands.

Historical Background

Origin. Oral traditions among the Evegbe-speaking peoples trace their origins to the early migrations of the Yoruba people, whose ancient kingdom existed as early as the 10th century along the northern edges of the rain forest of what is present-day eastern Nigeria. These pre-Ewe peoples were said to have joined the migrations of the Yoruba and Adja peoples during the great period of drought and famine to a place called Ketou, a walled town in ancient Dahomey, now the Republic of Benin.

Expansion. In the 13th century it is believed that overpopulation caused the pre-Ewe people to move from Ketou in search of fertile and protected territory. They migrated westward and split up into two groups. One group settled near the Mono River and founded the settlement of Tado. This group split and one subgroup migrated to the plateau region between the Mono and Haho rivers.

The second subgroup of the Tado settlement migrated farther eastward in Benin and founded the Adja kingdom of Alladah. This group is said to be the ancestors of the Anlo-Ewe who settled in Nuatja, a walled town where different peoples lived peaceably with each other. Each group established its own ward with its own chief, and the whole community came under the domain of one supreme king.

Sometime in the mid-17th century, however, peace came to an end under the brutal rule of King Agolkoli. Agolkoli's cruelty and the practice of human sacrifice caused many members of the community to flee Nuatja and form new groups. The northern group settled the uplands and the valley region, the southern group went to the lagoon and the coastal country, and the middle group settled the plateau near the Togo mountains. These areas came to be identified as Ewe country, but because of repeated migrations, subdivisions of clans, and intermarriage with other peoples, no one is quite certain if the original immigrants are directly related to the Ewe peoples of present-day Togo.

Independence. What is certain about the Ewe is that they continued, even when migrating and subdividing, to maintain themselves as a loose association of allied clans and subtribes who spoke different dialects of the same language. The essentially peaceful Ewe peoples refused to unite under one supreme ruler, a tendency no doubt borne from their experience under the cruel domination of King Agolkoli at Nuatja. After leaving Nuatja, the northern group pushed west and arrived near Palime, the section that now rests close to the western boundary of Ghana. Here the Ewe immigrants mingled with the pre-existing peoples of the Anum hills and founded 11 settlements. The middle group from Nuatja established nine separate towns of subtribes. The southern group founded the state of Anlo, several miles from the lagoon on the southern shores of present-day Ghana.

European traders. By the 1600s European penetration of the Gold Coast of West Africa had reached new heights. The traders who had dealt in gold now turned their attention to the more profitable trade in slaves. Slaves became the primary export; profits from slavery overshadowed the gold trade and caused the destruction of untold numbers of societies.

The European traders dealt for slaves with the more powerful coastal and inland tribes: the Akwamu, Denkyira, Akyema, and Ashanti (see ASHANTI). These people preyed upon the less stable and weaker states of the inland regions and exchanged their prisoners for guns and other European goods. The slave trade gave rise to a number of powerful Akan empires who competed with each other for a monopoly of the capture and sale of slaves.

Subjugation. In the 1700s the Ashanti conquered the Akyema, and their wars of expansion drove the Akwamu from their tribal lands into Ewe territory. The Akwamu forces invaded and captured tens of thousands of Ewe people, subjecting them to taxation and tribute payments in slaves and goods. The Ewe subtribes were thus drawn into the Akwamu economic orbit, which depended on the trade of raw materials and slaves to the European colonists who controlled the Gold Coast trade ports. Akwamu domination of the Ewe peoples lasted nearly 100 years, a period that resulted in deep division and strife among some of the Ewe groups. In 1833, however, after battling for their independence, the Ewe successfully broke away from their Akwamu overlords. Some of the Ewe sided with the Akwamu and their Ashanti allies and engaged in protracted warfare against the more independent Ewe subtribes. The warfare invited Ashanti invasion between 1868 and 1871 and resulted in the near ruin of Ewe territory.

The British. In 1874 the Ewe joined forces with the British who needed assistance in subduing the destructive Ashanti. After defeating the Ashanti with Ewe help, the British imposed a peace treaty and extended colonial rule over Ewe territory. This move helped to protect the Ewe from further assaults.

The Germans. Germany entered the fray in 1884, and pushed inland from the coastal area to take control of the country. A British-German pact in 1899 retained some of the Ewe under British rule, while the remaining Ewe territory came under German control.

German colonial rule of Togo lasted a mere 30 years, but that rule saw the development of a road system, a railway, a cash-crop economy, and a missionary educational system for the native population. Despite the attempted improvements, however, there was much opposition to German rule. Just before World War I many Ewe migrated to the Gold Coast, where they were welcomed by the allied powers.

In 1914 Germany was forced to surrender Togo. After the war ended, the country was redivided into the Gold Coast, French Togoland, and British Togoland, divisions that cut across Ewe territory.

Unification. The division of the Ewe gave rise to a nationalist movement for a reunification of Ewe lands and the formation of an independent state in 1951. This movement was led by Sylvanus Olympio. In 1956 elections were held, and a majority of the people in British Togoland voted to unify with the Gold Coast. The move was approved by the United Nations, and just before the Gold Coast won its independence and became the Republic of Ghana, British Togoland became part of the new country.

The remaining Ewe territory was still under other foreign control. In French Togoland, pressure from the Ewe peoples prompted a call for a general election supervised by the United Nations. The demand was granted in 1958 and Olympio's party won 60 percent of the vote. Sylvanus Olympio was named Prime Minister and negotiated with the French for self-rule. As a result, a date was set for independence, and in 1960 the French colony became the Republic of Togo with Olympio as its first president.

Olympio's leadership transformed Togo from a dependent state into a self-sufficient nation, but before long Togo's stability was threatened by Ghana's president Nkrumah over the issue of its border. Nkrumah falsely accused militants of plotting to redefine the Togo-Ghana border in order to reunify Ewe territory. The clash between Olympio and Nkrumah led to Ghana's arrest of Ewe residents in the area of question and the closing of the border.

Continuous pressure from Nkrumah's forces over border issues, combined with internal unrest, encouraged a new political faction to emerge from the ranks of Togo's small army. A young Togolese officer named Etienne Gnassingbe Eyadema rose to power in 1963. Reportedly Eyadema and his followers were responsible for the assassination of Olympio. In 1967, Eyadema removed the committee and assumed the presidency. In that same year unrest in Ghana resulted in the overthrow of President Nkrumah, and relations between the two nations improved. As Togo's head of state, Eyadema banned political parties, suspended elections, dissolved parliament and the constitution, and consolidated his power by forming a one-party system that has kept him in office.

Culture Today

The political history of Togo has left the country and its peoples in a poverty-stricken state. Generally, residents of the remote villages and towns fare better than their counterparts who reside in the urban areas and their shantytown suburbs. Western-style improvements are virtually nonexistent. Paved roads, running water, and electricity are available only to the privileged few who are employed by the government.

Village Life. The rural Ewe farm the land and live in compounds with their extended families in small kin-based villages. Ewe social order is determined by lineage; towns and villages consist of kinsmen and kinswomen who can trace their descent from a common male ancestor. The lineage of the people of a town, or *frome*, is headed by a chieftain, a male elder who oversees spiritual life and social rules and taboos, administers justice, allocates property, and settles disputes that are brought before him. Land belongs to the male lineage, which functions as a corporate unit and assumes collective responsibility for mutual aid and payment of debts incurred by its members.

Economy. Agriculture is the main source of income for the rural Ewe. Men farm the land for trade and food crops, and the women generally conduct all trade in the marketplace. The women also add to the family income by taking up other occupations—the sale of firewood, produce, crafts, and imported goods such as soap, liquor, cigarettes, and Western trinkets. Farmers depend on millet, maize, yam crops, cassava, beans, and groundnuts for trade and food. Farmland is cleared by burning the bush and trees, and cultivation is done by hand, typically with a crude hoe and cutlass. In recent times drought and poor soil conditions have resulted in near-famine conditions. In the coastal and lagoon areas the Ewe depend on fishing for their survival. Fish is generally dried and sold in the markets. Until recently the main cash crop was palm-oil, culled from the trees that grow wild in the region. Today the economy depends on cocoa farming for its trade, and this has become the mainstay of many Ewe villages. Government corruption has deprived even the educated Ewe of jobs in the cities. Consequently, there is no incentive to seek an education, and unemployment prevails in both urban and rural areas.

Food, clothing, and shelter. Ewe homes are constructed of mud-clay and twigs and have thatched grass or metal roofs and a few windows for light. The village consists of extended families who live within compounds. Each house has its own yard which opens into a courtyard shared by the occupants of the compound. Since the Ewe men practice polygyny (marriage to more than one wife) each wife and her children lives in a separate house. The husband, too, maintains a separate residence.

The men clear the land for their homes and farm. The women tend to their families and grow foodstuffs in their own garden plots for sale in the marketplace. Cooking is done indoors over a wood fire on a dome-shaped clay stove. The staple meal is *fou fou*, a doughy starch base made from yams. The yams are peeled and boiled and then pounded to a stiff consistency with a wooden pestle. The pounded yam is served swimming in a bowl of oil seasoned with hot chili-peppers. Another staple is a thick porridge of corn or millet. Sometimes, dried fish is added to vegetable sauces and eaten with rice or cooked bananas called plantain. Meat is rare, as are eggs and poultry. Since food is bland a popular addition is *Pili Pili*, a hot sauce made from Guinea peppers, onion and garlic. Typical beverages are a fermented millet beer and a homemade palm wine called *sodabi*.

Village women wear a *pagne*, a square of printed cotton that is wrapped like a skirt at the waist. They generally cover their hair with a turban and carry their infants on their backs. Men might wear a version of the *pagne* instead of trousers, but they most often wear khaki shorts and T-shirts purchased in the flea markets of the main towns. In the cities women wear a blouse or camisole. Children are encouraged to attend school and therefore wear khaki uniforms, first introduced by the French missionaries.

Religion. European missionaries converted many Ewe to Christianity. However, most Ewe continue to worship a High God called *Mawu*, "the all wise creator and giver of good things." Mawu is thought to have human form but to be invisible. Lesser spirits called *Trowo* act as go-betweens for God and man. Trowo are thought to take earthly forms such as wind, trees, fruit, rivers, animals, and human-made objects.

Although an Ewe compound may have a shrine for ancestor worship, these ancestors are linked to a larger family through the family's ancestral stool. Every family line keeps and worships a stool of its ancestors.

Witchcraft is believed to cause misfortune, illness, and death. An Ewe may hire a special soothsayer, an *Afakaka*, to rid the afflicted person of evil spirits.

Arts. Ewe culture is rich in crafts and weaving. Small village-based industries produce a variety of pottery, blacksmithing, cloth, and wood carvings. The Ewe are famous for sculpting wooden stools and drums. The women do basketwork for home and for sale, including mats for sleeping and kitchen use. Small clay figurines are sculpted for use as cult images by the priests in special ceremonies.

Ewe literature consists of educational texts and religious publications. There is one government-owned newspaper published in the Ewe's language.

For More Information

Boahen, Adu. *Topics in West African History.* London: Longman Group Ltd., 1966.

Oliver, Roland and A. Atmore. *The African Middle Ages.* New York: Cambridge University Press, 1981.

Packer, George. *The Villages of Waiting.* New York: Vintage Books, 1988.

The World and Its Peoples: Africa South and West. Vol. 2. New York: Greystone Press, 1967.

FALASHA
(fah lah' shaw)

Black Jews of Ethiopia.

Population: 25,000 (1986 est).
Location: Northern Ethiopia, Israel.
Languages: Amharic, Tigrinya, Ge'ez.

Geographical Setting

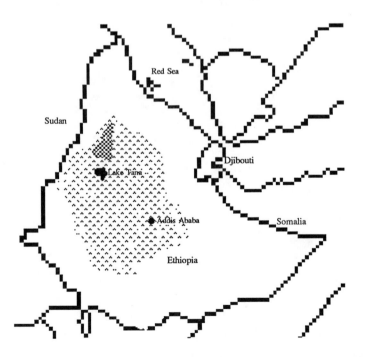

The Falasha have traditionally occupied northern Ethiopia's Simien Mountains, an area bounded to the north and east by the Tekeze River, to the south by Lake Tana and the Blue Nile, and to the west by the Ethiopia-Sudan border. The region forms the northwest section of the central plateau that is Ethiopia's main geographical feature. Bisecting it is the Great Rift Valley, which stretches along eastern Africa and has the lowest points of African land. Steep and rugged, with thin, rocky soil and hillside fields, the mountains offer poor prospects for farming. Rainfall is moderate, falling in soft, evenly spaced showers (with a slight concentration in the winter months). This puts the land of the Falasha in contrast to nearby parts of Ethiopia, where rain is torrential and marked by violent seasonal downpours. The Falasha part of Ethiopia is scrub woodland and thorny shrub land.

Historical Background

Ancient legends. Although the earliest documents mentioning Ethiopian Jews date from the 13th century, Falasha legend tells of events of biblical times. Often paralleling the stories in the Bible, these myths offer various explanations for the group's origins. In the most popular account, the Ethiopian Queen of Sheba visited the Jewish King Solomon and, returning to Ethiopia, gave birth to their son Menelik. Menelik eventually established a Jewish colony in Ethiopia. In another tale, Moses, at the head of an Egyptian army, defeated the Ethiopians in battle and took in marriage an Ethiopian princess to begin the Falasha.

In the 1970s, Israeli rabbis decided that the Ethiopian Jews represent the remnant of the "lost tribe of Dan," one of the 10 tribes lost when captured by the Assyrians in the eighth century B.C., but this view has no historical basis. Two explanations are possible. Some scholars suggest that the Falasha originated in the first few centuries A.D., when Jewish influence was strong in southern Arabia, and may have spread from there to Ethiopia. Others argue that they originated in the 9th to the 13th centuries as a countermovement among people resisting the expansion of the Christian culture of the Ethiopian kingdom of those times.

Conflict with Christians. Whatever their origins, the Falasha spread from their early stronghold in the Simien Mountains and developed their own independent state by the 13th century while struggling repeatedly against attempted Christian conquests. Falasha stories extend their independence back to the beautiful and warlike queen, Yehudit, who vanquished the Christian armies and drove back the Christian forces in the late 10th century.

For the next 300 years the Falasha lived in relative security, but in the 13th to 15th centuries a new era of Christian expansion, led by rulers who claimed descent from Solomon and therefore divine right to rule, slowly eroded Falasha independence. After a destructive invasion by Muslim forces from the Harar region led by Ahmad Grañm between 1527 and 1542, the Ethiopian Christian kingdom went through several decades of reconsolidation of its power. Led by emperors Sarsa Dengel (1563–1597) and Susneyos (1607–1632) the kingdom fought wars on several fronts, among them wars against the Falashas. After a series of bloody battles, the outmanned Ethiopian Jews became a downtrodden people, forbidden from owning land and often subject to enslavement and persecution. Although there is no clear idea of how many Falashas there once were, it is now clear that their population declined to the point that, in the 1800s, there may have been around 150,000.

Years of subjugation. It was probably after their subjugation by the Christians that the Ethiopian Jews became known as *Falashas*, a name that means "landless ones" or "aliens." The people themselves reject the term as derogatory, preferring instead the name Beta Israel (House of Israel), though *Falasha* remains in common usage among other peoples.

The decree that prevented the Beta Israel from owning land drove many of them to become craftsmen, employed, for example, by the Christian emperor Fasiladas in the 17th century to build elaborate castles at Gondar. Ethiopian society looks down on craftsmen, associating them with the evil eye, which brings bad luck. When imperial power waned in the 18th century, the Beta Israel lost much of their livelihood and were blamed for the country's troubles. Tens of thousands of Falasha were sold into slavery in the 18th and 19th centuries as the slave market boomed in the Middle East.

Falashas and world Jewry. In the late 19th century, European missionaries returned from Ethiopia with reports of the Falashas' situation. European Jews responded by sponsoring the 1868 journey to Ethiopia by Joseph Halévy, a French-Jewish professor from the Sorbonne Academy in Paris. Halévy informed the surprised Falashas of the larger Jewish community and exposed them to developments in Jewish practice unknown to them because of their long isolation. Halévy's student, Jacques Faitlovich, continued his work, living among the "Black Jews of Ethiopia" in 1904–5 and devoting the rest of his life to their cause. In the 1920s Faitlovich opened a school for Falashas in Addis Ababa and raised funds for Falasha students to study in Europe. By the 1950s, more than 30 schools had been established in Beta Israel villages; young Falashas were being sent to study in the new country of Israel, and Jewish tourists regularly exposed the Falasha to Western Jewish ways.

Operation Moses. Their exposure to the outside world led the Ethiopian Jews more and more to view Israel as their promised land. By the early 1970s most wished to emigrate to the Jewish state, a trend accelerated by hardship following the 1974 communist revolution in Ethiopia (See AMHARA). Jewish organizations campaigned to secure emigration rights for the group, which the government refused. Increasing numbers fled illegally, making their way through the deserts of Ethiopia and Sudan, at risk of capture and torture by Ethiopian soldiers. By the late 1970s a steady stream of Jewish and other refugees flowed westward, driven by oppression and famine. Makeshift camps sprang up near the Ethiopian-Sudanese border. By 1984, as many as 5,000 had reached Israel, most of them flown from Sudan by the Mossad (Israeli Intelligence), but more remained in the crowded, poorly supplied refugee camps. Disease and starvation killed many—2,000 Falashas died in the summer of 1984 alone. In late 1984 and early 1985, the Israeli government undertook a secret airlift ("Operation Moses"), which brought about 8,000 Falashas from the camps before being halted by worldwide publicity.

Culture Today

Operation Moses rescued those Falashas strong enough to reach the camps' young people, especially men. Of the 8-10,000 who remain in Ethiopia, many are elderly or infirm, or mothers with infants or small children. Widespread drought has compounded the difficulty of sowing and reaping crops without the help of the young men. Along with the resulting malnutrition, diseases such as malaria, tuberculosis, and dysentery have ravaged the population. Scarcity of pure and sanitary conditions adds to the difficulty of disease. Flies spread conjunctivitis, an eye disease that afflicts both adults and children and often leads to glaucoma and blindness. The Falashas remaining in rural Ethiopia have suffered increased hardship, but those in the cities often support themselves as small shopkeepers. Meanwhile, the shape of the culture is changing as those airlifted to Israel embrace a new way of life.

Food, clothing, and shelter. Falasha villages in Ethiopia consist of round houses with cone-shaped roofs. The structures are built of sapling poles, which support walls of mixed earth and dry dung. Often located on a hill by a river, the homes stand alongside the rustic, barren village synagogue.

The Falasha share certain customs and language with the Amhara (See AMHARA). The people of the village wear the *shamma*, the traditional Ethiopian white cotton toga worn by many Ethiopians— Jews, Christians, and Muslims alike. Men wear the shamma with cotton pants, women with a long cotton dress. Unlike the Amhara, Falasha women often embroider their dresses with Jewish symbols such as the Star of David. In the past, most men and women have gone barefoot. Before Operation Moses many Falashas, especially boys and men, had adopted Western-style dress, as have virtually all those now in Israel.

The Beta Israel have traditionally raised cash crops such as cotton, sesame, and sorghum. Dietary staples have been dairy products, grain, and fruit. Families raise livestock—chickens, goats, and perhaps a few cattle, in addition to growing vegetables, wheat, and the native grain called teff, a small-seeded grass that grows nearly three feet tall. A favorite dish is *injera*, a flat-bread made from fermented teff mixed with water and cooked like a pancake. Dinner for the Ethiopian Falasha family might consist of a spicy grain, a vegetable, and a red pepper stew (made on special occasions with meat) called *wot*, which is eaten with injera.

Language. The Falasha have no language of their own, speaking Amharic and Tigrinya, the languages of the two largest Christian groups in Ethiopia. They share Ge'ez, the Ethiopian traditional liturgical language in which their sacred texts are written, though few Falashas understand it today.

Religion and holidays. The Falashas base their Judaism on the Torah, or the Pentateuch, the Old Testament's first five books. From this sacred text they derive their dietary and cleanliness laws, ceremonies of birth, death, and marriage, prayers, festivals, and, most importantly, the observance of the sabbath. Isolated from later documents in Judaism (such as the Talmud), they have also evolved their own customs. Thus, while they shared with other Jews the holy days prescribed in the Torah—Rosh Hashanah, the Jewish New Year, and Yom Kippur—they did not observe Hannukah and Purim. Of the festivals unique to the Falashas, the most important is the Seged, held in late November in celebration of the return of the Jews from Babylonian captivity. At the time of the Seged, the Beta Israel priests lead a pilgrimage to a selected hilltop outside the village, where they hold prayer. Some customs reflect the influence of Christianity. The spiritual leader is not a rabbi, but a *kess* or priest. Monks have also played an important role in religious life.

In preparation for the Sabbath (*sanbat*), the village stops all work at noon on Friday. First the men and then the women wash their clothes and their bodies in the nearby river, purifying themselves for the next day's ritual. On Saturday everyone rests—no one works, cooks a meal, draws water from the well, or lights a fire. Every seventh Sabbath (called langato, seven) is specially celebrated with prayer and chanting from dusk on Friday to dusk on Saturday. Priests gather in a chosen village to hold the festive vigil, with *tallah*, a fermented barley drink similar to beer, served in the morning. Dancing concludes the Sabbath afternoon.

Family life. Falasha families are close-knit, with affection rather than discipline holding the unit together. Duties are divided between sexes, with boys helping their fathers in the fields or at work, and girls taking responsibility for household chores—fetching water, preparing meals, mending clothes. At mealtimes, the oldest daughter serves food to the parents first, then to herself and the other children.

Religion dictates most of the regular patterns of family life. Women are confined to special huts for 40 days after the birth of a son or 80 days after that of a daughter. Some customs are shared by both Jews and Christians in Ethiopia: confession to a monk or priest, funeral and memorial services for the dead, and the prohibition of work for seven days after the death of a relative.

Girls once were married from the age of 9, boys from 17, with a betrothal period of up to 3 years. In past times, the wedding lasted 10 days, but more recently the celebration has been reduced to 8 days, and the ages of the participants has increased. The groom's family invites friends and neighbors to his house, where priests beat a drum and recite prayers, tying a colored thread around the groom's forehead. He and his attendants then go to the bride's house for the night, from where they and two of her male relatives carry the new wife to the groom's house the next day.

Falasha crafts. Weaving, pottery, and especially metalworking have historically formed the basis of the Falasha economy. The association of such crafts with bad magic and the evil eye meant that the Falashas, already outcasts in society, became the blacksmiths of Ethiopia, supplying important metal tools such as axes, plow tips, and knives. Where once the smiths smelted metal from the abundant iron ore of the Simien highlands, now they more often rely on scrap metal. Since the airlift, weaving and pottery making have increased in importance, with women lining the streets of Beta Israel villages to sell their textiles or clay pots and figurines. Tourists, many of them American or Israeli Jews, who buy such crafts are now a vital source of income for the Falashas.

Time of adjustment. For those airlifted to Israel, the joy of arrival was tempered by their separation from family and friends and by the problems of adjusting to life in a new land. The new arrivals were sent to "absorption centers" called *ulpanim*, spartan camps in which the first task was to learn Hebrew, the language of Israel to which Ethiopian Jews had had no exposure. Along with classes in Hebrew, Israeli teachers instructed them in such matters as how to keep checking accounts, use the laundromat, shop in supermarkets, and look for a job. In religious practices, too, the Ethiopians have been brought more into line with other Jews. Adjustment has been difficult at times, particularly as some have questioned the Falasha's Jewishness. The process of assimilation promises to continue, as does concern for those still in Ethiopia.

For More Information

Gruber, Ruth. *Rescue: The Exodus of the Ethiopian Jews.* New York: Macmillan Publishing Company, 1987.

Rapoport, Louis. *Lost Jews: Last of the Ethiopian Falashas.* New York: Stein and Day, 1980.

Shelemay, Kay Kaufman. *Music, Ritual and Falasha History.* East Lansing, Michigan: Michigan State University, 1986.

FANG
(fang)

A relatively tall people of equatorial west Africa.

Population: 1,000,000 (1980 est.).
Location: Western Africa: the rain forest of southern Cameroon, eastern Equatorial Guinea, and northern Gabon.
Language: Fang, a Bantu language.

Geographical Setting

The land of the Fang lies just north of the equator where there is a fairly constant high temperature and heavy rainfall. Beginning at the

north, a dense, mixed evergreen and deciduous forest gives way to patches of open grassland and then to a tangle of vines, ferns, and shrubs nearer the equator. Mangrove forests spread across the swampy coastland. Runoff from the heavy rains flows to the Atlantic Ocean through the Sanago and Nyong rivers. These rivers expand into deltas as the rivers near the coast. Farther south the Campo River follows the border of Equatorial Guinea and Gabon. The main topographic feature of Gabon is the Ogooúe River that rises in the mountains of Congo and arcs through the center of Gabon before reaching the Atlantic Ocean. Year-round temperatures average above 82 degrees Fahrenheit, and annual rainfall varies between 60 and 100 inches.

Historical Background

Origins. According to oral tradition, the Fang came originally from southern Cameroon. However, little is known of the Fang until their first encounters with Europeans.

In the 1470s, Portuguese sailors established trade with Africans living on the west coast in a tropical rain forest where many rivers converged toward the Atlantic. Intent on trading in ivory and slaves, representatives of other European countries soon established footholds in what is now Cameroon, Rio Muni, and Gabon. British, Portuguese, French, and Dutch depended on the coastal chiefs to supply them with slaves captured inland. This trade in slaves continued even after the British had banned the practice for their citizens in 1807.

About the same time that the early Europeans appeared, another group arrived in the forest zone from elsewhere in Africa. Stories of this group spread through the European settlements. Called Pangwe or Pahouin, the African newcomers were thought to be fierce cannibals who wore frightening masks as they practiced witchcraft. Rumors that they ate human flesh helped prevent Europeans from penetrating the forest region. By 1820, this new people had settled in considerable numbers, their population increasing as other peoples migrated into the area. Coming from rain forests to the north, the newly forming Fang increased their numbers by adding the best warriors of the peoples they defeated.

Contact with the Europeans. In their northern land, the Fang had been farmers and had learned woodcarving and ironworking. In their new lands, they became elephant hunters, supplying ivory to other African groups who interacted with the Europeans. As the British and French vied for African trade and land, the Fang gradually absorbed or took the place of the middle groups in trade. By 1850 the Fang were attempting to trade directly with the Europeans. They did, however, refuse to submit to the French authority based at Libreville. The Fang instead pointed their war efforts toward the French, raiding French ships, taking merchandise, and capturing hostages to hold for ransom. The French refused Fang extortion. They struck back and, after several battles, succeeded in subduing the Fang. A period of cooperation followed. The Fang became respected among the French in Gabon for their language skills and intelligence, among the Germans in Cameroon for their strength and ability to work hard, and among the Spanish for their fighting ability. By 1900, the Fang were the largest society inhabiting the forest area. Their leaders, who valued most highly courage in battle, discouraged Fang interaction with the Europeans. In their limited relationships with Europeans, the Fang refrained from participating in the slave trade. They preferred instead to deal in ivory and forest products.

Germany controlled Cameroon until World War I. Following that war, the land was split between France and Great Britain, with France controlling most of Cameroon. Under its rules, the economy shifted from ivory and forest products to cash crops as the land was converted to agriculture. Slowly, the Fang adapted to the new economy. By 1920, the Fang had become farmers just as the French decided to exploit the timber resources of Gabon. The beginning Fang farmers found themselves conscripted to work in the lumber industry or on the construction of railroads. Crops were neglected and Fang groups became victims of famine, influenza, and smallpox. By 1933, more than half the Fang in two districts, Woleau-N'Tem and Okano, had died from disease. In the late 1930s, a renewed emphasis on agriculture returned the Fang to their farmland. But once again, they were forced to turn away from subsistence farming as the economy turned to cocoa and coffee cash crops after the second World War.

Independence. In the 1940s, the French set up local governments in Cameroon with the intent of native self-rule. To further this goal, schools were established in the cities of Douala and Yaounde. These cities were far from the Fang region around Libreville, so few Fang availed themselves of the schools. But beginning in 1947, the French expanded the school system. They also permitted native Africans to participate in the political life of Gabon. Fang groups began reorganizing their village according to clan ties in order to restore Fang unity and self-esteem. The French, seeing Fang action as a problem, called a government meeting. At this conference, Jean-Hilaire Aubame, a Fang, was elected to the French National Assembly. Under Aubame's leadership the regrouping movement, *alar ayong*, accelerated. Within the plan, each Fang village was to have its own elementary school, medical infirmary, sports arena, and public meeting place. Elections were established by the 1956 French Basic Law for the Colonies. In 1960 the Fang and others of Gabon approved a new constitution and the country became independent. One year later, the western British state united with the eastern French state to become the Federal Republic of Cameroon. Many Fang citizens were educated in public schools and found jobs in the government. However, the bulk of the old tribal complex remained in the southern region near the city of Yaounde. Shortly after independence, oil was discovered in Gabon and the economy turned to one of prosperity.

Surviving a coup attempt in 1964, the government of Gabon fell to President Omar Bongo, who established a one-party system that has survived since 1968.

Culture Today

Economy. Today, many Fang people in Cameroon and Gabon own their own coffee and cocoa enterprises and have a higher standard of living than the cultivators who till the land for food and shelter. In the urban areas, especially in Yaounde, many people are employed in both the private and public sector. Their social status varies according to their income.

The Fang in the upper-income group live in European-style homes, often multistoried structures constructed of brick. The house is cared for by servants. Aside from servants, wealthy families enjoy new cars, the latest European fashions, and expensive consumer goods such as stereos and kitchen appliances. Middle-income people live in more modestly priced homes, wear European-style clothes and ride motor scooters. Unskilled laborers lack adequate housing, use public transportation or bicycles, and because of the lack of jobs, compete for low wages, making them unable to deal with the demands of expensive city life. Another group, the civil servants and public employees, live in subsidized housing. They tend to eat imported foods and spend a good deal of their income on European-style clothing.

The cultivators of the rural south fare better than their poorer urban counterparts. If they are rich in landholdings, they live in modern houses with windows and shutters and with tin roofs. Families in the forest region build their own homes, usually rectangular wood frames with walls separating rooms and with thatched roofs.

While the cities of the south have high rise buildings and modern apartment complexes, most people cannot afford to live in the center of town. Instead they congregate in the overcrowded suburbs in houses made of wood and mud. The typical house for the poor city dweller has no running water or sanitation. Still, some houses have been upgraded with the addition of tile floors and tin roofs. The nearby villages are slowly being integrated into the suburban areas.

Farm families devote most of their time during the dry season to planting and harvesting food and cash crops. Men usually clear the land by burning, and the women raise cassava (a plant with a starchy root also called manioc), maize, groundnuts (peanuts), and plantain. With money earned through cash crops such as coffee, these farmers are able to purchase consumer goods at the local market.

Clothing. The European-style clothing favored by the educated city dwellers has found its way into rural areas. Typical Fang dress in the forest region combines European and traditional dress. Men wear European shorts and shirts with sandals or leather shoes. Women wear the traditional *pagne*, a colorful cloth skirt, and a blouse or tank top found in the secondhand clothing stores. Those with babies throw cotton scarfs across their backs to carry the young ones. Young children in the forest region usually wear no clothes except for decorative beads and amulets. School-aged children wear uniforms, usually a European shirt with shorts or skirts.

In the cities, women wear European cotton dresses and leather shoes. Men wear trousers and shirts or business suits. Most city dwellers spend a major portion of their incomes on clothing, and even in the rural areas most women are said to own a large variety of pagnes.

Fang men and women in the rural areas ornament themselves with tattoos and purposely inflicted scars in decorative designs. For tattoos a blue pigment is obtained from a tree fungus and applied by a professional native tattooer. Young men look forward to being tattooed as a sign of manhood, while women enjoy having their cheeks and abdomen tattooed. The scarring is usually done with a sharp blade or a nail, after which the juice of an herb is rubbed into the wound. All the designs are purely decorative, with no religious significance.

Food. The traditional Fang diet included meat obtained during the hunt and fish or crayfish caught by the women and children. Today, however, the diet is heavily reliant on cereal crops, forest roots, and tubers. When there is enough money from cash crops, Fang families buy smoked fish from door-to-door salesmen. Beef, bought from Arab herders and butchers in the city, is considered a luxury. Fowl and eggs are used for trade.

The chief dietary staple is *gari*, a flour prepared from cassava, which is used to make a thick porridge, then eaten with a spicily seasoned sauce of crushed gourd seeds, leaves, and insects such as grasshoppers, crickets, and termites. The poorer Fang eat almost any type of meat when it is available, including antelope and snake; during the rainy season the men sometimes trap monkeys, birds, and bush rats. Fresh meat is roasted over a log fire, or wrapped in leaves and covered with glowing embers, or smoked or dried for preservation. Plantains and yams are always eaten cooked, and the leaves are used for wrapping food and as plates for serving meals. Cooking oil is obtained from the palm or from the nuts of the shea butter tree, and the forest provides mushrooms and snails. Crayfish are caught by damming streams. Vegetables, fruits, rice, and corn are purchased from village markets. Typical beverages are home-brewed millet beer, palm and banana wine, and sugarcane juice.

The poor soil conditions in the forest have resulted in food shortages and heavy reliance on government stockpiles of cassava and cereals with little nutritional value. Furthermore, dietary taboos such as eggs, meat, and fruit for pregnant women have contributed to protein deficiency and malnutrition among infants and young children.

Unaccustomed to paying for food, the urban poor and newcomers from the rural areas spend most of their low wage earnings on clothes and consumer goods. Wealthier city dwellers, on the other hand, have access to more balanced and varied diets. They buy processed foods, canned vegetables, condensed milk, pasta, and potatoes, as well as meat, fowl, and fish.

Shelter. Fang villagers build houses of wooden or bamboo frames, with mud walls, and with a two-sided thatched roof. Within the village, the houses are constructed end-to-end on either side of the main road. Each village has an *abeng,* a special house for travelers that generally sits across one end of the main road. A central square is the site of a community meetinghouse, usually a roof supported by wooden poles.

The average house is divided into three to five rooms and is rectangular. Each family occupies its own houses, but the men's homes are nearer the village square, and women's dwellings behind them. Several villages, each with its own headman, make up a town. In recent times these towns have become adjuncts to the suburban sprawl that surrounds the cities.

In the coastal area fishing villages, the houses are of wood with corrugated iron roofs supported on piles. During the fishing season, men occupy small huts made of palm leaves laid over a frame of branches.

Family life. Women spend much of their time preparing and cooking food for their families. Young girls are taught how to cook at an early age and they assist their mothers in the tasks of grinding groundnuts to a fine powder, gathering logs for firewood, or carrying water from the rivers in calabashes and earthenware jugs. The Fang use cooking utensils—grindstones and boards, pots, spoons, plantain peelers, earthenware water jugs, calabashes, and gourds. They eat with spoons and wooden bowls, using broad palm and banana leaves as serving plates.

Fang society is male centered, and men have total authority over family life. Women tend to all domestic duties required for their husbands' well being—preparing meals, working around the house, and having children. Women may not provide such duties for anyone but their own husbands. To do so is considered criminal.

Religion. The Fang believe a spiritual form called *evus* consumes the soul of anyone who becomes sick, loses his material possessions, or dies. The Fang enlist the help of secret societies, *bieri,* to protect themselves against the forces of witchcraft. European missionaries in the 1800s converted many Fang to Christianity from their ancient religion, Bwiti. In the 1950s, those who did not seek the protection of the Christian church resorted to an antiwitchcraft movement called mademoiselle. To rid themselves of witches, the men attended a ceremony during which they planted trees or drove wooden stakes into the ground to purify the village and protect it against evil forces.

Arts. The Fang have a rich heritage in painting, sculpture, song, and poetry. Their artistic painted masks and statues are said to have influenced such Western artists as Pablo Picasso. Fang oral literature has been influenced in recent times by contact with Western society. A popular Fang festival, *esooulan*, still celebrates Fang unity with songs and a colorful dance called the *enyengue*. Wandering minstrels still repeat the official version of their migration from the north accompanied by a stringed instrument called the *mvet*. But the conversion of many Fang to Christianity has led to a combination of Bible stories and traditional mythology. Today most Fang literature is published in French and English.

Change. With new educational and job opportunities, some present-day Fang occupy high administrative posts in business and civil service. Others work in the professions, are prosperous commercial farmers, and form a part of the large bureaucracy of the Cameroon and Gabon governments. The distance between these well-to-do people and the poorer Fang of the city suburbs is growing. The change has greatly weakened the Fang traditional society, but the family remains important in the life of all Fang.

For More Information

Area Handbook for the United Republic of Cameroon. Washington, D. C.: American University, 1974.

Fegley, Randall. *Equatorial Guinea: An African Tragedy.* New York: Peter Lang Publishing, 1989.

Weinstein, Brian. *Gabon: Nation-Building on the Ogooué.* Cambridge, Mass.: Massachusetts Institute of Technology, 1966.

The World and Its Peoples, Africa South and West. Vol. 1. New York: Greystone Press, 1967.

FON
(fawn)

People who migrated from southwest Nigeria and established
an empire in the southern region of Benin.

Population: 1,000,000 (1980 est.).
Location: Benin, formerly called Dahomey.
Language: Fon, a tonal language very closely related to the language
of the Ewe.

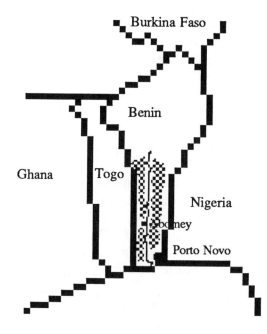

Geographical Setting

The Oueme, Benin's principal river, rises in the north at the Atakora mountains and travels to the coastal area. There it divides and empties into Lake Nohoue and the Porto-Novo lagoon. On the southern coastline, along the Gulf of Guinea, a flat sandy beach extends inland to a series of mangrove swamps and lagoons. This hot, humid marsh zone of interlocking creeks and pools, the most important of which is Lake Nokoue, has been formed by large sandbars that redirect the southward flow of the Oueme River as it winds towards the sea. Beyond the 50-mile-wide coastal zone is a clay plateau broken by occasional sandstone hills. Farther north, the plateau meets a plain of savanna grasses and strips of light forest along the riverbanks. In the southern zones, the climate includes monsoon winds and heavy rainy seasons; the northeast region is hot and dry and subject to the dusty harmattan winds that blow in from the desert. Average temperatures range from 68 to nearly 100 degrees Fahrenheit.

Historical Background

Origin. The Fon of Dahomey were probably a late part of the migration from the Oyo Empire during a great period of drought and famine that gripped the savanna region south of the river Niger. These migrations, which are said to have occurred sometime in the 13th century, reached the kingdom of Ketou, a Yoruba and Adja settlement in modern Benin. Overpopulation stimulated migration farther west and people spread out and settled territories of present-day Ghana, Togo and Benin.

Upon leaving Ketou, the Adja, Fon, and Arada (Allada) peoples went to settle a region in southern Dahomey. In 1575 these migrants founded the kingdom of Allada. Leaders from the core group went on to found smaller kingdoms along the coastal and lagoon areas: the Whydah, Jakin, Za, and Tori. These kingdoms developed trade economies. They built a key port at Whydah and a harbor, which later came to be known as Porto-Novo.

The Allada Kingdom of the Fon and its offshoots remained tributary states of the Oyo Empire. On their own, however, they flourished as slave traders to the Europeans, the Dutch and the French who had followed the Portuguese and built trading posts along the West African coast.

Before long, economic and political rivalry erupted and weakened the Allada Kingdom. After the death of a Fon king, two of his younger sons competed for the Allada throne. When the younger of the two was installed as king, the elder brother was forced into exile. Later this brother returned and claimed the throne, and the young king and his supporters were compelled to migrate inland and build the city state of Abomey. There they formed the new Fon kingdom of Dahomey in 1625.

Fon Kingdom. Legend tells of a quarrel between Dogbagrigenu, the exiled Allada leader, and King Dan of Abomey, who had granted the migrants some land. King Dan chafed when the Allada leaders demanded more land to build their royal compound and accused the migrants of trespassing "upon his belly." When Dan refused their request, he was killed, and the royal house was built on his grave—thus the name Dahomey, "upon Dan's belly."

The Fon Kingdom was not as well organized as its parent and neighboring Allada states. It had manpower but no wealth and turned to slave raids to bolster the economy. To ensure their economic fortunes, the Fon indulged in religious rites that sometimes included offering human sacrifice to the spirits of dead ancestors.

The Fon monarchy established an elaborate and expensive court that included a female counterpart for each of its officers, from the palace ministers down to the chieftains. These ministers reported to a king, one of the strongest of whom was Wegbaja. The system was supported by a large army, equipped with muskets and weapons that they received in exchange for slaves from the Europeans. The government was expensive to maintain and the need for wealth led to a policy of slow expansion. By the end of his reign in 1680, Wegbaja's tactics had proven successful; Dahomean territory had expanded to 18 towns and villages and had set the foundations for its fearsome military might.

A warrior nation. Dahomey rose from being a tributary Oyo state into a powerful independent nation. It engaged in civil wars with the states of Alladah and Whydah to gain a monopoly of the slave trade. These conflicts enraged the Oyo, who entered the fray to protect the tribute paid them by these small states. When the old Empire took political control over Dahomey territory, its forces nearly destroyed the Fon kingdom, but the Dahomeans survived.

In 1685 King Akaba began the task of rebuilding the weak Fon kingdom. He is credited with restoring the power and wealth of Dahomey using the same policies as his predecessor. By the time King Akaba died in 1708, Dahomean territory had grown to some 40 towns and villages.

Once again Dahomey rose, this time under King Agaja, a shrewd military leader whose strategies built the Fon reputation as a mighty warrior state. Agaja instituted military training for all young men, established a vast spy network that kept track of Dahomey's enemies and engaged his powerful armies in constant warfare. In the 1720s the Fon Kingdom conquered Alladah and Whydah and gained control of the slave trade. Agaja established a strong relationship with the European slavers and they ensured Dahomean domination over other states.

These conquests set into motion another wave of invasions from the Oyo Kingdom, and by 1730 they had succeeded in returning Dahomey to a tribute paying status. The desperate Fon leader, Agaja, his armies depleted and the kingdom beaten into submission, sought help from the Portuguese at Fort Whydah. This assistance resulted in negotiations and a treaty with the Oyo. The Fon Kingdom agreed to pay tribute to the Oyo and in return it was allowed to keep its armies and to govern itself.

While the Fon resented Oyo domination and felt oppressed because they were forbidden to engage in any wars, King Agaja showed his good faith by sending Prince Tegbesu to live with the Oyo. Agaja died a broken man. By this time, Dahomey was poverty stricken and rife with internal chaos.

In 1740 Tegbesu was chosen as the king's successor to rule the bankrupt and floundering kingdom. Tegbesu set about to restore the glory of the once-powerful monarchy. One of his first acts was to eliminate all those who had contested his throne. Then he did away with any potential rivals and sold their supporters into slavery to prevent revolt. He instituted new laws of succession, allowing only a direct son of the king to ascend the throne. The reorganization completed, Tegbesu decided to promote economic progress rather than make war.

Slaves and Amazons. Tegbesu was faced with a great challenge; Dahomean economy was based solely on the capture of slaves, and its armies had been depleted in the Oyo wars. He beefed up the sagging army by adding female warriors, the legendary "Amazon" military corps of Dahomey. In truth, Tegbesu's strict policies had left the king at odds with his own people. He conscripted the wives and daughters of his many sons into the female militia because they were the only people he could trust.

As the 18th century wore on, slave raids increased to ensure Dahomey's wealth. But at the same time the market for slaves on the coast had dwindled so Dahomey was unable to make its tribute payments to the Oyo. Facing poverty and uncertainty, the Fon Kingdom signed another peace treaty with its overlords and from that time until the 1830s Dahomey abstained from provoking the Oyo. When Tegbesu died in 1774, King Kpengla attempted to restore the slave economy, but his measures proved fruitless, and the Fon of Dahomey finally lost their position in the slave trade.

Renewal of the Fon Kingdom began when Oyo domination was thrown off in 1818 under King Ghezo, a direct descendant of the Adja lineage. Fon power rose under King Glele, who ascended the throne in 1858. Glele refused to end the slave trade or the ritual practice of human sacrifice. He outfitted his armies, one third of which were female "Amazons," with guns and fancy uniforms and continued to raid and plunder smaller tribes. Glele's aggressive campaigns set him at odds with the French who had begun to colonize West Africa. The conflicts continued under the rule of King Behanzin, and they finally erupted into war with the French in 1892.

French rule. When Dahomey fell and the king surrendered in 1894, it was proclaimed a French protectorate. Agoli-Agbo, the king's brother, assumed the throne under the French and became a puppet ruler.

The French puppet-regime lasted until after World War II, a period that introduced a missionary educational system as well as attempts to develop an agricultural economy. With education, Dahomey became an intellectual center that spawned a social elite of writers, artists, authors, and professionals. In 1946 Dahomey was granted two seats in the French National Assembly, and the Fon played a significant role in the nation's politics. Dahomey became an independent state within the French Union in 1959.

Independence. The nation gained its independence in 1960, but its weak economy and regional rivalry divided Dahomey along ethnic lines. The three major cultural groups, the Fon, the Yoruba, and the northern peoples, clashed over control of political power (see YO-

RUBA). Despite efforts to unite the splintered nation under a single political party, regional differences and power grabs continued. In 1963 the first republic collapsed and ushered in a wave of military coups. The army, unable to resolve regional conflicts, created a new government in 1964 under the dual leadership of Justin Ahomadegbe, a descendant of one of the Fon royal families, and Sourou Apithy, a Yoruba leader. The civilian coalition was short-lived, and by 1973 Dahomey experienced a sixth bloodless coup d'etat led by army Colonel Mathieu Kerekou.

In 1975 the country changed its name to the People's Republic of Benin, and after a serious coup attempt in 1977 a new constitution with more moderate policies was instituted. Kerekou remained in power, and in 1980 formed a new cabinet, including many former civil servants. The Fon showed a keen ability as administrators.

In 1984 Kerekou was re-elected as President for a second time. However, the bloated bureaucracy and poor agricultural economy has rendered the nation dependent on foreign aid. A new economic policy has been instituted in order to shift from a single cash crop to more staple resources such as cotton, coffee, cocoa, and palm products.

Culture Today

The Fon are the single largest ethnic group of Benin. They make up the bulk of the peasant population that is found in the rural towns and villages of the lower coastal areas. In contrast to the farmers of the southern region, the Fon in the European-influenced coastal cities are often dependent on a social-welfare system based on government employment and foreign aid.

Social structure. Fon society is patrilineal and polygamy is practiced among those men wealthy enough to purchase more than one wife. Land is inherited by the children through the father, and marriages are arranged by the families of both partners, often based on a price for the bride's purchase that is established well in advance of the actual marriage.

Economy. Government control of the economy, which depends almost entirely on palm products for export, has created difficult conditions in Benin. Many Fon seek employment in the palm-oil industry on the European-owned plantations near the cities of Abomey, Porto-

Novo, and Whydah. Others find work in related service industries along the shipping ports, and still others attempt to find jobs in the newly created agricultural projects.

Most Fon are reputed to be excellent farmers. They raise corn, a variety of manioc, yams, and other vegetables for income and food. They also raise poultry and are fishermen.

The Fon of the Cotonou live in the lake village of Ganvie. All the town's structures are supported on the water by wooden stilts and are built of bamboo and palm branches with thatched roofs. Everyone in the village works and all activity takes place on board the dugout canoes that navigate through the waters between Ganvie and the mainland. The main economic pursuit of the Cotonou Fon is fishing; the men catch the fish in nets, and the women conduct trade. The fish is smoked and dried, then sold in the floating-boat market of Ganvie. Profits are used to buy cereal grains, fresh drinking water, and imported household and personal goods.

Food, clothing, and shelter. In the cities it is common to see a mixture of European clothes and traditional costume, sometimes even worn by the same person. Men often don short-sleeved sport shirts and trousers or shorts. Women generally wear a knee-length, sarong-style dress of printed cotton fabric. Most women tie their hair up with colorful bandannas or turbans. In the villages, men are some-times seen in a traditional tunic and shorts, or bare chested with a length of fabric wrapped around their hips. Chieftains are normally identified by the highly ornamented parasols they carry. These um-brellas are normally used at large ceremonial gatherings and are dec-orated with appliqué fabrics.

As in most of West Africa, diet consists mainly of a starch base served with a variety of stews and sauces seasoned with *pili pili*, the hot chili pepper condiment found in most homes. Starches such as *fou fou* are made from yams that are pounded to a doughlike con-sistency. *Dun dun* is boiled, sliced, and deep-fried yams. A stiff fer-mented corn or millet porridge is the mainstay of most rural diets; the addition of meat, poultry, or fish is determined by economic status. Okra pods, "lady fingers," appear alone as a vegetable or as a thickener for sauces. A favorite special occasion stew, *Ago Glain*, is made from shellfish or fresh fish that is cooked with tomatoes and onions and spiked with pili pili. Plantains are eaten boiled or as highly spiced chips. All Fon dishes are eaten with the hands from bowls or calabashes. The Fon drink a fermented millet beer, and *sodabi*, the potent palm wine of the region.

Fon dwellings consist of mud-wattle houses arranged in rectangular family compounds. Each compound has an open courtyard and contains a shrine that houses the cult symbols of the family.

Religion. Fon religion is animist; that is, the people believe objects in nature have spirits. Fon deities are symbolized by animals; *Lisa* is the female creator who takes the shape of a chameleon. Lesser gods, *Vodu*, are symbolized by common objects. In fact *Vodu* has been interpreted as voodoo by Western culture, and rites practiced by fetishist priests and secret societies are magical in nature.

The arts. Marking the body with scars into which colors are worked is an ancient Fon method of beautification. Other art can be seen in the ancient city at Abomey, where the restored palaces of King Ghezo and King Glele stand. Inside, great thrones and objects of the old

Fon Dance of the Women Warriors. *Photo by Eliot Elisofon. Courtesy of National Museum of African Art.*

dynasty depict Fon history: paintings and tapestries attest to epic battles and sacred scenes, cult sculptures symbolize kings and ancestors, relief carvings portray historical events. The most notable objects are the wooden sculptures and statues, often decorated with metalwork; brass statuettes cast in the "lost wax" process; and the production of *Ase*, the portable alters used in the practice of ancestor cult.

Fon literature consists of oral tradition, songs, legends, riddles, and proverbs, often delivered in an archaic language difficult to translate. Many folktales are fantasies built around local animals. One story, for example, tells why the lizard chooses not to talk. Modern literature, written in French, includes the work of the poet Ajagba,

Five-foot-tall iron statue of the Fon god of war.

the short stories of Maxmillian Quenum, author of "In the Land of the Fon," as well as historical novels that take place in the ancient kingdom of Dahomey.

Music and dance is popular among the peasant population and their songs depict village life. Traditional songs include such titles as *To the Sun-God* and *For the Earth God*—typical tunes of nature and the old Fon religion.

For More Information

Argyle, W. J. *The Fon of Dahomey.* Oxford: Clarendon Press, 1966.

Benin. New York: Chelsea House, 1989.

July, Robert W. *A History of the African People.* New York: Charles Scribners Sons, 1974.

Scholefield, Alan. *The Dark Kingdoms: Impact of White Civilization on Three Monarchies.* New York: William Morrow & Co., 1975.

FULANI
(foo lah' nee)

Cattle-raising people living in various areas of the inland
grasslands of West Africa.

Population: 7,000,000 (1985 est.).
Location: West Africa, with the largest group bridging the border of
Nigeria and Niger.
Language: Fulfulde.

Geographical Setting

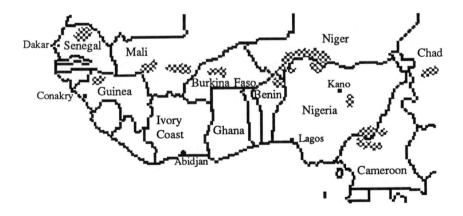

West Africa includes the countries of Benin, Togo, Ghana, Ivory Coast, Burkina Faso, Liberia, and Sierra Leone. The region lies just north of the equator and is a plateau tilted toward the Atlantic Ocean to the south. Flat and sandy, the coastline is marked by lagoons and mangrove swamps. Farther from the coast, the land rises to elevations of 1,000–2,000 feet. Still farther inland, spots of the plateau rise to more than 3,000 feet. Here forest and grasslands cover the terrain. Major rivers such as the Niger cut through the region on the way to the Atlantic Ocean.

The Fulani live in several groups scattered through different countries on the higher plateaus. Here the rainfall is more than 100 inches a year. Although near the equator, the land's high altitude provides mild temperatures. Fulani cattle herders have cleared much of the land of trees, used it heavily for grazing, and now mix agriculture and other occupations in order to earn livings in the overused land.

Historical Background

Origin. According to Fulani folk stories, a villager was forced to flee his home and, after much wandering and suffering, was rescued by a water spirit. The wanderer had watered animals along his way and was rewarded for this kindness with a gift of cattle from the spirit. Thus, the way of life of the Fulani was established. From that beginning, the Fulani became cattle herders and grew dependent on dairy products for food.

The actual history of the Fulani (who call themselves Foula or Pullo) is one of a people loosely formed into nomadic groups. They originated in the far west of the desert region of Africa as specialists in livestock-raising who coexisted with settled farmers in the Takrur Kingdom of 11th century Senegal. Making use of marginal lands on the edge of the Sahara Desert, they began to expand westward, establishing similar patterns of economic coexistence with cultivators as far east as northern Nigeria by the 17th and 18th centuries.

Muslim Fulani. The Fulani expansion took place during eras when Islam was gradually spreading in the West African savannas, and many of the Fulani were Muslim. In the early 1800s many Fulani flocked to the support of a *jihad*, or holy war, proclaimed by Uthman dan Fodio, a Fulani who was a Muslim cleric. The jihad was directed against the nominally Muslim kings of the major Hausa (see HAUSA) city-states of what is today eastern Niger and northern Nigeria. Many

Hausa also supported the successful campaigns of the next decade. The victories of dan Fodio's forces and those of his allies resulted in the blending of Fulani and Hausa people to form a Fulani-Hausa empire, the Sultanate of Sokoto, which survived until the area was conquered by the British and French in the early 20th century.

Scattered throughout much of West Africa, the Fulani became subjects of many countries, undergoing colonization by various European powers before beginning to regain their independence during the 1950s and 1960s. Survival under different rulers and the widespread drought of the 1970s, which resulted in the loss of many cattle, has forced the Fulani into other lifestyles. Today nomadic, settled, and partly settled Fulani inhabit the countries of West Africa. Scattered as they are under different governments, the Fulani are bound by shared values such as their high regard for cattle and their proud pastoral history.

Culture Today

Appearance. The Fulani tend to be dark-brown skinned with a greater frequency of slender noses and thin lips than most of their neighbors, probably having a mixed ancestry of Berbers from the Sahara and Tukolors of the ancient Takrur Kingdom. The Fulani culture came to place great importance on beauty. Adults would modify the shape of a newborn baby's head, for example, to improve its appearance. Brass anklets were worn for beauty, and leather trousers were fringed with beads by the different groups. Today, however, such traditional dress is more often seen among the Fulani Boro (cattle Fulani) than among the Fulani Gida (house Fulani)—those who live in towns and on settled farms.

Herders. The Fulani Boro have been described as comparatively shy and poorly educated in terms of formal training. However, living in small bands and wandering with their herds, they maintain their traditional way of life. In search of grazing land, these Fulani change homes with the seasons. A family of the Niger delta region may find abundant water and grazing in dry weather and move to the higher plains in the rainy season, where they are dependent on deep wells for water. Since abundant grasses grow on the plains in the dry season, this is the best time for feeding livestock. It is also a time when herders can visit markets in the Niger River valley to sell animals or buy weapons, grain, and cloth.

Although they are different from settled Fulani, the Fulani Boro are not considered poor. Owning cattle is a symbol of health and well-being among all Fulani. Cattle provide food, clothing, and purpose in life. Moreover, the Fulani Boro play an important role for various nearby people, trading milk products for other foods on the journey from pasture to pasture. In addition, the Fulani herds are often allowed to graze on the fields after the harvest because the dung of the animals fertilizes the fields for next year's crops.

Farmers. The Fulani Gida are a settled people who grow crops such as pulses (seeds of pod-bearing plants) and maize, and who live in farm villages or towns. Most of them adhere to Muslim beliefs. Some

Fulani woman with gold earrings.

have grown wealthy, and some have gained high esteem in the Muslim world for their high levels of education. Today these wealthy or educated Fulani still own cattle but hire laborers to tend the herds. Also hired for labor are the poorer Fulani whose loss of cattle has resulted in their moving into towns where they become craftspeople such as potters. These poor Fulani often suffer their misfortunes in silence, since the ability to bear pain without complaint is one of their people's values.

Farmer-Herders. In addition to the Fulani Gida and the Fulani Boro there are the seminomadic Fulani who limit their movement to the savanna, an area they can also farm. A present-day family of this group may divide its labors, with some family members attending to farming and others herding cattle. For food or trade, cattle provide milk, butter, cheese, and blood to accompany the food crops of maize and pulses.

The three lifestyles have helped the Fulani adjust to population growth. They have, however, led to some conflict among the people.

A typical market in West Africa. *Photo by Barbara Neibel.*

The land that is valuable for grazing is also the prime soil for raising rice and sorghum. So while farmers and herders depend on each other for food, they compete for land.

Family life. A Fulani girl is given a cow at age 9 and the calves it produces are usually given to her when she marries by entering her husband's home. There are no formal marriage ceremonies but there are formal marriage rules to follow when the bride leaves her father's home to join her husband. She may then transfer the care of the cows to her husband, but she retains milking rights to a number of cows the husband has reserved for her. If a woman later divorces her husband, she takes the cows with her.

Food and shelter. The traditional Fulani diet centered on cattle products—milk, butter, cheese, and blood. As farming became more common, vegetable products became more popular in the daily diet. The various groups of Fulani began eating more maize and other edible plant seeds, pulses, along with yams and other vegetable products.

Fulani homes differ according to their various lifestyles. Settled Fulani live in thatched, earthen structures of cone-cylinder shape or in rectangular houses with brick walls, flat roofs, and inner courtyards. The nomadic Fulani occupy homes built with poles and mats of leaves or grass. A Fulani homestead has two parts—the permanent living area and the temporary corral for cattle. Together they form the *wuro*, or household. Houses always face west to protect from sun, rain and wind. Historically, a Fulani man could take many wives into his home, but today the typical Fulani family includes only one wife. Still, the Fulani household made of earth with a woven grass roof has a house for the man, and a house for each wife, with a nearby kitchen. Among the settled Fulani, it is the husband who holds title to the property.

Religion. The Fulani had begun to leave the region of Senegal by the 11th century and had reached northern Nigeria by the 16th century. At first the Fulani religion was animist, the belief that objects in the environment have souls. By the 14th century Islam had arrived in Fulani-Hausa territory, and many Fulani converted to the new religion. Farther west, however, the Fulani people were at first hostile to the Muslims. The kingdoms at Fouta Djalon and Fouta Senegal persecuted members of the new religion. Gradually, the religion of

Islam won favor with many of the Fulani. It was not until that religion added fervor to their forays against other people that the Fulani began to unify as a people and to establish empires. Today the Muslim religion is the dominant religion among the Fulani.

Values. The literature of the Fulani, expressed in song, poetry, and oral folklore tells stories of Fulani achievements and values. One love story in the poetry of the past tells of a romantic interest who is "light of skin" and with "straight hair." This ideal "never stinks of fish," "never breathes sweat" and has no bald spot from carrying heavy loads on her head. (See Beier 1966, p. 50.)

For More Information

Beier, Ulli. *African Poetry.* Cambridge, Massachussets: Cambridge University Press, 1966.

Mountjoy, Alan B. and Clifford Embleton. *Africa, A New Geographical Survey.* New York: Frederick A. Praeger, 1967.

Osae, T. S., S. N. Nwabara, and A. T. O. Odunsi. *A Short History of West Africa—A.D. 1000 to the Present.* New York: Hill and Wang, 1973.

Fulani home.

HAUSA

(how' suh)

A predominantly rural West African people who built large cities and whose culture reveals a strong Arab Muslim influence.

Population: 7,000,000 (1987 est.).
Location: Nigeria, within the Sudan desert.
Language: Hausa, probably the widest-spoken language in sub-Saharan Africa, with estimates of nearly 20 million speakers.

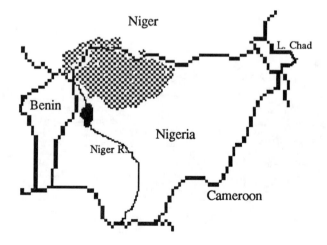

Geographical Setting

Hausaland lies in the plateau and plains areas of northern Nigeria and southeastern Niger. Bordered on the northeast by Lake Chad, it extends eastward almost to the Niger River in Niger. Here the elevation is between 2,000 and 2,400 feet. Hausaland, however, is less of a tribal territory or actual physical place than a cultural entity and mind set. Today, Hausa peoples are linked and divided from other groups more by language than by geographical borders. Still, climate and the cycle of the seasons play a very important role in the lives of the Hausa, particularly the rural Hausa, who make up about four-fifths of the total Hausa population. During the wet season, which is mostly between June and September, as much as 30–40 inches of rain may fall. Farmers are extremely busy in this period tending their crops as the heavy rains can easily endanger their livelihood. During the dry season between October and May virtually no rain falls. The people spend this time in other activities, such as building houses or engaging in craftwork.

Historical Background

Origin. According to folk stories, there were originally seven true Hausa kingdoms, each of which had a walled city called *birni* that dominated the surrounding countryside. These seven kingdoms may have developed from family-linked groups into the territory-based system the Hausa now have. They had already come into existence by the 11th or 12th centuries as centers of commerce and rural production.

Trade. The inter-regional trade of West Africa that has existed since prehistory had a profound effect on the Hausa, as has the trans-Saharan trade that began to reach the Hausa between 500 and 1000 A.D. Along with the desperately needed salt that Berber and Kanuri traders brought came the religion of Islam. Trade routes also allowed religious and worldly scholars to bring their knowledge of script and law to the courts of the Hausa rulers. Gradually these Hausa leaders adopted Muslim ways. By the end of the 15th century, Islam and the traditional religions were equally popular in Hausaland.

In 1591, a war in the Arab section of North Africa led to the collapse of a major empire there. One result of this was the creation of a new trade route that passed directly through Hausaland. Over time, this trade shift boosted the economy and population, which, in turn, led to a political change from smaller chiefdoms into larger kingdoms. Hausa rulers, or *Ha'be*, became very powerful and increasingly oppressive towards the peasantry. They demanded heavy taxes and labor, appointed officers unfairly, and allowed a mixture of Islamic practices with pre-Islamic religion, a situation that conflicted with Koranic law.

The Jihad. In the late 18th and early 19th centuries, discontent with the standard of living and the exhortations of persuasive leaders encouraged a rural population that included both Hausa farmers and nomadic Fulani herders to join in revolt (See FULANI). The movement was led by a scholar named Shehu Uthman dan Fodio and became known as a holy war, or *jihad*, against the corruption and excesses of the Hausa elite. The war began as a scholarly revolt but soon escalated into a military one with victims who were both Hausa and Fulani. A lieutenant to dan Fodio named Muhammed Bello eventually oversaw the establishment of peace and Muslim reform in the region, with the Fulani frequently assuming positions of political dominance. The end of the *jihad* brought political and religious confederation of Hausa and Fulani in a loosely unified sultanate that survived until its conquest by the British at the beginning of the 20th century. The capital was established in the Hausa city Sokoto.

European influence. As the end of the 19th century approached, the pattern and volume of trade changed drastically, accompanied by occupation of most of West Africa by the French and British. European countries had been involved in trade with West Africa since the mid-15th century. In the 17th and 18th centuries, several million slaves were transported to the New World from these regions. However, in the 19th century slave trade was gradually suppressed, and other products, especially palm oil, became the major exports. Competition and commercial interest among the different European nations led, in the late 19th century, to the partitioning of West Africa. The Europeans created borders to better control the colonies but also ended up splitting people culturally. The Hausa homeland was divided and became more isolated from the rest of the region. In Hausa regions claimed by them, the British decided to rule through the established authorities, as it was the least costly way to maintain their overall control. The French ruled in a more direct fashion over the Hausa on their side of the colonial borders.

In the 20th century, the Hausa-Fulani territory was caught up in the general unrest in Nigeria. Living in countries whose boundaries had been arbitrarily set by British and French overlords, the Hausa were among those who sought and achieved independence for Nigeria in 1960. Various governments attempted to unify the many groups that make up Nigeria. Although the Nigerian prime minister in the early 1960s was a Hausa, southern Nigerians, such as the Ibo and Yoruba, held most of the economic and educational advantages in the new country. In 1966 a military coup deposed the elected government. The country was then led by a northerner, but not one of the Hausa-Fulani people.

After a series of military coups, the establishment of a second republic took place in 1979. This republic survived until 1983, when it was replaced once more by military government. By 1989, plans were under way to develop a third republic to rule over the Hausa, Fulani, Yoruba, Ibo, and other groups, each wanting a voice in the government. One of these groups, the Ibo, has long sought its own nation (see IBO). Today the Hausa live a cooperative life with their once-dominating neighbors, the Fulani. Hausa people reside in cities and towns such as Sokoto (population 145,000) and Kano (475,000) and farm the outskirts of the towns, while the Fulani raise cattle in the countryside and come to town to trade. Through the many efforts to change them, the Hausa people have continued in their older Islamic traditions, resisting change.

Culture Today

Village life. Traditional Hausa live in towns, or *gari*, composed of households or compounds called *gida*. Surrounding the village are farms belonging to the various households, and beyond that are the uncultivated bush lands, called the *daji*. Most Hausa from this rural world do not travel much farther than the limits of their villages, perhaps to trade with the Fulani herders who live on the outskirts of their villages. On market days, people come from all over to trade, sell their wares, and exchange information and current news. Most activities, such as farm work, visiting, or ceremonies, take place during the early morning hours when the sun is not so strong. In the hottest part of the day, the village settles down, and then it comes alive again in the late afternoon and evening when most socializing is done.

While the village is basic to the rural Hausa experience, the real focal point of social organization is the *gida*. A typical gida includes separate dwellings for the head of the household, his wife (or wives), and perhaps his married son(s). With a fence of earth and grainstalks, it usually has an open courtyard with a cooking area, a well, a shelter for the animals, and a shop on the street side for selling goods. Among the well-to-do classes, several compounds may be connected by walled passages, fences, and entryways. These are used by the women to reach friends and neighbors since Islamic belief prohibits them from being seen in public, a practice called *purdah*. However, this

A Kongo refugee from Angola. *Photo by Eliot Elisofon. Courtesy of National Museum of African Art.*

restrictive custom is not usually followed by poorer Hausa or by rural Fulani. The gida is always controlled by the husband of the family, who may share his household with his married sons or brothers. Hausaland, according to Islamic custom, is dominated by men.

Children. Children play a very important role in Hausa society, which values them highly as investments in the future. Rarely punished physically, young people enjoy considerable freedom. They run errands, serve as messengers for their family, and often sell products for their mothers, who are secluded. When they are older, the boys often help with the harvest or the cattle. Some children attend West-

Building a Hausa granary using coils of mud and straw. *Photo by Eliot Elisofon. Courtesy of National Museum of African Art.*

ern-style schools, while others (mostly boys) spend time studying the Koran, the book of Muslim scriptures. Although the marriage value increases for educated females, girls are less often encouraged to go to school than to stay home and help their mothers. Traditional education for both sexes more often involves a combination of informal observation of elders and formal instruction.

Women and marriage. Women are sometimes married at the age of 13 or 14, especially among well-to-do Hausa. This can be a very traumatic experience as it entails a complete change of lifestyle. Freedom is sharply curtailed, and the expectations of a wife are quite numerous. She must move to the home of her husband's family and can only see her family occasionally. In addition, she may encounter a jealous first wife. Polygyny (having more than one wife) is an accepted practice of Islam, as well as a symbol of prestige. However, a new wife is usually welcomed as an extra helper. Once married, the women are responsible for reproducing and nurturing the children, and for providing and preparing the meals for the family in the compound. They obtain luxury items by making and selling goods, and are otherwise materially supported by their husbands.

Economy. The farming village is a base for trade and agriculture. Families serve as the basic farming unit. Many men also pursue other trades and crafts. In the wet season, men become drummers, praise-singers, butchers, leather workers, blacksmiths, bicycle mechanics, or carpenters, along with many other occupations. Hausa people are rarely judged on occupation alone, but rather on their performance as a member of the farming community.

The main foods are sorghum (*dawa*) and bulrush millet (*gero*), but other crops are grown for commercial value or to let the land regenerate. Crops planted in rotation with others to help regenerate the soil include cassava, okra, red peppers, and cowpeas. Some of the Hausa land in the eastern plains area is periodically flooded. Sugarcane, maize, and sweet potatoes are grown in this region. Where irrigation is possible from streams and wells, water is drawn into small bags pulled up by ropes in a process called *shaduf*. Farmers raise onions and rice in these areas for higher profits. Crops grown to sell also include cotton, tobacco, henna, hemp, and groundnuts.

Religion. Hausaland has been officially Muslim for at least two hundred years. In some areas, though, traditional religions are still practiced, especially by women who are generally thought to have evil powers as a natural trait. The devout Hausa Muslims perform five prayers daily, as dictated by Islam, starting before sunrise and ending after sunset. Men and boys pray together in groups wherever they may be—during market or perhaps in the fields. This ensures strict observance by the males. On the other hand, women are allowed to pray individually in their own compounds, which suggests that their observance is considered less important.

The Hausa express most things in terms of God's will. Islam is a religion of submission to God, with reward promised in the next life. Those who obey Allah's will and show patience in suffering expect to have everything they desire upon leaving the physical body. Those who do not, at least publicly, are scorned and called "nonbelievers," which is the worst profanity thinkable.

Ceremonies. Aside from the five daily prayers performed by the Muslim Hausa, there are two major religious events that take place

Men and horses in quilted cloth armor. *Photo by Eliot Elisofon. Courtesy of National Museum of African Art.*

during the course of a year. The "Lesser" and "Greater" festivals, as they are called, involve both hard work and great enjoyment for the devout followers. For an entire lunar month, these followers fast and study the Koran, the holy text. Following the fast, there is a great celebration including a feast (*biki*), gift-giving, and for those who can afford it, the highly esteemed pilgrimage to Mecca, which bestows great honor and virtue on a man.

One of the more commonly performed rituals is the naming ceremony. It occurs seven days after a child is born and is a way of officially recognizing a child in the community and congratulating the family on the continuation of the lineage. The baby is named, after which its head is shaved and tribal marks or tattoos are imprinted on it. The people perform this and other ceremonies, such as circumcision, funerals, and marriage, in the early morning and celebrate afterward with feasts when possible.

Philosophy. The Hausa put great stress on moral excellence and personal character. Wisdom, justice, fairness, and honesty are highly valued in individuals. On the social level, safety, security, balance, and order are considered the ideal and are represented in the Hausa concept of *lafiya*. This concept is crucial in understanding their thoughts and culture and has been said to encompass morality, economy, interpersonal relationships, and the relationship between people to the spirit world and God. A strong belief among the Hausa is that if people adhere to the social and religious requirements of Islam, their relationships with each other will be fruitful. For men, this entails submission to God, and for women, submission to men.

For More Information

Wall, L. Lewis. *Hausa Medicine: Illness and Well-Being in a West African Culture.* Durham, North Carolina: Duke University Press, 1988.

Hill, Polly. *Rural Hausa: A Village and a Setting.* Cambridge: The University Press, 1972.

Webster, J. B. and A. A. Boahen. *History of West Africa.* New York: Praeger Publishers, 1967.

HERERO
(her eh' roh)

Bantu people of Namibia who were among the leaders pressing for Namibian independence.

Population: 55,000 (1985 est.).
Location: Namibia, Angola.
Language: Herero, a Bantu dialect.

Geographical Setting

The land of the Herero lies along the coast of Africa north and west of the Republic of South Africa. It is bounded on the south by the Orange River. Except for mountain ranges inland in Namibia and again in Angola, the land is flat and arid. Before Europeans settled on farms there, the land mostly supported cattle grazing. A low desert, the Namib Desert, lies along the Atlantic Ocean and extends a few miles inland where the terrain rises slightly to support a scrub woodland. Still farther inland, the scrub growth gives way to savanna—the grasslands of Africa. The Khomas Highlands and other mountain areas separate the brush land of Namibia and Angola from the Kalahari Desert, which dominates the interior of southern Africa.

Historical Background

Origin. Portuguese sailors traveled along the coast of what is now Namibia as early as 1484 but found the desert coastland undesirable. The region inland was inhabited by the Nama people, who were left undisturbed by the early explorers. Before the 1800s, a new group migrating from central Africa had begun to share the land with the Nama. These newcomers, the Herero, were cattle herders who led a wandering life for part of each year. The older residents considered the unsettled newcomers to be of lesser status and called them "ant-diggers." Nevertheless, the Herero settled themselves just north of the Cape of Good Hope and began to trade cattle with the Europeans who were colonizing the Cape. In the 1840s, missionaries from Holland, Great Britain, and Germany began attempts to Christianize the Herero. Germany and Great Britain began to claim territories that would split the Herero-occupied lands.

Conflicts over land. Competition for grazing land with other settlers of the Cape and farming efforts of the Europeans grew in the second half of the 1800s. The 1860s and 1870s saw considerable fighting over land in the area. Starting in 1884, the German settlers claimed South Africa (in which Namibia was then included), and soon these settlers began to take up land for their own purposes. Tensions over European dominance grew until war erupted again in the early 1900s—this time between the Nama and mixed-race residents and the Germans. The Herero soon rose, too, in revolt. This rebellion was quickly suppressed by the Germans, who treated the Nama leniently but proceeded to destroy the Herero. Under extermination orders from General von Trotha, the Herero population was reduced, in 1903, from

80,000 to less than 20,000. The ruling government confiscated all Herero land and reduced the remaining Herero people to slavery. In 1908 diamonds were discovered in the mountainous areas of the country, increasing the influx of German settlers and the pressure on the earlier inhabitants. After defeat in World War I, the Germans yielded control of the country to the League of Nations, which gave the responsibility of government to Great Britain.

An independent Namibia. Eventually, control of the Herero people fell to the government of South Africa. In 1946, under Chief Hosea Kutake, the Herero lead a movement requesting the United Nations to intercede and provide freedom for the black peoples under South African domination. That plea failed, and South Africa responded with the policy of *apartheid*, a policy of racial separation that the Herero were leaders in opposing. By 1975, South Africa had been pressed to convene a meeting of leaders of all the black reserves in Namibia. This conference adopted a resolution for an independent Namibia and set a time line for final independence in 1978. Meanwhile, a long guerrilla war against South Africa was led by the Southwest African Peoples Organization after it became clear that South Africa was not willing to grant independence. Finally, in 1989, the country of Namibia was recognized as a separate nation. Hereroland lies in the northeast section of Namibia, a country the Herero share with the Nama, Kaoko, Ovambo, Kavango, Bushmen, and Damara.

Culture Today

Government. Once, the Herero lived in small communities of extended families, each with a village chief, and with one dominant chief over all the Herero. Through the turmoils of their own movements, and their differences with the Nama and then the Europeans, the role of the head chief declined until the position became largely symbolic. In recent years, the Herero Chief Kuaima Rimako grew in strength as he led the movement for a separate nation of Namibia. Chief Rimako became the main spokesman for this movement and a prominent political leader in southern Africa. With Namibian independence, the Herero began a strong role in the government of the new nation.

Social structure. Many Herero were educated in missionary schools and some attended colleges in Europe. As a result the Herero began to adopt many Western attitudes. Still remaining is a clan system of members of related families. Each Herero can claim support from both a matrilineal (mother-related) clan and a patrilineal one. The clan of the father plays a responsible role in spiritual affairs, while the clan of the mother controls the land and other properties.

Food, clothing, and shelter. Earlier, as cattle herders, Herero dressed simply in a leather apron and a goatskin cloak. Women added beads and copper or brass jewelry for arms and legs. However, contact with the Europeans resulted in change. Today Herero workers wear European-style clothes, and Herero businessmen wear suits and ties much like their European counterparts.

Homes, too, reflect the European influence. Once the Herero lived in dome-shaped houses constructed by bending saplings and fixing them to a central post. The resulting framework was then covered with bark, twigs, or hides and surfaced with clay. Today many Herero homes are rectangular structures of brick. Few Herero cling to the nomadic cattle-herding lifestyle. Where once the Herero were dependent on their cattle, sheep, and goats, today's Herero frequently work as hired hands on a larger cattle enterprise or farm, or as workers in the mines and factories controlled by Europeans. They buy their food and other necessities from stores. Windhoek, near the edge of Hereroland, is a modern city with a great deal of German-style architecture. It is the capital of Namibia.

As nomads, Herero families subsisted on soured milk, some meat, and wild fruits and vegetables. Corn has since been introduced on Namibian farms, and the Herero have changed their diets to include more of this grain.

Religion. As with most African people, the Herero believe in a supreme deity and lesser gods. And as many Africans, they also believe in ancestor spirits who intercede for the living with the godhood. During their dominance by Europeans, many Herero were converted to Christianity, which they blend with their traditional beliefs. Christian events are often accompanied by ceremonies designed to win the good offices of the ancestor spirits. Still today, the old religious organizations continue to practice through such groups as the Cult of the Sacred Fire.

Politics. Herero people join other groups in securing their newly won right to self-determination in Namibia. They are searching for ways to win a greater share of the wealth of the large agricultural units and mining riches that have long been dominated by the white population. However, as in other emerging nations of Africa, old ethnic differences must first be resolved before black Africans can join in effective new country organizations.

For More Information

Hodgson, Bryan. "Namibia: Nearly a Nation?" *National Geographic*, June 1982, pp. 755–797.

Saunders, Christopher. *Historical Dictionary of South Africa.* Metuchen, New Jersey: Scarecrow, 1983.

South Africa 1984: Official Yearbook of the Republic of South Africa, 10th ed. Johannesburg, Republic of South Africa: Chris van Rensburg Publications, 1984.

IBO
(ee' boh)

Also called Igbo; a group of over 200 culturally related peoples, speaking dialects of the Igbo language.

Population: 8,000,000 (1980 est.)
Location: Southeastern Nigeria.
Languages: Igbo, English.

Geographical Setting

The traditional Ibo homeland forms a roughly circular region to the northeast of the Niger delta, where the Niger River flows south

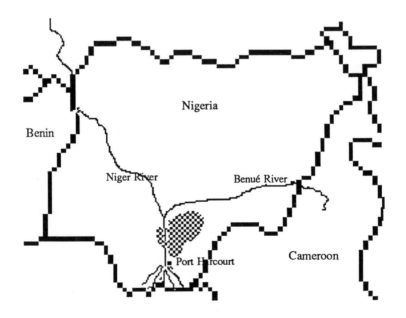

through Nigeria to meet the Atlantic Ocean. In the 1950s, before many moved to other areas in Nigeria, about 12 percent of the Ibo lived alongside the river's western bank. However, most of Iboland (as the area is known) lies between the Niger to the west and the Cross River to the east, about 200 miles. It extends inland about 300 miles, from the delta town of Port Harcourt north, past the town of Enugu. Among the highest in Africa, the population density in Ibo country exceeds 2,500 individuals per square mile in some areas.

The delta region is heavily forested, as are places along the rivers. Other areas, particularly to the north, are mainly grassland with scattered forest. Most of the land is low, measuring under 1,000 feet in altitude. Featuring a tropical climate, the region experiences alternating wet and dry seasons. Rains begin in February and increase through July, then break in August. They resume from September to November. Rainfall is heaviest in the south, which receives about 100 inches per year.

Historical Background

Ancient origins. Iboland has been inhabited for at least 5,000 years, and its first settlers are considered ancestors of its current people. Pottery made there today resembles that made 4,500 years ago, suggesting remarkable cultural continuity. Around the same time, the Igbo languages began to break away from nearby relatives such as the Yoruba (see YORUBA) and Edo. Before 1000 B.C. the people of this region were already cultivating native yams, which became central in economic and ritual life. Knowledge of ironworking reached Iboland shortly after 500 B.C., probably from the northern Nigerian center of Nok (see NOK).

The bronzes of Nri. Over the next thousand years, Ibo metalworkers improved their skills, transforming agriculture and hunting practices. By 800 A.D. they had already developed an impressive artistic tradition as well. This tradition centered around the site of Nri in north Iboland. Expeditions have uncovered a series of sites near Nri. These sites have provided bronze objects—elaborately decorated bowls and bells, as well as sculpted human and animal figures—that reveal a brilliant age of Ibo artistry. Other finds include iron weapons, copper jewelry, and elephant tusks, suggesting ivory was important in the local economy.

Democracy and commerce. While archeology provides a vivid glimpse of Iboland in the 800s, less is known about the next thousand years. It was during this time, however, that the Ibo peoples developed a society that spread political power throughout the villages rather than concentrating it in the hands of a central ruler as other societies had (see KONGO). The village became the basic unit of social life. Led by elders and others with proven ability, each village made decisions collectively in what Westerners would describe as a participatory democracy. Early European visitors to Iboland remarked on the freedom and liberty the people enjoyed. Trade also developed and was closely connected with a high level of craftwork. Ibo blacksmiths produced hoes, bolts, hinges, swords, axes, razors, and other iron tools, which they exchanged with neighbors to the north for beads and copper jewelry. Villages in the south traded farm produce for salt and fish from coastal and delta peoples. A system of markets arose, using different types of currency, from cowrie shells to copper bracelets and brass rods for money.

Slave trade. The last three hundred years of this period, from about 1520 to the early 1800s, saw the slave trade grow to dominate commerce. Continued by the Dutch in the 17th and by the English in the 17th and 18th centuries, this trade in human cargo took a huge toll on the Ibos. Scholars today estimate that during the 18th and 19th centuries more than 400,000 Ibo people were transported from the coasts of eastern Nigeria. Many of these were interior neighbors of the Ibo taken by Ibo merchants to be sold, but many others were Ibo who were shipped to the American colonies and the West Indies.

The colonial period. By the mid-1800s the slave trade had fallen into disfavor; Europeans sought other African riches. Soon palm oil, used as a lubricant and fuel in Europe's growing centers of industry, became Iboland's main export. Slavery continued in the region itself, however, so that Ibo slaves both produced and transported the palm oil. In the late 1800s, the British began bringing Iboland under colonial rule as part of Nigeria. In 1889, British forces sacked the prosperous Ibo town Onitsha, and six years later the Royal Niger Company began campaigns to subdue the Ibo, who resisted fiercely. Greatly handicapped in weaponry and other resources, the Ibo nonetheless defied British occupation for many years. From various areas, they rose up against the occupiers again and again, prompting repeated British military expeditions. With the 1914 outbreak of World War I (and the related withdrawal of some local British garrisons) new uprisings spread throughout Iboland.

Women's War. The discovery of coal in Iboland during the early 1900s increased the number of British in the region. They imposed their own system of rule, appointing Warrant Chiefs (local governors) from among the village populations. The system led to widespread corruption among these Chiefs. Led by bands of Ibo women, the Women's War of 1929 began in protest against the Warrant Chiefs. It rapidly escalated into rebellion against colonial rule. The women protested in groups through a small area of Iboland. British troops fired on them in eight different locations, killing 55 and wounding 50. Though brief and bloody, the war forced the British to take greater heed of the Ibo's existing institutions of self-rule.

Nigerian nation. From the 1920s to independence in 1960, Ibo and other African leaders pressed for an end to colonial rule in Nigeria. Competition between Nigeria's three main ethnic groups complicated the effort, as each became tied to a single political party. The Ibos became the main force in the National Council of Nigerian Citizens, the Yoruba in the Action Group, and the Hausa and Fulani in the Northern People's Congress. Although leaders of these parties sought to reduce ethnic divisions in politics, their efforts met with little success.

Tensions grew after independence. A coup d'etat by some Ibo army officers in 1966 led to a military government and mounting anti-Ibo feeling by other Nigerians. In the north, attacks on the Ibos in late 1966 caused thousands of deaths, and over a million Ibos fled to the Eastern Region (which was designated for the Ibo, in contrast to the Yoruba who resided in the west and the Hausa and Fulani in the North.)

Biafra and its aftermath. On May 30, 1967, the Ibo military governor, Lieutenant Colonel Chukwuemeka Ojukwu, declared the Eastern Region independent of Nigeria and formed it into the Republic of Biafra. Nigeria attacked the rebels. While the federal government's firepower was superior, the Ibo began with high morale and effective leadership. Several foreign states recognized Biafra, and world sympathy leaned toward the Ibos, many of whom died from starvation and disease during the 30-month war. Gradually worn down, the Ibos finally surrendered in 1970. Over a million Nigerians, the majority of them Ibos, are estimated to have perished in the Eastern Region during the conflict.

Surprisingly, the bitterness of the war gave way to generosity and good will afterwards. Nigeria's government strove deliberately and successfully to blend the Ibos back into Nigerian life, and the end result was a major easing of ethnic differences. Oil and coal deposits in Nigeria have contributed to the well-being and peacefulness of its peoples in postwar years. As Ibos have returned to jobs in the north and west, Nigeria's goal of a multiethnic society seems reachable. The government plans to complete in 1992 the process, begun over a decade earlier, of doing away with military rule.

Culture Today

Local differences among the more than 200 Ibo groups call for caution in making overall statements about culture. In fact, before colonial times, the Ibos had no reason to identify themselves as such. Instead they gave their loyalty to local units such as family, lineage, or village. Only in reaction to outsiders such as the British, Yoruba, and Hausa did the Ibos develop a sense of collective identity (an experience common to many African societies). Therefore, while the practices described below are widespread, they vary to some degree from group to group.

Family life. Traditional Ibo society places great value on marriage and children. While a man may marry more than one wife, estimates indicate that most men from the colonial period until now have had a single wife. Marriage includes a long period of negotiation between the two families, involving payment from the groom's family to the bride's family. The ideal number of children is nine, though most families are smaller. Between marriage partners, the husband provides the dwelling and some land for his wife and her children. (An Ibo woman marries outside her village, and thus does not inherit land.) As for the wife, her main tasks include collecting firewood and water so that she can cook for the family. She controls the household. For help in cooking, she turns to young girls or boys. Meals are haphazardly eaten. A mother and her young children may eat together; boys and girls may eat separately followed by their parents;

a husband may have food sent to a room of his choice. Family meals are common only in households that have adopted Western or European habits.

Food, clothing, and shelter. Grown exclusively by the men, the many types of yam provide the Ibo with their single most important food. (The people consider yam stealing a serious offense, in some places punishable by death.) Other staples include cassava, corn, melons, beans, okra, and peppers, and fruits such as bananas, pineapples, oranges, and papaw. Most meals include yam or cassava *fufuu*, which is prepared by boiling pieces of the vegetable, then mashing them into a sticky dough. Main dishes are soups and stews, with a base

Wedding of Joe and Bath. *Photo by Barbara Neibel.*

with vegetables and palm oil, for example. Boiled yam thickens the mixture, to which meat or fish is added. Generous amounts of raw pepper spice the stew, which is eaten with fufuu. The people still use extracts of the palm plant: palm oil for cooking and palm wine to accompany meals.

Once Ibo women wove fine cotton or palm cloth for trade and coarser material for their own use, but spinning and weaving have become rarer today. Mass-produced cotton prints are now available at local markets. Like Westerners, many present-day Ibo men dress in pants and shirts while women may wear simple cotton dresses or shifts.

The layout of a village changes with the area, but houses are usually made of clay. The Ibo paint their dwellings in bright patterns of red, yellow, and black, covering them with thatch or tin roofing. In the past, a husband and wife often had separate houses, but today's family typically occupies a single house. The buildings each have a front "yard," or clean open space, swept daily, where children play. Surrounded by vegetable gardens and shady trees, they border broad, carefully planned streets.

A nursery school graduation in Nigeria. *Photo by Barbara Neibel.*

Ibo society. The Ibos place high value on group as well as individual achievement. Villages compete with one another in building schools, hospitals, and other public amenities. There are age groups (associations restricted to villagers of similar ages and mostly to men). These age-groups help maintain law and order and arrange activities for the benefit of the public. Besides age groups, secret societies exist. They discourage crime and promote community welfare while keeping up a pretense of hiding members' identities. (They are "secret" in the same way as Masons in America are supposedly secret.) Members may appear masked in the night to frighten offenders. Performing social services, wealthy men of the village form other societies. The Okonko society, for example, maintains roads in southern Iboland.

Outside the home, women have a place in larger society. They perform many economic tasks, from raising vegetables to refining palm oil and selling products in local markets. Colorful and competitive, these daily markets are avenues for profit and for meeting friends from neighboring villages. It has been suggested that women have lost some of the power they once wielded in Ibo society. The Women's War of 1929 was perhaps an attempt to regain it. If they lost power due to outside influences, their experience was similar to that of their Hausa countrywomen (see HAUSA).

Religion and health. The Ibos were little attracted to Christian beliefs until the early 1900s, after the British conquest of Iboland. Many Ibos today combine Christian beliefs with their own traditional beliefs. Traditionally, the people worship a great many gods, representing the different forces they perceive in the natural world. The supreme god has three names that reveal his qualities: *Chukwu*, the ever-present spirit; *Chineke*, the spirit who creates; and *Osebuluwa*, the spirit who upholds the world. Ibos also practice ancestor worship, believing the deceased members of their family to still be a part of daily life. They are invited to share meals, and it is thought that ancestors safeguard the family and its property. Their immortal quality rests on the Ibo belief that every living person has a *chi*, a spirit that does not die.

Health is closely related to religious beliefs. Traditional *dibia*, or herbalists (people who prescribe herbs as medicine), still practice their cures.

Education. In Ibo society, individuals succeed on their own merits rather than by inheriting power from a parent. It is said that this prompted many to enroll in mission schools during the colonial era. So many Ibos have learned to read and write that they are now one of the most literate people in Black Africa. Using their abilities, they are helping the Nigerian government reshape education in the country. The goal is to replace old education programs from Europe with ones that better represent peoples and customs in Nigeria.

Arts and literature. Education has helped the Ibo produce a remarkable body of literature in both the Igbo and English languages. The first writer in English, Olaudah Equiano (circa 1745–1797), was sold into slavery as a child. After learning English, arithmetic, and navigation, he bought his freedom at age 19, then went to work ending slavery in the Americas and in England. In England he wrote his best-selling autobiography. In 1933, Pita Nwana, writing in Igbo, published the prize-winning novel *Omenuko.* Novelist Chinua Achebe (author of *Things Fall Apart* and *A Man of the People*) achieved great success in novels on early colonial and present-day life in Nigeria.

An Ibo nun. *Photo by Barbara Neibel.*

The Ibo celebrate their culture through other arts as well, such as dance, painting, and sculpture. Like many other Africans, the Ibo have a great love of proverbs. Dances and masquerades require the community to participate, as illustrated by the proverb, "You do not stand in one place to watch a masquerade." There is a festival called *mbari* that puts the artists to work. A village chooses a few artists to honor the Ibo gods and goddesses by creating a a home of statues. These large statues are modeled in clay and painted in earthy tones such as black, red, and brown. Other statues capture in wood or clay scenes from village events.

For More Information

Amadiume, Ifi. *Male Daughters, Female Husbands: Gender and Sex in an African Society.* London: Zed Books, 1987.

Cole, Herbert M. *Mbari: Art and Life Among the Owerri Igbo.* Bloomington: Indiana University Press, 1982.

Isichei, Elizabeth. *History of the Igbo People.* London: Macmillan Press, 1976.

KAMBA
(kahm' ba)

Traders and farmers of western Kenya; called A-Kamba by the people themselves.

Population: 1,500,000 (1985 est.).
Location: Kenya, northern Tanzania.
Languages: Kikamba, Kiswahili, English.

Geographical Setting

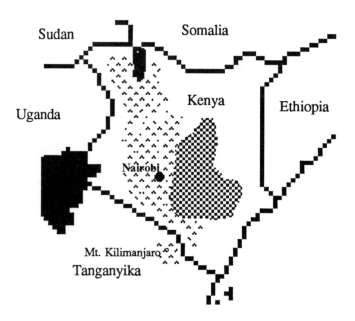

The land of the Kamba lies in eastern Kenya, stretching southeastward from near Nairobi to within about a hundred miles of the Indian Ocean coast. In the west, the land consists of dry rolling steppe between 1500 and 3000 feet in elevation and reaching in one area to above 6000 feet. It is a land of frequent droughts in which the many streams dry up nearly completely for part of each year. At higher elevations there are some forests, but most of Kambaland is bush land or grassland in the highlands around Mt. Kilimanjaro.

Historical Background

Trading and raiding. The Kamba developed into a distinct society in the 16th century and subsisted especially by cattle-raising in the plains around Mt. Kilimanjaro. In the early 17th century, facing Maasai competition for grazing land, they emigrated northeastward over a period of two or three centuries. By the late 1600s, they had settled in the higher, hilly parts of their present-day country, where many built terraced fields and irrigation ditches and became skilled farmers. But as populations grew, many Kamba moved into the drier steppelands to the east, cultivating crops, but especially emphasizing livestock-raising. Some of those who settled in eastern Kambaland began in the 1790s to make their living as merchants. They acquired goods from tribes of the interior, such as the Maasai, and exchanged them at the coast with Swahili merchants. Major items for exchange were ivory, slaves, food, poisoned arrows, and medicines, the last two of which were expertly manufactured by the Kamba themselves. From the 1790s through the 1840s, the Kamba monopolized trade in the area, traveling on weekly journeys across the desert to the coast in caravans of three to four hundred people. When competition from Swahili caravans cut the Kamba traders out of the carrying trade by the 1850s, the Kamba became ivory collectors and sold ivory and foodstuffs to rival caravans.

Disputes and complaints among the people were settled by older members of the group. The Kamba had no formal chiefs in precolonial times and were loosely organized into hundreds of local, independent village-sized communities. The political power was in the hands of older married men (*atumia*), who gathered in conferences to discuss issues and decide on actions.

British rule. The lack of a central government made resistance to the British difficult. The British took control of the region in the last two decades of the 19th century. The British divided Kambaland into several administrative districts. In World Wars I and II, the Kamba men frequently served in the British army. This experience gave some Kamba and other residents of Kenya an awareness of the outside world and contributed to a desire for freedom.

Independence. Freedom from colonial rule and independence for Kenya came in 1963. The government then began to persuade the Kamba to give loyalty to the country in which they form the fourth-largest ethnic group. To accomplish this, the government of Kenya encouraged the traditional clans (extended families of up to 50,000 members) to form legal associations with elected officers with whom the government could deal. Young Kamba men responded by becoming active in the political life of Kenya. Today government of the Kamba is conducted by the group's local councils, which regulate affairs according to tradition, and by representatives of Kenya. The representatives are chiefs and headmen appointed by the national government to work with the councils.

Culture Today

Organization. The social organization of the Kamba is based on family relationships. Several related families form a "gate" (*muvia*); several gates make up a clan (*mbae*). There are as many as 40 clans, each with its own totem, or symbol. Villages are made up of related families. Within a village, the Kamba live in homesteads that may consist of 12 or more houses for an extended family—a husband and one or more wives, along with other relatives.

Food, clothing, and shelter. The traditional home is built of mud over a branch frame, with a thatched roof that nearly reaches the ground. The house stands about four feet tall and has two fireplaces inside: one by the door and the other behind a partition that sets off an inner room for parents. Several such houses including a separate house for each of a man's wives, and grain stores belonging to these wives make up a family homestead. Homesteads of the husband's brothers lie nearby in the village. At one time, a wooden fence surrounded each homestead, but this practice is being largely abandoned. In the center of each homestead, there is a courtyard and a cattle shed. New styles have appeared in the recent past. Some have now discarded the more traditional structure for rectangular houses made of brick with grass or iron roofs.

Inside the house, there is a central fireplace with stones around it holding pots and pans and various tools such as barrels, knives, wooden spoons, grinding stones, and baskets. Beds are separated from this cooking area by thin walls of sticks and earth or by blankets.

Traditionally Kamba men dressed in a skirt of cloth or hide tied around the waist and reaching below the knees, and women wore hide or cloth wraparounds, tied at one shoulder. At the beginning of the 20th century, young women wore a leather apron studded with brass beads. Often they, as well as young men, added a type of corset made from strings of beads. Most of the men draped themselves in

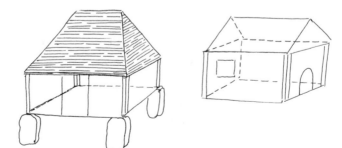

Kamba houses.

trade blankets. The Kamba wore all manner of jewelry, from copper ring necklaces to bracelets and finger rings. There is a custom among some Kamba of filing teeth; that is, chiseling a triangle shaped space between the two upper middle teeth. Today they wear dresses, shirts, and shorts in the styles of European people or blankets made from cloth and animal skins, although other European-style dress is rapidly pushing the traditional dress aside.

Along with trading, traditional activities are herding and hunting. Sheep, goats, and cattle are raised for food, trade, and as exchange for brides. Hunting, done with bow and arrows, provides hides for sale and for clothing. Farming has long been a significant part of the Kamba economy. Crops raised for food are bulrush millet, maize, peas, beans, potatoes, cassava, sorghum, and pumpkins; cash crops include cotton, coffee, and tobacco. Some customary dishes are porridge, pieces of meat, honey mixed with gruel, and cooked green bananas. However, soil erosion and overpopulation has driven many Kamba to the cities in search of employment, and diets are changing with this movement.

Family and social life. The Kamba recognize definite states of male and female life.

Kamba "Age Sets"

Boy	Girl
Young man/warrior	Single young woman
Middle-aged man	Married woman
Old man	Old woman
	Childless woman

These "age sets" are marked with appropriate rituals. According to tradition, formal entrance into adulthood occurs in these stages. In their teenage years, young Kamba undergo the most elaborate ritual. Boys and girls are divided into separate groups, each with 10 to 15 members. There is a "tutor" who teaches each group their duties in life. Among the old rituals are a hunting expedition and also a mock cattle raid for the boys. Someone shouts words such as "Beware, the Maasai with their cattle are coming to attack you." The boys then rush to surround the cattle and hurl dry cow dung at the enemy. Boys and girls might also be given a picture riddle to interpret as part of the ceremony.

Language. The Kamba vocabulary includes words to express past and present, but since no future cycle or event has yet occurred, there was no Kamba expression for distantly future events. This is changing as a result of the growing awareness of world events. A new language to express the future is growing today.

Religion. Religion among the Kamba is closely integrated into most aspects of life. Missionaries visited the Kamba as early as 1849, and today at least two-thirds of the people are Christian, often blending the newer religion with more ancient beliefs that include ancestor spirits, as well as one central creator god. Dance and song become part of the religious activity on special occasions such as for the driving away of the dangerous spirits (*aimu*). Some of these aimu are the departed dead of up to five generations who are thought to take an active interest in family affairs. Aimu who have been dead for longer periods become nameless and take less interest in current affairs. In Kamba religion, death is a passage from one life into another, where the dead person rejoins relatives and friends.

Both male and female medicine "men" still practice their trade. Belief in magic is common. Magic is thought to be the cause of most events that cause harm. Harmful magic is brought about, it is believed, by "witches," people with envious or hateful feelings toward others. Useful magic may come from Kamba medicine men or be the result of using amulets or charms.

Arts. More in keeping with their heritage, many work as wandering traders selling woodcarvings. Since World War II, the Kamba have become famous for these carvings. Standard versions of pieces in traditional style are now sold in the United States and Europe.

Other art forms among the Kamba are dancing, music, storytelling, riddles, and games. Their storytelling involves animals, proverbs, and word puzzles. Their musical instruments include drums, bells, rattles, and gourds. Kamba people are fond of singing. Folk songs and Christian songs are sung at home and in the fields. Poets recite in the form of songs, many of which they create as they sing them. The best of these songs are remembered as part of the musical heritage.

One story tells of a hare and an eagle who both wanted to marry a beautiful girl. Her father set the conditions. Whoever won the girl must start at daybreak for the coast and return before nightfall with sea salt. The tortoise persuaded the eagle to delay the event for several months, during which, with the help of other tortoises, it secured the salt and laid plans for the race. The tortoises lined up along the route and tricked the eagle. Meanwhile, the first tortoise delivered the salt and won the girl.

Sometimes, the songs offer advice. For example
I am not a fool;
I know writing is better than memory
But the book will not forget.
Our past is forgotten,
But the Europeans don't forget because of writing.
Let me ask the children to read day and night.
Let them learn in school;
We are trying to get wisdom for them.

(Kavyu 1977, pp. 28–29.)

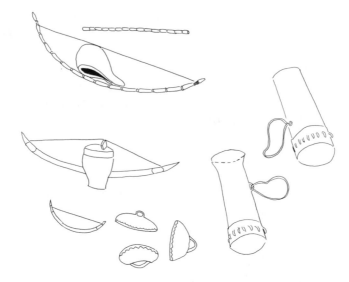

Counterclockwise—Kamba drums, bells worn on wrists and ankles, fiddles, playing baton.

Change. Today Kamba parents want their children to attend school. They also want to replace the traditional hoe with plows and mechanized farming. Meanwhile, trading posts and shopping centers have already become popular. The Kamba people are moving away from the uncertain farm life to seek employment in the cities.

For More Information

Hobley, C. W. *Ethnology of A-Kamba and Other East African Tribes.* London: Frank Cass and Company, Limited, 1971.

Kavyu, P. N. *An Introduction to Kamba Music.* Nairobi: East African Literature Bureau, 1977.

Mbiti, Reverend John S. *Akamba Stories.* Oxford: Clarendon Press, 1966.

KHOISAN

(koy' sawn)

Descendants of the ancient inhabitants of South Africa.

Population: 55,000 (1980 est.).
Location: South Africa, Namibia, and the Kalahari Desert of Botswana.
Language: Many different languages belonging to the Khoisan language family, having the unusual feature of click consonants.

Geographical Setting

The southwestern tip of Africa varies from windswept, green-belted coastlines to the dry climate and sparse vegetation of the Kalahari Desert. The Kalahari Desert is not actual desert, but steppe (dry, wooded grassland). South and west of the Kalahari the vegetation becomes scrub forests, and a drier and hotter true desert lines the coast of Namibia. The interior region is mostly a flat land, 1,000 to 2,000 feet above sea level, that has an average rainfall of less than 20 inches a year.

Historical Background

Migration. The Khoisan of today are the remnants of an ancient hunting and gathering people that once lived from Ethiopia south to the Cape of Good Hope. A trail of cave and rock paintings of these people can be found as far east as Ethiopia and south into what is now South Africa and Namibia. The cave and rock paintings tell of a people who survived by hunting and gathering, supplemented by raids on neighboring cattle herds, and entertained themselves and practiced healing with dances. These nomadic people were moving south, at about the same time the Bantu of West Africa were expanding eastward and southward. By the 15th century, the old Khoisan traditions survived only in the southwestern parts of Africa.

Toward the coast, the people who call themselves Khoi-khoin (men of men) had found land suitable for cattle grazing and had become herders. Those nearer the Kalahari Desert continued to hunt and gather the materials available in their surroundings for food. The two groups, coastal herders and desert hunters, became independent of one another. The life styles varied so greatly that some began to treat the San of the coast and the Khoi of the desert as separate peoples. Distinctions were further clouded by the unions of some of the Khoi people with Bantu neighbors. As the groups grew, the desert dwellers found themselves edging closer to their cattle-herding kinsmen and frequently supplemented their hunting and gathering by hiring themselves out as cattle and sheep tenders. Thus the Khoisan lived in small bands throughout the southern tip of Africa.

Europeans. In the 1400s, the Cape region was visited by Portuguese sailors who sought to trade with the Khoisan. The cattle-herding natives were willing to trade their cattle and fruit for scarce materials such as iron, copper, beads, and brandy. They traded for a while with the Portuguese. The desert people, however, had learned to survive by sharing. Their survival often depended on cooperative actions, so these "San" had little interest in private ownership. Those items needed for survival were the property of everyone. They had little in the way of goods to trade, and little need for trade. But in 1510, the Portuguese envoy to the Far East, Francisco de Almeida and 60 of his followers tried to cheat the Khoisan and were driven in disarray back to their ships. Discouraged by this final violence, the Portuguese abandoned their trade with the cattle herders.

A century passed before Dutch, English, and French sailors again appeared in the area. They established a trading post on the coast. The success of the trading center near what is now Cape Town encouraged the Dutch to settle near there starting in 1652. As the Europeans began farming and herding for themselves and their towns grew, first the Khoikhoi, and then the other Khoisan, began to lose their lands and their independence. People of mixed Khoisan-European ancestry began to grow in numbers, and some of these moved north to Namibia from the 1780s onward. Today about 20,000 descendants from intermarriages between the Khoisan and Europeans live in a separate community in Namibia.

Division of Khoisan. One-third of the Khoisan have clung to the hunting and gathering lifestyles in the desert. But most of the Khoisan today have intermarried with other native peoples or with Europeans. Those who have intermarried live as herders, herd tenders, farmers and fishers in Namibia and South Africa. The lifestyles of the hunters and gatherers has grown increasingly difficult to sustain as the population of other people has increased.

Culture Today

The desert dwellers. Land development and ownership has encroached on the ancient hunting and foraging territory of the Khoisan so that today few people live in the traditional ways. This minority resides in small units at watering holes and along the few rivers in the Kalahari Desert.

Food, clothing, and shelter. Around the Kalahari the people live in dome-shaped shelters made of woven grass mats that are easy to pick up and move. In warm, fair weather the mats dry, leaving holes between the leaves for air circulation. But in damp weather the leaves swell to seal the home against rain. From clusters of these dome-shaped houses, the Khoisan venture out to hunt such game as the antelope using arrows tipped with poison made from venomous snakes, beetle larvae, or plants.

Among the nomadic members of the Khoisan, the men hunt, while the women are responsible for packing and carrying the family's goods, picking fruit, tending children, and digging for edible roots to eat. They gather water from wherever it can be found and carry it in ostrich eggs.

The desert provides little water so babies are supplied with liquid by being nursed for long periods, sometimes as long as two or three years. Since having another baby during this nursing period would reduce the supply of the mother's milk, births in rapid succession are discouraged. This, along with the diminishing resources as the nomads are pushed deeper and deeper into the desert, has forced a decline in the traditional life patterns of the Khoisan.

Appearance. The Khoisan are brown-skinned people of generally small stature. They average less than five feet six inches in height, although some Khoisan are taller than six feet. Their heredity has left a tendency to accumulate fat in the thighs and buttocks. In the subtropical climate, there is little need for clothes. Traditional dress among the Khoisan is a loincloth for the men and an apron for the women, to which the women sometimes add a shoulder strap for carrying babies or household goods.

Family life. Families hunt nine or ten months of the year, then join other families at an annual gathering. Led by an elder, the larger group provides an opportunity for the Khoisan to celebrate rites of growing into adulthood. Marriages within a family are unpopular, so the annual gathering is also an important time for arranging marriages. In addition, it is the time of year for telling and retelling the ancient stories.

Arts. The Khoisan enjoy music played on their traditional instruments—a five-stringed guitarlike instrument known as the //gwashi, a mouth organ, and a thumb piano. The ancient art of painting has been lost, but at festivals women decorate their foreheads, cheeks, and chins with dots of red paint made from animal fat and a red mineral. Called *buchu,* this paint is carried constantly by the people along with sweet-smelling herbs in a small leather pouch.

Language and literature. The Khoisan speak a language that is dotted with clicking sounds. They have no written language, but a rich oral literature, with many stories based on natural elements. For example, the praying mantis is a common hero who is often accompanied by her daughter, the porcupine. Attempting to simulate their animal characters, storytellers have often added new sounds to the language. Khoisan mythology also includes many stories about the sun, the moon, and the stars. One story tells of the sun falling to earth every evening, changing into an elephant and being killed for food by a special people, the Knee Knee None.

The herders. South and west of the Kalahari, the Khoisan have become herders. Here the lifestyles vary according to the proximity of European neighbors. Away from the European settlements, the Khoisan herder lives in a settlement of family members. Those who have gathered some wealth (in numbers of cattle or sheep) may keep a few servants. In the past these servants mostly were drawn from war captives. They are not held as slaves, being free to leave if they wish. Servants are not considered goods to be sold.

Nearer the Europeans, Khoisan people have come to dress and live more like their neighbors. Today the Khoisan in the Cape region dress in Western clothes and work at many occupations from herding to fishing.

For More Information

"Bushmen of the Kalahari." *National Geographic.* May 1974, pp. 732–732B.

Schapera, I. *The Khoisan Peoples of South Africa.* London: Routledge and Kegan Paul, 1930.

Thomas, Elizabeth M. *Harmless People.* New York: Random House, 1989.

Vossen, Rainier and Klaus Keuthmann, editors. *Contemporary Studies On Koisan, Parts I and II.* Hamburg: Helmut Buske Verlag, 1986.

KIKUYU

(kee koo' yoo)

A people of Kenya who provided early leaders in the formation of the country, some of whom were involved in the Mau Mau revolt.

Population: 2,200,000 (1984 est.).
Location: The Kikuyu Highlands in Kenya northwest of Nairobi.
Languages: Kikuyu (a Bantu dialect), English.

Geographical Setting

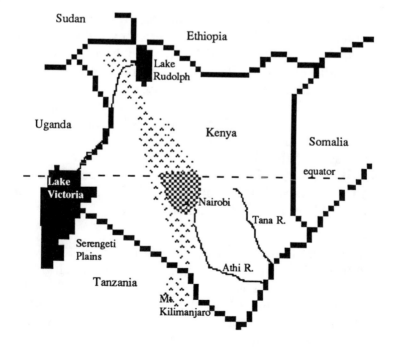

Extending from Lake Rudolf in the north to Lake Victoria in the south, the Great Rift Valley crosses through the center of Kenya. North of Nairobi and east of the Rift, the land is marked by high plateaus, hills, and the 17,000-foot peak of Mount Kenya. This region has been a land of much geological activity. Volcanos have spread ash over much of the plateau area, providing fertile soil for crops. Water, too, is abundant. Many streams cross through the land, and the average annual rainfall is 30-50 inches. In the past, extensive forest covered the region. Today maize, coffee, and tea are grown, mostly on small family-owned plots. To the west, the land drops abruptly to the floor of the Rift Valley. This region has for centuries been used for cattle grazing.

Historical Background

Origin. According to myth, the Kikuyu originated from a woman named Muumbi. The nine daughters of Muumbi and her husband Gikuyu evolved into the nine Kikuyu clans that bear their names.

Kikuyu historical traditions indicate that in the 16th century the clans began to expand from a home area in the northern edges of their present-day territory. As they spread south into the then forested country between modern Murang'a and Nairobi, they purchased land piece by piece from the Athi people. Here they followed the farming practices already established in their earlier home. Each purchased piece was a ridge of land, settled on by a pioneer and his family whose descendants then formed a *mbari*, or lineage, which became the local community unit. The pioneer and then his oldest living descendant became responsible for distributing land within the community as it grew. Distribution of land was to become the single most important historical issue for the Kikuyu.

The Kikuyu established relations with other peoples in the area, trading their crops with the Kamba for tobacco, gourds, and honey and with the Maasai for hides and sheepskins.

Troubles with the Maasai. During the 18th century, Kikuyuland was subjected to frequent raids by the Maasai, even though the two peoples traded goods and intermarried regularly. By the 1860s, however, Maasai power had begun to decline. The Kikuyu responded by expanding their agricultural territory, but disaster followed. The numbers and influence of the Kikuyu were diminished by an epidemic of smallpox in the 1860s and by a famine in 1884 during which the mortality rate of undernourished Kikuyu soared.

British rule. Meanwhile, the British claimed Kenya in the 1890s and, applying superior military power, began annexing Kikuyu territory, starting a colonial era that was to continue for more than 70 years. Weakened by disease and famine, the Kikuyu retreated as the British advanced. By 1948, 20,000 Europeans had settled in Kenya, some of them on land claimed by the Kikuyu. As a result, these people experienced a land shortage that prompted quarrels among themselves as well as opposition to the Europeans. During World War II, however, the Kikuyu fought in the British army on the side of the Allies. The years after the war saw unemployment, housing shortages, and rising African dissatisfaction with the government. In 1952, dissident Kikuyu formed themselves into armed bands and began a rebellion. Fighting between these "Mau Mau" units and British government forces ended in 1955, although small units of Mau Mau continued to raid towns and white farms after that date. At least 3,000 Kikuyu warriors were killed by the British government's army between 1952 and 1956. The rebellion was a contributing factor resulting in a British decision to place Kenya under self-rule, although the peaceful efforts of African national leaders were also important. A constitution was drawn up and a two-house parliament was initiated with African participation. One of the outspoken representatives for independence in this congress was Jomo Kenyatta, himself a Kikuyu.

Independence. In order to silence Kenyatta, charges of misconduct were brought in 1955, and he was imprisoned to be released later by court order. Kenya finally became independent in 1963. In the first presidential election, Jomo Kenyatta was chosen president of the new nation. Repossession of land by the Kikuyu became a major issue. It was finally addressed by the Million Acres Settlement Scheme, which enlarged the territory available to the Kikuyu. As part of this land reform the government began a program under which one-third of the land acquired by European farmers was purchased and redistributed to the Kikuyu.

Government. The Kikuyu today comprise 16 percent of Kenya's population and are the most powerful people in Kenya's single political party, the Kenya African National Union. As the most numerous, the best educated, and the most politically active people, except possibly for the Luo, they have been feared and challenged by others in the country. Furthermore, there has been internal conflict due to a new inequality between wealthy Kikuyu business leaders and less prosperous Kikuyu peasants. Its violent nature is reflected in the 1975 assassination of J. M. Kariuki, who opposed President Kenyatta and the wealthy Kikuyu elite.

Although much land reform has been accomplished, population growth has far outstripped the increase in available land. Landlessness remains one of the most serious issues in Kenya today.

Culture Today

Economy. Two-thirds of the people of Kenya earn a living through farming—either as independent small farmers or as farm workers on larger agricultural units. The soil in Kikuyu country is fertile, streams abound, and the air of the hills and forests is crisp and sweet. The traditional economy rests on crops raised on the fertile soil. Maize, beans, sweet potatoes, and other vegetables are grown for food; European potatoes, coffee, and bananas are among the cash crops, with tea becoming an important crop in the 1970s. Vegetables rather than animals are regarded as the primary source of food; cattle are kept for milk, and goats, sheep, and chickens for meat.

Landownership. Because of patrilineal landownership and division of land through many intermarriages, the average farmer in the 1960s might have possessed many acres, but his land was scattered over a wide area and fragmented into small plots. Consequently, a Kikuyu farmer was likely to spend more time traveling to his farm areas than working the land. In the late 1960s, a consolidation program was initiated that divided the land among the current owners but concentrated the acreage so that one man's farm was in a single unit. The idea was to provide each farmer with a single plot of at least ten acres on which to raise food for his family, and enough surplus to be sold that the farmer would have an annual income potential of about 70 dollars. Drought, changes in governmental policy, and changes in leadership have resulted in a slower land reform than was anticipated. Today a typical farmer owns only an acre or two of land, which is used to produce a small offering of cash as well as food crops. Many Kikuyu have responded to the land shortage by migrating to farms of Europeans and to towns, where they are employed as laborers. On large commercially owned farms, Kikuyu are granted a plot of land on which to build homes. The houses are often built of cedar posts covered with branches and thatch. In the towns, the Kikuyu have displayed the aptitude for business developed through their precolonial history of bartering with other Africans and the early Europeans for items such as beads, copper wire, and salt. Kikuyu businessmen have become involved in light industry and import businesses as well as in small trade.

Food, clothing, and shelter. As in the past, homesteads of the Kikuyu are grouped to form local communities along a ridge or part of a ridge. This neighborhood of family homesteads ranges in size from several dozen to several hundred related people. In addition, groups of unrelated tenants or clients of the community may attach themselves to it. The typical Kikuyu house was once a round structure with wood walls and a grass-thatched roof. Today it is usually a rectangular earthen-walled building with a thatch or corrugated iron roof. An extended family typically occupies several houses for related family units. If a husband has more than one wife, each lives in her own separate dwelling. Together the houses of the extended family form a homestead that is customarily surrounded by a hedge or wooden fence. More prosperous families own items such as bicycles and automobiles.

Maize is the staple crop of the Kikuyu and most Kenyans, although formerly the staple grain was sorghum. It is supplemented with sweet potatoes, beans, potatoes, and bananas. Like their neighbors, the Kikuyu do not use their cattle for meat. Rather, goats, chickens, and sheep are raised for meat and for hides used in clothing. Cattle are valued for their milk, which forms an important part of the Kikuyu diet.

Few Kikuyu today, even in very rural areas, can be found wearing the traditional-style dress of goatskin clothing. In the past both men and women wore metal ornaments decorating the neck, arms, legs, and ears. The hair was shaped into various styles with string, feathers, and mud. For dress-up occasions, ornate headdresses of feathers, cloth, beads, and leather were worn. Heads were shaved for certain rituals. This colorful dress has rapidly disappeared as the Kikuyu seek employment in the larger towns and become accustomed to western-style clothing. Kikuyu living in Nairobi, for example, wear shirts, pants, dresses, and suits similar to those worn by people in the large cities of Europe. However, on national holidays, some people dress up in traditional attire for dances and other celebrations.

Religion and education. Missionaries attempted to convert the Kikuyu with varying degrees of success. Many Kikuyu rejected Christianity in favor of their traditional religion, which calls for worship of one creator-god, Ngai, and the spirits of ancestors. Others sought to combine their older customs with Christianity.

In 1924, rather than send their children to Christian mission schools, the Kikuyu set up independent schools. Since then they have placed a continuing emphasis on education, becoming doctors, lawyers, and teachers and devising sophisticated games for amusement.

Individuals are divided into age grades, which are successive stages of life from birth through adulthood, with six age grades for males and eight age grades for females. The politics of the people before British rule was based on their age organization. Males were initiated into age sets at adolescence. The members of an age set moved together through the successive stages or age grades of life. Grouped together, a number of successive age sets formed a generation set. According to tradition, the male members of an age set ruled for about 30 years, after which a formal ceremony marked the passage of power to the next generation.

Literature. Much of the folk literature of the Kikuyu tells in story and song about their encounters with neighboring peoples. One internationally recognized book *My People of the Kikuyu* tells of the wars between the Kikuyu and Maasai in the 17th and 18th centuries. This book was written by Jomo Kenyatta, the early nationalist leader who became the first president of the republic of Kenya.

Another well-known nonfiction work, *Longing for Darkness*, written by Kamante, tells of Kikuyu labor on a white woman's farm. The Kikuyu experiences are also portrayed in the recent motion picture *Out of Africa*.

For More Information

Balandier, Georges, and Jacques Maquet. *Dictionary of Black African Civilization*. New York: Leon Amiel, 1974.

Bethwell A. *Historical Dictionary of Kenya*. Metuchen, New Jersey: Scarecrow, 1981.

Kamante. *Longing for Darkness: Kamante's Tales from Out of Africa*. New York: Harcourt Brace Jovanovich, 1975.

Stager, Curt. "Africa's Great Rift." *National Geographic*, May 1990, pp. 2–41.

KONGO
(kon'go)

Called BaKongo by the people themselves; a Bantu-speaking
tribal group concentrated around the
lower Zaire (formerly Congo) River.

Population: 6,000,000 (1987 est.).
Location: Angola, the Republic of Zaire, and the
Republic of the Congo.
Languages: KiKongo, French.

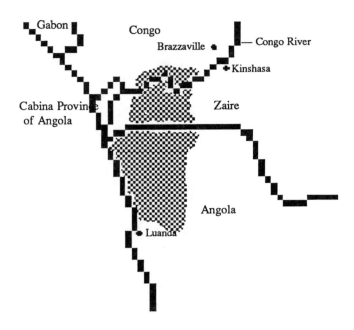

Geographical Setting

The Congo River, called the Zaire River in the country of Zaire, the seventh longest in the world and second only to the Amazon River in the volume of water it delivers to the sea, cuts a 2,600-mile arc from the heart of Africa to the Atlantic Ocean. For the last 200 miles of this journey, the river passes through the Kongo people's homeland, an area near the Atlantic coast divided among western Zaire, northwestern Angola, and southwestern Congo. In much of its passage through the region, the river drops through gorges and ravines that churn the river into spectacular whirlpools and high waves.

The northern section of the Kongo lands, in the Angolan sector north of the Congo mouth called Cabinda, has patches of rain forest; to the south of the river lie the savannas of far northern Angola. There the coastal lowlands quickly give way to grasslands with wooded areas. The terrain's elevation increases as one moves east. Rolling central hills lead up to rugged mountain forests, carved into north-south ranges by a series of river valleys. In the lower coastal and central regions, the equatorial climate offers even temperatures and generous rainfall; patterns of agriculture depend mostly on the uneven quality of the soil, which is rich in river valleys and thin and sandy elsewhere.

Historical Background

Kongo kingdom. The Kongo people arose from among the various Bantu farming groups that had settled the woodlands and forest of the lower Congo River region during the last millennium B.C. Several small kingdoms had formed by about 1300 A.D. near the lower Zaire River. According to Kongo legend, Ntinu Lukeni, the son of a king from one such kingdom, led a group south across the river, conquering the people there and expanding his realm, probably in the late 14th century. The Kingdom of Kongo, centered around its capital Mbanza Kongo (later Sao Salvador) in modern Angola, grew into one of the most powerful African states. Two factors seem to have contributed to this success: the absorption (rather than mere domination) of conquered groups, to form one people; and the control of trade between the coast and the interior on the one hand and the southern savanna and northern rain forests on the other.

Power resided in the king, who controlled both military and religious affairs. His court included pages, slaves, and a harem of wives.

The king appointed provincial governors, who in turn appointed district officials. Through these officers he administered legal and judicial institutions and collected taxes from the villages, in the form of labor, goods (raffia palm cloth, hides, etc.), or currency. The currency consisted of shells found only in the king's fishery so, unlike other African kings, he alone controlled it.

The Portuguese and Christianity. Thus, when their ships arrived in 1483, Portuguese explorers encountered a centralized state. The Portuguese soon entered into friendly relations with the king, and during the 1480s several trips were made and diplomatic exchanges developed between Portugal and the Kingdom of Kongo. Catholic missionaries traveled to the Kongo court, and Kongo nobles visited Portugal. Trade began in the 1490s, the Kongo king Nzinga Nkuwu exchanging ivory and copper products for missionaries and military assistance. The king and several Kongo nobles converted to Christianity in 1491, in an apparent attempt to strengthen the power of the court in the face of threats by rebellious local nobility. Nzinga Nkuwu renounced Christianity a few years later, but his successor, baptized Afonso by the Portuguese, remained Christian, as did later kings.

The reign of Afonso (1506 to about 1545) established a pattern that continued until the 1670s and would influence life for 200 years beyond. The Kongo kings used Christianity to reinforce their power, at the same time relying on Portuguese military assistance to maintain the frontiers of Kongo territory. In the 16th century, the kingdom controlled a region half the size of England. In exchange, they supplied Portugal with ivory, copper, and valuable slaves for her trade, first with the Gold Coast in West Africa and later with the Mediterranean area and the Americas. No fixed procedure for succession existed, so a new king often spent years strengthening his position. Also, this increased his reliance on guns and the proceeds of trade with Portuguese to subdue threats to his kingship. Kings grew increasingly dependent on the slave trade as well, entrusting their own security to personal slaves and earning revenues from sales of captives. Meanwhile, the Portuguese needed a strong central authority like the king to act as their middleman.

Decentralization and conflict. During the 1600s, however, changing circumstances ended the kings' strong position in relation to local powers. The kings lost control of the slave trade as other dealers, responding to increasing demand for slaves, were sometimes forced to take captives even from within Kongo people. Other factors contributed, such as new trade routes that bypassed Mbanza Kongo. While the local chiefs grew wealthier, the Portuguese had already shifted the focus of their colonial efforts to the areas just south of Kongo, operating from a base in Luanda and spreading their commercial influence inland from the 1570s onward. Their efforts led to the detaching of the tributary kingdom of Ngola (from which modern Angola takes its name) from the overrule of Kongo, to the rise of a number of other African kingdoms that benefited politically from the new trade focus, and to increasing conflict between Portugal and Kongo. The Portuguese governor of Angola mounted an unsuccessful attack in 1622, followed by a war that ended in the defeat of the Kongo army at the Battle of Mbwila in 1665. Mbanza Kongo was sacked and destroyed. Though reoccupied (and renamed Sao Salvador), the one-time capital eventually declined to no more than a very large village in the 1700s.

Slave dealers. Over the next 200 years, Kongo broke up into small, independent chiefdoms. Though his office still held prestige, the king lost power to the local chiefs. Because much of the chiefs' wealth came from trade in slaves, the period from about 1700 to 1885 has been called "the era of the slave trade" (MacGaffey 1986, p.200). New ports, built and controlled mostly by Europeans, sprang up to accommodate the burgeoning traffic. The Africans who supplied captives for the trade formed a nobility, while the wars for captives kept the kingdom in constant turmoil.

Colonialism and independence. The slave trade began declining in the mid-1800s, by which time it had been outlawed by all European countries. There was illegal traffic, but the outcome of the American Civil War in 1865 ended the bulk of this illegal traffic. While the area of the Kongo had been among those most ravaged by the 400-year slave trade, unlike other areas it had not yet been claimed as a colony by any European power. However, Belgium's King Leopold, who had so far been unsuccessful in partaking in the quest for riches from Africa, began to colonize the region. In 1885, under the General Act of Berlin, European powers agreed to recognize his authority over the Congo (Zaire) River basin, calling the territory the Congo Free State. This later became a protectorate of Belgium known as the Belgian Congo. To the north (in the current Republic of the Congo), there was French colonial rule. French cocoa and coffee plantation owners used the Kongo as laborers and porters on caravan routes. Farther south, in Angola, Portuguese rule continued, demanding forced labor and land from the Kongo.

An unsuccessful rebellion against the Portuguese in Angola (1913–1914) drove many Kongo to Belgian territory. Here an epidemic of sleeping sickness had weakened the local chiefdoms, killing many in the previous generation. The people spent a few generations gathering their strength, then gained independence later in the century. African nationalism grew after World War II, the Kongo becoming active in wars against colonial rule from 1961 to 1974. The Belgian Congo achieved independence in 1964, becoming the Republic of Zaire in 1971. Three years later in 1974, Angola gained its independence and became a Marxist state.

Culture Today

Scholars have studied the Kongo people more intensively than many other African cultures. In the process, they have uncovered some preconceptions of their own. The missionaries, administrators, and others who wrote about the people imposed their own ideas (of, for example, "customs" and "tribes") on a lifestyle and continent that were less clearly defined than they imaged. Thus, they divided the inhabitants of the kingdom into separate groups (BaKongo, BaSundi, BaBwende, and so on), which failed to reflect the unity of the region's people and their society.

Food, clothing, and shelter. The Kongo have been mainly an agricultural people. Two modern staples, maize and manioc, were introduced from America through the trade with Europeans. These crops replaced the earlier millets and sorghums, which Kongo nobles continued to favor as better-tasting well into the 1700s. The people eat the manioc leaves boiled; they dry and pound the roots into flour, then boil it to make a gruel called *nfundi*. Another popular dish, *moambe*, contains meat or fish mixed with palm nut extract and is highly spiced with the hot pepper *pili-pili*. The people also grow rice, peanuts, beans, bananas, peas, tomatoes, eggplant, and peppers, and they collect wild fruits, herbs, roots, honey, and nuts. Palm groves supply oil and ingredients for palm wine. The Kongo raise few cattle. Men hunt for meat, and everyone fishes.

Kongo cloth was a valuable export in the days of the old kingdom. Weavers used raffia palm fibers to produce highly-prized textiles, comparable in quality to silk, on vertical looms. The nobles owned the finest materials; villagers wore a plain cloth called a *tanga* wrapped around the waist, with women sometimes wrapping a second piece around their upper bodies. In villages today, men tend to wear European-style clothing, while women have adopted brightly patterned cotton cloth, either wrapped around the body or tailored as a blouse or dress.

Kongo villages, usually housing about 60–80 families, fall into an orderly grid pattern. Today the rectangular houses are built of sun- or kiln-baked brick, with roofs of straw and palm thatch or, more commonly, corrugated tin. In the past, wood poles and stakes supported a covering of tightly woven straw or palm leaves. The houses of the common people were small, low rectangular structures with a single, narrow opening for light and access. Like their clothes, the nobles' houses, made of boards or other material, set them apart, making visible their greater wealth and prestige.

Village, town, and city. Recently, many Kongo have found employment in two large cities, Kinshasa (formerly called Leopoldville, capital of the Belgian Congo) and Brazzaville (capital of the former French Congo). Located on opposite sides of the Zaire River, these cities have prospered as origins of land routes that bypass the unnavigable parts of the waterway. Kongo men have also taken part in the national building of road and rail routes.

However, most Kongo still live in villages. Organized around clans and landownership, the social structure in these villages remains close to that of earlier times. The clans are matrilineal (a child joins the clan of its mother). Also, they divide into "houses" (*nzo*), which control land and smaller lineages (*futa*) that own portable property. A village shelters members of a central clan in several houses and lineages, along with incomers (relatives by marriage).

In the kingdom, the fundamental cultural division was between the *mabata*, or small villages, and the *mbanza*, or towns. People who inhabited the mabata formed what amounts to almost a separate ethnic group from those of the mbanza. Towns dominated villages. Both produced a surplus of food and other products. Although towns produced more, they could demand part of village surpluses, or an equivalent in money. Nobles lived in the towns, and the high number of their slaves accounted for production there. The villages, by contrast, produced food and goods themselves. Called the *nkuluntu*, a village headman would deal with a town's nobles, collecting and passing on the surplus they demanded.

Family life. Households are based on the division of labor between men and women. The women perform most farming tasks, working the fields and preparing the family's food. Men help with heavy field work, but their main responsibility is to build and maintain the houses, to hunt, and to collect and produce various tree products, such as palm wine. Traditionally boys and girls were separated from the ages of about six, with each receiving training from the parent of the same sex. Since households relied on cooperation between husband and wife, a trial marriage period allowed couples to see if they were compatible. It also provided time to work out the sum (bride-wealth) that the groom and his family would pay to that of the bride.

Religion. The Kongo people's rapid conversion to Christianity masked the survival of pre-Christian beliefs. Often, "believers" simply translated Christian ideas into terms used in Kongo religion. Kongo and Christian priests were both *nganga*, for example, and the Christians used the word *loka* (curse, bewitch) to mean excommunicate. Many practices continued, including rainmaking, puberty rites for girls, initiation for boys, and the purchase of charms to secure personal gain. In particular, ancestor veneration remains central to Kongo religion. The dead (whose world is believed to mirror that of the living) are thought to have a strong interest in the affairs of the living. Since the Kongo aim to cultivate their ancestors' goodwill, their homes contain ancestor shrines where the family offers prayers.

Health. Both national governments and various religious missions provide health care. They have controlled, but not eliminated, tropical illnesses such as sleeping sickness, malaria, intestinal parasites, tuberculosis, and bilharziasis. Alongside formal health centers, the people observe traditional religious and magical practices. The Kongo distinguish between illness caused by nature and by humans. If humans are the cause, a patient will consult an herbalist *nganga*, whose treatment rests on the idea that the body is a container for the soul. The remedy is protection through charms or blessings to strengthen either body or soul, or through attacks on the witch accused of causing the illness.

Arts and crafts. Religious ideas help define the most important craftsman of the Kongo, the blacksmith, whose skills rank him with chiefs and priests. As the producer of weapons used in hunting and war, he is believed to possess the power to deflect evil threats. Aside from iron, Kongo artisans also work in lead and copper, producing rings and anklets that display social status. Weaving is no longer practiced as widely as in the past, but household items such as woven mats provide both bedding and decoration. Sculpture has been a major art form. In the past, statuettes called *mintadi* (guardians) were carved of soft stone to represent a dead or absent chief. These statuettes include symbolic features—headdresses, knives, and necklaces—to represent the ruler's rank and power. Other statuettes, to promote fertility, portray a mother holding a child to her chest. Still others have been made by Kongo religious sculptors, who work in metal or wood and, for example, grace a cross with designs that link the African and Christian traditions.

For More Information

Hilton, Anne. *The Kingdom of Kongo.* Oxford: Oxford University Press, 1985.

Kaplan, Irving. *Zaire: A Country Study.* Washington D.C.: American University, 1979.

MacGaffey, Wyatt. *Religion and Society in Central Africa: The Bakongo of Lower Zaire.* Chicago: University of Chicago Press, 1986.

KRU
(crew)

Fishers of west Africa now living mostly in Liberia.

Population: 85,000 (1980 est.).
Location: Liberia and the Ivory Coast.
Languages: Kru, English.

Geographical Setting

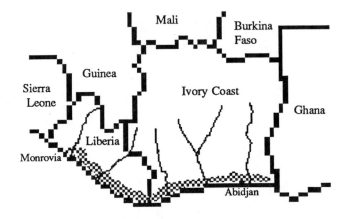

Liberia, the home of the Kru, lies on the west coast of Africa between Sierra Leone, Guinea, and the Ivory Coast. In the southwest, the Atlantic Ocean coastal area is a maze of inlets, lagoons, and marshes, which lie in a sandy, lowland that stretches inland for 50 miles. Beyond the marshes and sand the land rises until it eventually reaches an altitude of 2,000 feet. The higher land is covered with tropical forest that is dense at lower altitudes but thins farther inland and at higher altitudes. Six major streams cross the region. Most of them are not navigable, since sand bars close them at their mouths. The weathering of the land has resulted in some small natural harbors, to which the early 19th-century settlers from America added a harbor carved out of the sand and rock, Monrovia.

The Kru live along the coast, where they have learned to build large canoes and navigate the difficult waters along the coast.

Historical Background

Origin. According to Kru stories, their people migrated to the coast of West Africa in the 16th century and became sailors and fishermen. There they settled in isolated townships that were nestled among the palm trees and sat behind sandy beaches dotted with rocks. By the 18th century, the generally short and stocky Kru seamen were a common sight aboard European sailing ships that trafficked in slaves.

The Kru and slavery. According to oral tradition, the Kru escaped slavery themselves by making a bargain with the Europeans: slaves could be transported across Kru territory to the coast without interference if the Kru themselves would not be taken into captivity. Therefore, the Kru wore a tattoo—a vertical line down the center of the forehead so that the slave trader might identify and bypass them. Soon the Kru were involved in securing slaves for the Europeans. Slavery was already common among African peoples; some societies even had individuals who willingly became slaves (see MALINKE). Now a larger market demanded slaves from everywhere on the continent for shipment abroad. The Kru received slaves from inland societies and transferred them to the Europeans, then became sailors on the slave ships.

Gaining a reputation as skillful and dependable workers on board and around ships, the Kru acted as stevedores, sailors, cooks, and interpreters. The banning of the slave trade by the British in the late 19th century prompted a change in the merchandise handled by the

Kru. Still, they maintained their maritime role, now loading cargo such as palm oil, peppers, and ivory on ships and becoming skillful pilots of British mailboats that traveled along their coast.

Independence. In the 1820s–1840s a group called the American National Colonization Society offered freed slaves of the United States the opportunity to return to Africa and choose what is now Liberia as the place to settle. About 6,000 black Americans chose to move to the new settlement. These people became leaders in establishing a new country. In 1847, Liberia became independent and the American-Liberians assumed a dominant role in the government of the country. A worldwide depression reduced the amount of trade with the Europeans, and hardship fell upon all the black populations of Liberia. Only the Germans displayed interest in trade with Liberia. Their interest waned, however, with the onset of World War I, and Liberians were left to fend for themselves.

Meanwhile, the country was experiencing internal conflict between the American-Liberians and native African peoples, who felt they lacked political representation. In 1915 the Kru revolted, largely because of a tax imposed by the government. They viewed the tax as the last in a series of injustices at the hands of merchants who had neglected to pay wages as promised and who had continually raised prices of the goods they sold to native peoples. The revolt continued until 1916, by which time government forces had succeeded in burning several Kru towns to the ground. The 1930s saw a second Kru uprising followed by voluntary resettlement of many Kru outside traditional territory. For a time, Kru workers were employed in the coastal stores and warehouses of the Germans, the British, the Dutch, and the Swiss. However, after World War II European trade on the Kru-dominated south coast of Liberia was largely abandoned in favor of trade at Monrovia, the major port on the north coast of Liberia. In 1944 Liberian President William Tubman adopted a unification policy for the peoples of Liberia. Subsequently, various peoples of Liberia gained political representation and became involved in the country's governmental structure.

Still the economy of Liberia is not strong. For 60 years, one or two companies such as the Firestone Company, which exploited forest rubber sources, supported the government. But the holdings of these companies have been sold to the Liberian government or to private interests. The economy, mostly based on agriculture and fishing, has grown, but not as fast as government expenditures. Liberia became poorer as the result of a change of government to military rule, which was forced on the people in 1980. Government violence followed, though there was a return to civilian rule in the elections of the mid-1980s. Since then, Liberia has been struggling to gain economic health.

Culture Today

Assimilation. In recent years, the government of Liberia has encouraged country unity, and has successfully merged the various peoples of Liberia into one with a national identity. Although many cling to some aspects of their traditional life, people in the cities have been exposed to education and to Western clothing and lifestyles.

Village life. Traditional Kru towns and villages are isolated from one another by unbridged rivers. About 20 subgroups of the Kru people are scattered through these towns and villages, the subgroups speaking different dialects and following different lifestyles. Located in the older sections of towns are one-story rectangular-shaped houses with mud or plaited-mat walls and thatched or corrugated-iron roofs. Concrete block two-story houses appear in the newer part of a town.

In search of education and employment many of the young people have migrated to larger towns such as Monrovia, where a sizeable Kru community has developed, and where the Kru have adopted lifestyles like their neighbors.

Food and clothing. Many Kru continue to earn their livelihood in the traditional manner, becoming fishermen who both consume and trade their catch. Capable sailors and shipbuilders, those who still fish build large canoe-shaped boats. They fish using a variety of methods, including the old ways of catching fish in basket fish traps.

Kru women raise crops—rice, cassava, peanuts, and vegetables— then trade their crops in towns along the coast. Those who have migrated to the larger towns are wage earners on ships, in shipyards, and in occupations such as teaching, medicine, the civil service, and politics. Some find employment on the local rubber plantations just north of Monrovia.

Liberia is a tropical country, warm most of the time. The Kru people, like other Liberians, adapt to this weather by wearing loose-fitting cotton dresses or cotton shirts and shorts. In business, the men may be seen in shirts and ties.

Organization. The traditional Kru town is politically organized around clans. Clan heads are included in the council of the town chief. In the past, the townships operated independently, but today they are part of the country wide governmental system with a Kru governor and councilors who represent the various subtribes of Kru. Social organization is maintained even in the larger towns, where the Kru have formed separate communities and established the Kru Corporation, an organization that addresses the people's needs as they arise, handling disputes and welfare activities.

Religion. Most of the people along the Liberian coast profess Christianity, while one group, the Mandingo, are Muslims (see MALINKE). Kru identity is maintained by their practice of traditional religion, which involves belief in a supreme deity, various nature deities, and ancestor worship. In addition, the Kru have a rich oral literature that includes folktales, proverbs, and humorous stories. As with other societies, the Kru folklore suggests the values they place on elements of their culture. For example, Liberian proverbs stress the importance of children ("There is no wealth where there are not children"), and of seizing opportunities ("One doesn't throw a stick after the snake has gone"). These aspects of their culture help perpetuate their distinctiveness as a people and their pride in their maritime heritage.

For More Information

Drachler, Jacob, editor. *African Heritage.* New York: Crowell-Collier Press, 1963.

Dunn, D. Elwood and Svend E. Holsoe. *Historical Dictionary of Liberia.* Metuchen, New Jersey: Scarecrow, 1985.

Osae, T. S., S. N. Nwabara, and A. T. O. Odunsi. *A Short History of West Africa—A. D. 1000 to the Present.* New York: Hill and Wang, 1973.

MAASAI

(mah' sigh)

Pastoral people of Kenya known for their skill as warriors.

Population: 100,000 (1989 est.).
Location: Kenya and Tanzania, an area known as Maasailand.
Language: Maasai, a Nilotic (from the Nile region) language.

Geographical Setting

Eastern Africa is quite varied topographically. It is an area of scattered rain forests, grassy highland plains, and savannas. The area that is

home to the Maasai features several natural wonders, including Mount Kilimanjaro, the Ngorongoro Crater, and Olduvai Gorge, where some of the earliest human remains have been found. Except for the high mountain peaks, the elevation here ranges from 3,000 to 10,000 feet above sea level. In the highlands, rainfall is sufficient to support agriculture with fertile soil. It is the place where most of the regional population lives. In the lower, semiarid plains there is not enough rainfall for crops, but the grasses provide food for grazing cattle. While some Maasai move from place to place depending on the season, others live permanently in homesteads.

Historical Background

Origin. Ancestors of the Maasai have been traced back to the ancient people of southern Sudan near the Nile River. The more recent origins of the Maasai were in far northern Kenya, where their ancestors took in a migrant people from southern Ethiopia. They spread southward to Tanzania. Maasai folk stories explain that during this migration the Maasai encountered the first *Great Loibon*, or seer, a warrior-prophet with supernatural powers. He predicted that they would meet with their messiah, *Kidong'oi*, in the Loibon hills of their clansmen.

According to their mythology, when the pastoral Maasai met *Kidong'oi* he brought cattle from the sky to the earth and gave them to the Maasai. This event is the basis of many of their beliefs, including the one that all cattle is rightfully theirs, justifying the many cattle-raids they made and creating the need for fearless warriors.

Maasai and the trade routes. The Maasai achieved a reputation as skillful spear warriors and were feared by all of their neighbors who owned cattle. At the height of their power in the mid-19th Century, Maasai controlled approximately ten million acres in Eastern Africa. Winding through some of this land were routes that were very valuable to traders and explorers. Using their strategic position, the Maasai exacted generous amounts of cloth, tobacco, and beads from European explorers and trading caravans that tried to pass through their country. Their strength and independence also kept them from enslavement by the Arabs and religious conversion by the Christian missionaries. They had a strong distaste for change and a belief of supremacy over other peoples that kept modern-world intruders and their customs at bay for much longer than other ethnic groups in Africa.

Colonialism. With the approach of the 20th century, the British and Germans had gained control over a great deal of Eastern Africa. Germany claimed an area from the Indian Ocean to the east of the lakes along the Great Rift of Africa. Britain controlled Kenya, Zanzibar, and Uganda. The British held Kenya as a protectorate until Kenya became a colony in 1920. During their rule they enacted laws to stop cattle-raiding, recruited Maasai warriors for military service to oppose other Africans, and tried to persuade the Maasai to put their children into British and missionary schools. As a result of such rapid and profound changes, a strong anticolonial sentiment built up among the Maasai. Cattle-raiding declined, but military recruitment among these peoples was low, as was Maasai attendance in schools. The Maasai refused to participate any more than absolutely necessary because they feared the more involved they became with "civiliza-

Maasai on the road, trading hides with Arab merchants. *Photo by Eliot Elisofon. Courtesy of National Museum of African Art.*

tion," the more they would lose their traditional ways and be exploited by the state. A popular theory is that Maasai wealth and power (in terms of land and cattle) insulated them from the demands of the government, thus making full cooperation easier to avoid. Their world view, value system, and distaste for anything non-Maasai must have also played a large part in this.

In any case, the power of the British began to fade with the rise of the African Independence movement in the 1950s and 1960s. At that time, the East African Community (EAC) was established to unite those who experienced British colonialism and to attempt to reduce differences among the various societies. In 1977, though, the EAC fell apart, and the border between Kenya and Tanzania, which composed part of Maasailand, was closed. The Maasai, however, paid no attention to political differences, only to kinship bonds, and they continued to live and move according to custom. They slowly began to partake of the modern world in small ways, and eventually complied with the government and allowed their children to attend school.

Culture Today

Appearance and clothing. The Maasai are a relatively tall people with skin color varying from black to copper-tone.

Their most common garment is a cotton togalike material wrapped around the body. Red ocher and animal fat are often smeared over their skin to insulate them from heat and cold. Young men wear their hair in elaborate braid and bead mixtures and wear copper wire jewelry.

Food and shelter. The traditional pastoral Maasai live sparsely without the use of modern conveniences. They rely almost completely on the products of their cattle for subsistence. From the herds they get meat, milk, cheese, blood (which they use as an emergency protein supplement and in some rituals), dung for fuel and plaster, cow hides for bedding and clothing, urine for cleansing, and butterfat for baby food and other rituals. It is not surprising that because they rely so heavily on these animals, deep bonds exist between the people and their cattle. The Maasai know each cow's voice, color, and name. In recent years, and to a great extent in the highlands where White influence was strongest, they consume products that don't come from their herds, such as sugar, tea, soft drinks, and beer.

Traditional shelter is a house made from branches and a plaster of earth and cow dung. Each house is built according to a specific hierarchical structure of the settlement. The framework of a hut is built by the men, and the women fill in the plaster. After it is properly blessed, it contains a family hearth, beds and benches for one family of children, mother and father, with elders and warriors living separately. Usually, cattle are housed in a kraal, or fenced area, nearby.

Family life. Clusters of families (between one and thirteen) occupy the relatively small settlement referred to as a *boma*. It is surrounded by a fence made of branches that has an entrance for each direction. Inside, the houses line the fence. The cattle are kept in a corral in the center of the settlement.

It is customary for Maasai men to practice polygyny, that is to have more than one wife. Each wife usually lives with her children in her own house and the husband splits his time equally between each wife. The wives often develop very close relationships and support each other in daily duties, which include child care, cooking, and feeding and milking the herds. The children usually take the herds out for the day to graze, sometimes supervised by their fathers. The Maasai complete all of their chores between the hours of sunrise and sunset.

Social life. Loosely assembled groups based on kinship and tribe form the Maasai settlements, but age-sets organize people across settlements and throughout society. For men especially, life is a progression of strictly set stages accompanied by specific duties and privileges. Elaborate rituals and celebrations revolve around reaching certain life-stages, the most important being the achievement of warrior status. This stage brings respect and the responsibility for defense of the community and herd to the adolescent male. While the qualities of bravery, loyalty, and independence are still highly valued, they are put to less practice than in earlier days when cattle-raiding and defense were so important.

Celebrations and rituals. The Maasai celebrate a great many events. Some of the rituals are as painful as they are important; for instance, the ceremonial cutting of the flesh (circumcision) experienced by both adolescent females and males. Others are more lighthearted, for example, the naming ceremony for babies. Once every 15 years, the largest celebration of all occurs. It is the promotion of junior warriors to senior warriors. Called *E Unoto*, this event is attended by thousands of people and takes place over four days. At the end of it, the new generation of warriors, or *murrani*, gets their heads shaved by their mothers, a privilege considered to be the peak of a moral life.

The arts. Dancing is practiced ritually, sometimes causing the dancers to become so mesmerized they go into ecstatic trances, and have to be helped by their friends. Long and descriptive songs praising their warriors' prowess or the beauty of the women usually accompany these dances. They are sung by everyone, with one or two exceptional storytellers singing solos. The Maasai are extremely adept at storytelling, and their tradition of oral literature stretches back for generations. Story topics often involve ancient warrior heroes who displayed the discipline and endurance of pain that the Maasai admire so much. One story relates how a warrior killed a lion and lioness singlehandedly on a steamy hot day in the Great Rift Valley.

Recent change. In the late 20th century, the unique Maasai identity has been increasingly difficult to maintain. The military purpose that originally guided the group now has no place, since cattle-raiding was outlawed and there are no longer any enemies to fight. Today their struggle is against the land-hungry members of "civilization" and the continual drought that has vastly depleted their cattle stock. Increased population pressure and limited resources have weakened and strained the traditional pastoral system, forcing the herds into smaller space, which is rapidly deteriorating the environment. Since the Maasai have less space to wander in, there is less time for the land to renew itself after being used.

Despite continuing failure by their government to integrate them into the modern society, gradual integration and modernization is occurring. One successful example of the slow change is the school system. Maasai children dressed in the traditional *lubegas* (robelike long dresses) sit side by side with Maasai children in Western dress as they are all taught arithmetic using cattle instead of numbers.

For More Information

Beckwith, C. and Tepilit Ole Saitoti. *Maasai*. New York: Abrams, 1980.

Ole, Saibull Solomon and Rachel Carr. *Herd and Spear: The Maasai of East Africa.* London: Collins and Harvill Press, 1981.

Ole Saitoti, Tepilit. *The Worlds of a Maasai Warrior: An Autobiography.* New York: Random House, 1986.

MALINKE
(mah lean' key)

Residents of West Africa whose ancestors once were part of the powerful kingdom of Mali.

Population: 700,000 (1983 est.).
Location: Mali, Senegal, and Guinea.
Languages: Malinke (Mandingo), a Mande dialect; French.

Geographical Setting

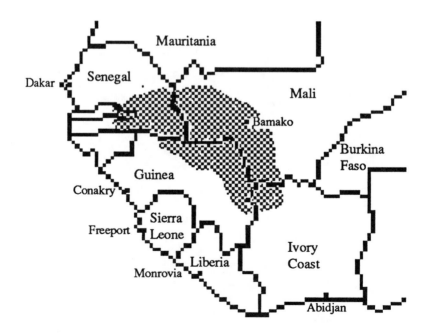

The Malinke, or Mandingo, people are spread through nine countries of West Africa, but the most concentrated populations are along the rivers of Mali, Senegal, and Guinea. The most world-famous Malinke town, Juffure (made famous by Alex Haley's story of the leading family of the village, Kinte), lies along the Gambia River a hundred miles from the coast. Most of the country of the Malinke is bush land, covered by scrub forests and thorny bush. Along the rivers, this changes to tropical forest with many kinds of wildlife supported by the dense plant life. In the rainy season from June to October, the forest becomes a mass of palms and other trees and shrubs. Average rainfall is more than 40 inches.

Historical Background

In the 10th century, the Malinke occupied a small state near the Niger River in modern Mali. They are part of a people spread throughout West Africa, all speaking dialects of the same language, Manding. Over the centuries the people grew into separate chiefdoms whose wealth lay in gold and iron deposits found in the territory.

Islam. In the 11th century, the *mansa* (king) of the chiefdom Kangaba was converted to Islam and embarked on a pilgrimage to Mecca during which he established new trading relations with outside peoples. In the 11th and 12th centuries, succeeding kings made other religious pilgrimages, conquering more and more territory, and solidifying trade relations so that the Malinke mines became the main source of gold for caravans from Morocco. Although the local people prospered, they were under the control of the foreign King Sumanguru. The Malinke leader Sundyata waged a successful war for the independence of his people in the 13th century. Known as the lion king, Sundyata united the Malinke chiefdoms to fight Sumanguru. Spreading his people's way of life, their language, and their goods through a vast region, Sundyata turned a small chiefdom into the largest and one of the most powerful of all African empires, the Empire of Mali.

This empire flourished in the 14th century under the leadership of Mansa Gongo-Musa. Sundyata had established the empire, and Mansa Gongo-Musa shaped it into an Islamic stronghold, bringing it widespread fame. In 1324, Mansa Gongo-Musa made the most renowned pilgrimage of all. The camels in his caravan carried 12 tons of gold, and the monarch traveled with 60,000 companions who helped him conquer the territories of Timbuktu and Gao along the way, bringing the empire to the pinnacle of power. During the 15th century, the empire controlled much of the area that today makes up Senegal and Mali.

The king was the supreme power; those who came before him were required to kneel and place dust or ashes on their heads. No one was permitted to wear sandals in his presence or to sneeze before him. This monarch lived in near seclusion, which preserved the idea that he was of divine origin. No one was permitted to see him eating. To begin each harvest, the king hoed the first ground to bless the crop. He kept many slaves, but gave them responsible tasks involving the administration of the empire. His bards (poets called *jeli*), however, played even more significant roles as his advisers and spokesmen and as arbiters settling disputes between clans and peoples. Each princely family, in fact, had a jeli to preserve tradition. In a society without books, the jeli was an important personage who recorded events, customs, and government principles in story and song.

Following King Mansa Gongo-Musa's death, a series of weaker rulers encouraged unrest among the Malinke. In Timbuktu, Malinke rule was replaced by the government of the Tuareg people from 1433 to 1439. Later, a war that continued from 1501 to 1513 resulted in conquest of the many Malinke areas by the Songhay people. Throughout these years the authority of Mali kings persisted in a few areas. But by the time the Moroccans overran the area in 1591, the Mali empire had ceased to exist. A cluster of small but strong Malinke kingdoms succeeded Mali between 1500 and 1900, most notably Kuarta and Segu in central Mali, but also a number of smaller states in the southern and western parts of the old empire's domain.

With colonial conquest Malinke became subjects of French West Africa. This region attained independence in 1960, when Mali was proclaimed a self-governing republic. In Mali, Malinke people share the government with other groups such as the Bambara, Fulani (see FULANI), and Tuareg. More than 200,000 Malinke, known there as Mandingos, live in Senegal, where the Wolof (see WOLOF) and Fulani-Tukulor are dominant groups. About a half million Malinke live in eastern Guinea, sharing territory with the Fulani and other peoples. Thus the Malinke remain divided among the countries arbitrarily defined during the European scramble for African land in the late 1800s. By that time, Malinke settlements were spread among those of other peoples along the Gambia River, usually in swampy areas suitable for growing rice.

Change. Today the people living in the region of the Malinke have the possibility of more unity through a Senegal-Gambia agreement to share some elements of government and to work together on some of the region's most critical issues. However, living under various rules and in close contact with other cultures, the Malinke/Mandingo have become a diverse group, with cultural aspects adopted from their rulers and their neighbors.

Culture Today

Organization. The Malinke live in independent states ruled by kings who claim hereditary rights. Kangaba, for example, is now ruled by descendants of the ancient empire in a line that has held power for 13 centuries and is one of the oldest dynasties in the world. Priest chiefs lead districts within each village. While Islam is the predominant religion, the Malinke combine its tenets with more traditional beliefs and practices. Both a Malinke bard and a Muslim priest take part in ceremonies such as the naming of babies.

Malinke of the same ancestry generally enjoy warm and friendly relations with one another, recognizing their kinship as a social bond. In addition to sharing a common name, they observe the same prohibitions. A taboo on eating a certain animal is respected by all members of the group.

Related families live in a group of mud-walled homes. However, the Malinke family is more than the husband-wife and children unit that is so familiar to Europeans. Rather, the head of a Malinke family is the eldest male, perhaps a grandfather. This family head makes many of the decisions for members of the family. For example, the family head must be consulted before a marriage is arranged. In some regions, the bride is married to the family head and then given to the groom.

Malinke are grouped in classes based on ancestry. The highest class is royalty, followed by nobles, commoners, and artisans or craftspeople. A particular craft is associated with related families whose ancestors practiced the craft.

Economy. Like other Manding-speaking people, the Malinke are farmers and fishers. Living on relatively fertile ground, they raise sorghum and other millet grains, along with rice, for food and for trade with the Fulani or Berber peoples of the north. In exchange, the Malinke acquire dairy products from their neighbors. Those near the rivers or the many mangrove swamps carve boats from logs and make fiber nets with which to fish. Shaped like large canoes, these pirogues are often highly decorated by their owners. A particular group, the Dyula—a people of Malinke origin—have become noted traders. They sell dyed cloth and decorative leatherwork, material used to clothe the Malinke. Leather work is produced by Malinke craftspeople, who are descendants of an occupational caste of workers in ancient Mali society. In addition to the leather workers, there are ironsmiths, goldsmiths, and silversmiths.

Clothing and shelter. The Malinke house is usually round and thatched with a cone-shaped roof; newer homes are square, made of earthen blocks in some areas and of woven grasses in others. Today some homes are roofed with corrugated iron. Combinations of old and new include earthen walls and thatched roofs. Large grain-storing baskets, wooden mortars and pestles, and large bowls, cooking pots, and pans are normal equipment for the Malinke house in the town or village. Those Malinke in the larger cities live in more European-style housing.

Customary clothing for women includes batik and tie-dyed dresses or skirts and blouses, while men wear loose-fitting gowns, shorts, or Western-style trousers. On special occasions, women wear head ties and fine gold jewelry, which is kept for sale should circumstances demand it.

Malinke men form hunter's associations, each with its distinctive shirt. A typical hunters shirt is a long-sleeved cotton shirt made from seven strips of cotton. The sleeves are open on the underside as is the side shirt seam, which is the length of an arm from elbow to armpit. Each shirt has loops sewn at the chest for hanging short-bladed knives or hunters' whistles.

Religion. The Muslim religion is predominant throughout the area in which the Malinke live. However, the Malinke add ancient, animistic rituals (rituals involving spirits of natural objects) to their religious activities. The Malinke bard works with the Muslim religious leader, for example, in rituals concerned with birth, naming babies, circumcision, the harvest, and encouraging the fertility of the soil. In addition, Malinke religion demands great respect, if not reverence, for ancestor spirits along with the Muslim God.

Arts. Craftspeople among the Malinke are traditionally of lower status. However, a special regard is given to the bards in keeping with their favored position just as in the ancient kingdoms. Today, jeli (in French, griots) recount their folk history in song while they play Malinke instruments such as the 21-string harp-lute and the xylophone. Once, large Malinke drums, made from tree trunks, carried messages throughout the land. Today these drums are used in many rituals, while much of the music is listened to on portable radios. The continuing popularity of their music is reflected in the fact that several Malinke themes have been adopted by other African nations for use in their national anthems. Despite such fame, some have referred to dance rather than music as the "national art." Dance is part of most rituals and is a chief entertainment in the villages.

For More Information

Imperato, Pascal James. *Historical Dictionary of Mali.* Metuchen, New Jersey: Scarecrow, 1977.

Quinn, Charlotte A. *Mandingo Kingdoms of the Senegambia.* Evanston, Illinois: Northwestern University Press, 1972.

Volmer, Jurgen. *Black Genesis: African Roots.* New York: St. Martin's Press, 1980.

MBUTI

(mm boo' tee)

The longest-term residents of the equatorial rain forests of
central Africa; a people who are generally short in
stature (mostly under five feet).

Population: 50,000 (1984 est.).
Location: The Ituri Forest of northeast Zaire.
Languages: Various dialects of MButi, a Bantu language, and Efe,
a Central Sudanic language; also other languages of the Congo Basin.

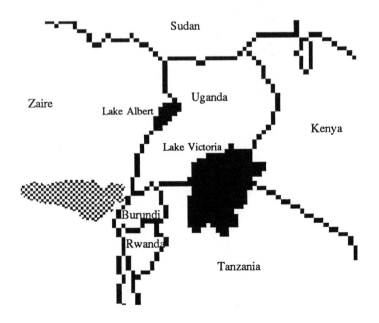

Geographical Setting

Zaire is a large expanse of flat basin country, straddling the equator and dominated by the Zaire (Congo) River that flows north across the equator from the southeast and empties into the Atlantic Ocean in the southwest. The basin is rimmed by high mountains in the east and plateaus in the north and south. The northeastern border, an area of the Great Rift Valley, is dotted with lakes. More than half of the basin is covered by dense tropical rain forests. Here, the soil and air are perpetually humid as the treetops meet to form an overhead canopy through which little direct sunlight penetrates.

Historical Background

Origin. The existence of a short, brown-skinned people in Africa was recorded as early as 2250 B.C. by Egyptians. Later descriptions appear in the writings of ancient Greek scholars. It is believed that these "pygmy" people roamed the forests in nomadic hunting bands, each speaking a separate language. They lived this way for thousands of years before the Bantu began, about 3000-2000 B.C., to move in from Nigeria and the Cameroon highlands. Central Sudanic people also moved into the eastern pygmy country by perhaps 3,000 years ago.

The precise time and length of these migrations has never been established, but oral history of the people of the forests tells of the impact of the immigrants on the hunters of the Ituri Forest. It was the penetration of large numbers of Bantu agriculturists, who possessed metal working and tool making skills, that had the most profound influence on the pygmy nomads.

Associations with Bantu. The Bantu, as well as other immigrants to the region, felled the giant trees to build villages and gardens in the forest. They were at odds with the forest because it hindered farming. The forest dwellers welcomed the farmers and were happy to trade with them. They learned the language of the Bantu villagers and traded meat and honey for farm products. The villagers, however, considered the small people an inferior race and treated them as subordinates. At the same time, they relied on the pygmies' abilities to master the forest.

In time, each Bantu village came to have a retinue of pygmy vassals who were paid farm products and manufactured goods to act as scouts and guides. As more groups of Bantu immigrants arrived and battles began between groups, the services of pygmy forest guides became invaluable. The pygmies were also used as spies and sometimes as soldiers. The associations between village masters and pygmy serfs developed into an interdependence.

By the mid-1600s, the long-established associations had given way to a beginning pygmy acculturation. Each of the three Ituri Forest groups, who prefer to be collectively identified as MButi, gave up its own language and learned to communicate in a tongue understandable by their villagers. Occasional marriages of pygmies and villagers occurred but were not favored by the MButi. Long-held customs included the custom of sister-exchange between MButi hunting bands. Intermarriage, when it occurred between male villagers and female pygmies, was most often accompanied by a bride price paid by the villagers. Children of these unions remained in the village with the father's family, even though the mother frequently elected to return to the forest.

The MButi became adept at leading a dual life, that of the dependent village serf and of the independent forest hunter. To maintain good standing in the village, they embraced such Bantu customs as initiation rites for the youth, weddings, and funeral ceremonies. But the MButi scorned the villagers' reverence for spirits of the dead and their practice of witchcraft and sorcery.

The MButi did not believe in the power of spirits of dead ancestors to do good or evil. The MButi god was the god of the forest; the forest spirit represented both a father and a mother who nurtured and educated its forest children. The bounties of the forest provided for all their needs—safety and security from others, clean drinking water, plenty of game, fish, wild fruits, and honey, as well as unlimited shelter. They protected the forest by playing on the fears of the villagers. Wild tales of evil ghosts and demonic spirits that haunted the forest kept the villagers away.

Non-Africans and the MButi. Early non-African explorers passed through MButi territory, as did Arab traders in search of gold and ivory. Unable to understand the MButi language, these visitors observed the small people at a distance and created stories about pygmies who could kill elephants and collect ivory. Owing to their short stature and mysterious way of life, the Ituri pygmies became the subjects of study.

In 1699, an English physician named Edward Tyson wrote a book in which he tried to demonstrate that the pygmies were apes or monkeys and not human. This view was challenged by studies in the early 19th century. German scientist Georg Schweinfurth wrote about his first meeting with a pygmy man named Adimokoo. The Italian explorer Miani captured two pygmies and sent them to Italy to be studied scientifically.

While some stories described the capture of pygmy slaves, the MButi never engaged in the European slave trade. But about the 1870s, Swahili and Arab traders began to penetrate to the Ituri Forest region from the east and employed Africans to attack villages and capture slaves, sometimes destroying entire groups.

In the late 1800s, the explorers' stories of riches in ivory and gold reached Europe and stirred the Belgian monarch King Leopold II's interest in the region. The then-Congo River basin was claimed and a Belgian colony developed. In 1887, the traveler Morton Stanley, acting for the Belgian government, investigated the Ituri Forest still unknown to Europeans. When Stanley's party became lost and suffered from near-starvation, they were rescued by the MButi. Stanley credited the MButi with teaching his men how to survive in the wild by eating wild foods.

In the 20th century, the MButi again became the subject of scholarly studies. In 1953, the American anthropologist Patrick Putnam and his wife Anne went to live among the MButi. Putnam built a field camp and hospital on the edge of the forest and a village gradually grew around it. Camp Putnam came to be used as a trading post where the MButi exchanged meat for farm foods with the villagers. The MButi still cling to their ancient lifestyle, trading with villagers and returning to the forest to hunt and forage.

Culture Today

Social structure. The MButi are democratic and cooperative nomadic bands, each operating within clearly defined territories. Each band consists of several families who live in temporary camp settlements in the forest. All tool making efforts and most of the effort of the settlement is devoted to hunting and picking food. The band moves from camp to camp as the hunt proceeds.

The MButi have no social hierarchy, chieftains, or class structure. Each band forms a small egalitarian society where decisions are reached by mutual consent. Respected elders whose good judgement is esteemed by the band are often consulted on matters of major importance such as when and where to set up camp, when to start the hunt, and when to move on to the village settlement.

Family life. The MButi are monogamous and live in nuclear family units. Related families usually live side by side in separate huts, but intermarriage between related kin is forbidden. Sister-exchange, a practice between hunting bands of trading sisters in marriage, is common. The wife joins her husband's band and her children automatically gain membership in the band. Marriage is made by a combination of mutual consent and prearrangement. However, if either partner is dissatisfied or unhappy, that partner can dissolve the union.

Men and women are considered equal and all work and division of food is shared. The men hunt and make tools. The women erect the huts, forage for fruit and other edible vegetation, and do the cooking. In some bands the women assist in the hunting and fishing, and the men gather termites and honey, and butcher and smoke the meat to preserve it for trade in the village. Both parents play an active role in the care and development of the children.

The MButi family does not keep or raise animals, except for the Basenji dog, which does not bark and is useful in hunting. The different MButi groups have different hunting habits. Some are archers who use arrows dipped in poison. Others are net hunters, using spears to kill the animals that are driven into nets by the shouting and bush-beating of the wives. The MButi are known for their production of poison and for their skill in preparing effective medicines from the plants of the forest. They claim to be able to cure such afflictions as headaches, dysentery, fever, cuts, wounds, stomachaches, and tooth problems using these medicines.

Families live in a main settlement built on the outskirts of the village with which the group is associated. The symbiotic relationship with the village has made the MButi dependent on farm foods, metal tools, cookware, and modern utensils. MButi build their settlements in shade on the edge of the forest near the village. The villagers grow manioc, yams, plantain, corn, peanuts, rice, and beans. For these products, the MButi trade meat and forest products.

Food, clothing, and shelter. Even though hunting is a full-time job, meat makes up only a small part of the MButi diet. The hunters search for wild boar, forest buffalo, antelope, monkey, elephant, and rhinoceros. These they butcher and distribute equally among the members of the band. Pygmies either cook the meat or preserve it by drying and smoking it to use in trade. Their own diets consist mainly of forest roots and tubers, fruits, nuts, and fungi. For protein, the MButi forage for snails, fish, termites, and snakes. Seasonal honey gathering expeditions are of particular importance because honey is considered a delicacy. It is gathered by men using a special axe to climb the tree to the hive. The bees are smoked out using embers wrapped in tree leaves, leaving the hive to be raided for honey by hand.

In the forest, clothing is minimal. Both men and women are bare to the waists. Men wear a length of bark cloth that is pulled between the legs and tucked in at the waist. Women wrap bark cloth around their hips or wear a thin loincloth strip. Children remain naked until they reach puberty. Older clan members sometimes wear a cape made from animal skins around their shoulders. Men, women, and children wear bark or fiber bracelets to which are attached wood, teeth, nuts, and feathers. Dyes of white, red, and black are obtained from clay and bark and applied to faces and bodies. MButi are also fond of rubbing their skins with plant oils.

Mbuti people of the Ituri Forest. *Photo by Eliot Elisofon. Courtesy of National Museum of African Art.*

MButi settlements consist of clusters of dome-shapped huts form-ing a circle with the entrances facing the center of the camp complex. A separate hut houses each family and is built cooperatively by the women. The huts are constructed by twisting and bending saplings to make frames, then covering the frame with large tree leaves ar-ranged in an overlapping pattern. Furniture and possessions of each family are kept to a bare minimum because the camp moves as soon as game and vegetation are exhausted. Logs are used for seating. Food is eaten immediately, so there is no need for storage. However the women weave baskets from fibers to carry fruits and vegetables they have gathered and to transport cooking.

The intimate nature of MButi life is such that there is no "private business." All disagreements and disputes, even marital squabbles, involve the entire band until they are resolved to everyone's satis-faction.

Religion. The god of the MButi is *molimo*, spirit of the forest. Molimo is believed to be a benevolent spirit. In special festivals, dancers move through a fire lit for the molimo. In other celebrations, trumpets are blown in the hopes of awakening the forest spirit. The MButi believe in the goodness of the forest, and that evil events occur because the forest spirit is sleeping. Their religion leads them to treat criminal offenses in four different ways. First, they look for the supernatural to punish through disease or accident. Or they might expect the mol-imo to damage the perpetrators' home. For offenses such as theft, the band may join in thrashing the culprit. Lesser offenses can be settled by fights between the people involved.

Arts. Storytelling, singing, and dancing are important methods of expression for the MButi. Music is performed on a notched flute or with a stringed instrument, the *lukembi,* which sounds something like a zither. Singing is often associated with religion. The men per-form a religious song to molimo, in which the voice reverberates throughout the forest. Women belong to their own religious associ-ation, the *elima*, in which songs are important expressions. Dances are often performed by the men.

Artistic expression is also found in graphic body painting and in the beating of resonant sticks, hand clapping, and foot stomping to accompany dances. The MButi have no known written literature, painting, or craftwork. Legends about pygmy life and the world of nature make up the general folklore. Many of the pygmy stories are created spontaneously during storytelling sessions.

For More Information

Duffy, Kevin. *Children of the Forest.* New York: Dodd, Mead and Company, 1984.

Putnam, Anne Eisner. "Mbuti: My Life with Africa's Little People," *National Geographic*, February 1960, pp. 278–302.

Turnbull, Colin M. *The Forest People.* New York: Simon and Schuster, 1968.

Vlahos, Olivia. *African Beginnings.* New York: Viking Press, 1967.

NDEBELE
(nn day bay' lay)

An offshoot of the Zulu people who broke with them and
migrated to Zimbabwe in the mid-19th century;
called AmaNdebele by the people themselves.

Population: 2,500,000 (1986 est.).
Location: Zimbabwe (formerly Rhodesia), the Republic of
South Africa.
Languages: Ndebele, English.

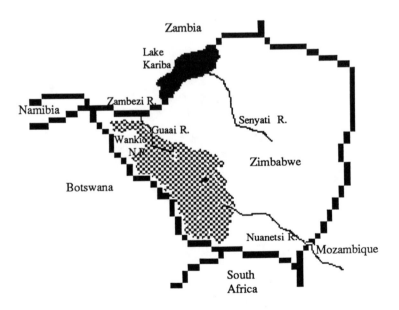

Geographical Setting

Zimbabwe's Ndebele live mostly in the southwestern part of the country, particularly in and around the major city Bulawayo. Numbering about 1.5 million, they occupy much of the western portion of the High Veld (or "plain"), which stretches in a broad band through Zimbabwe. Approximately 400 miles wide and in most places 4,000–5,000 feet high, this grassland runs northwest to southwest. It separates Zimbabwe's major river basins, the Limpopo to the south and the Zambezi to the north. The terrain varies from flat land to rolling hills to rougher, rocky hills, and includes grassland, woods, and fields. On either side lie narrower bands of Middle Veld (3,000–4,000 feet), parts of which the Ndebele also inhabit.

Historical Background

The word *ndebele* is a Sotho (the language of the country of Lesotho) term meaning "strangers." It has been applied to several different groups. The society of Ndebele described below live in Zimbabwe. These are distinct people with their own language, history, and artistic traditions.

Breakaway kingdom. The Ndebele (the *N* should be sounded, not said) are an offshoot of the Zulu people (see ZULU). Founded around 1821, the offshoot group traces its origin to the military commander Chief Mzilikazi. A one-time subordinate chief of the powerful Zulu monarch, King Shaka, Mzilikazi broke with the king and led about 300 of his men north, moving through several temporary settlements, and arriving in the area around present-day Pretoria (in South Africa) in the early 1830s. Beginning in the late 1830s, conflicts with pursuing Zulus, with mixed-race cattle-farmers called Griqua, and with Afrikaners convinced Mzilikazi to move once more, this time across the Limpopo River. Here Mzilikazi and his followers established themselves in a kingdom that became known to Europeans as Matabeleland (the Sotho pronunciation of Ndebele is "Matabele"). Gradually they came to dominate the area's previous inhabitants, the Shona. Unable to resist the warlike newcomers, these agricultural people paid tribute to and served the Ndebele by cultivating their fields and manufacturing their tools and weapons.

Under Mzilikazi, the Ndebele maintained their control of the Shona by centering their society around the army. Each *induna*, or chief, commanded a regiment, with the regiments grouped into four divisions, each of these controlled by a senior induna. The various headquarters for the regiments later evolved into towns, a town taking its name from the regiment that first settled there. In the beginning Mzilikazi appointed the senior chiefs; later the positions became hereditary. After Mzilikazi's death in 1868, the senior chiefs moved to increase their own power at the expense of the central leader's. Mzilikazi's son Lobengula eventually became king, but his monarchy proved to be more limited than his father's.

Growing European presence. External events also weakened the Ndebele monarch. From about 1850, small numbers of European missionaries had trekked through the region. Some, such as John Smith Moffat, a Scot, started mission schools and settled in the area. Others, like Moffat's brother-in-law David Livingstone, traveled and wrote books about their discoveries. Then, beginning in the 1860s and 1870s, European hunters arrived in the region in search of the valuable substance of elephants' tusks—ivory. Both the missionaries and hunters had limited contact with the Africans. Few of the Ndebele converted to Christianity, and the elephant population was soon reduced to a paltry few. Yet the returning Europeans brought reports of supposedly huge gold deposits in Ndebele territory. Agents of British financier and developer Cecil Rhodes were able to gain from the Ndebele king Lobengula concessions to exploit areas to the north of the kingdom and not actually ruled by Lobengula. Interpreting the concessions in ways not agreed to by the king and bringing superior weapons, whites began arriving in the 1890s. This ended the isolation upon which the Ndebele had relied.

British company rule. At first, the Ndebele resisted the white invasion. Some of their subject Shona defected from the Ndebele cause. In 1893, Ndebele raids against Shona defectors killed servants of the whites and disrupted white mining operations. Also, there was an inflammatory incident. Some Ndebele delegates to Cecil Rhodes' operation, the British South African Company (BSAC), were shot by mistake. The British sent three armed expeditions against the Ndebele. In two "battles," British machine guns routed the enemy warriors, killing several hundred Ndebele. Lobengula fled his kingdom at Bulawayo, escaping to the north with his remaining supporters. Soon after he died, the British declared an end to the Ndebele kingdom. They uprooted the Ndebele and the subject Shona from their homes and confined them to Native Reserves. A period of hardship followed. Both the Ndebele and the Shona suffered forced labor, heavy taxes, land seizures, and confiscation of their cattle under BSAC rule. In 1896, the two groups rebelled. They surrounded Bulawayo and killed white settlers, staging a bloody revolt.

Colonial years. During most of the colonial period, the Ndebele and other Africans had no part in the political development of Rhodesia (the country was named after Cecil Rhodes). They had lost over half their land and cattle, their villages had been dismantled, and they were taxed even though they lived on the least productive areas of a land they had once controlled. The Africans of Rhodesia became a subject people. Under threat of criminal penalties, they had to register themselves and obtain passes to enter white urban areas. Many Africans supported themselves by meeting the needs of the white communities; unable by law to live in those communities, they occupied impoverished townships outside them. The Land Apportionment Act of 1930 slightly increased the area of the black reserves, and offered some land for sale to Africans. As with the reserves, however, the land Africans could purchase was usually drier and tended to be isolated from the many routes of transport. Meanwhile, white-controlled businesses relied on unskilled black labor but blocked blacks' access to higher education and professional achievement in the segregated society.

Independence and majority rule. In 1953, under British rule, the colonial territories of Southern and Northern Rhodesia joined with Nyasaland (now called Malawi) to form the short-lived Central African Federation. White Rhodesian independence movements led in 1965 to the country's unilateral (that is, unrecognized by the British) separation from Britain, with the continuation of white minority rule. The world community, attempting to force the whites to adopt majority rule, refused to trade with or send diplomats to Rhodesia.

In the 1970s black African guerrilla movements, led by Joshua Nkomo, an Ndebele, and Robert Mugabe, a Shona, mounted an increasingly fierce campaign to win political rights. In 1979, British intervention, spurred by guerrilla victories, brought about the capitulation of Rhodesia's white government. Prime Minister Ian Smith forfeited his rule. Elections held in April 1980 made the one-time guerrilla leader Robert Mugabe prime minister of the new black-ruled Republic of Zimbabwe. Friction followed. In 1982, controversy over land, along with severe drought, led to a revolt by some citizens in Matabeleland. Prime Minister Mugabe used military force to suppress the revolt, the friction leading to a considerable loss of Ndebele lives.

While the majority of Ndebele have continued to live in Zimbabwe, they are a minority in the country. The Shona make up 80 percent of its population, the Ndebele 14 percent, and other black Africans 5 percent. Today whites, who are mostly of British origin, form only about 1 percent.

Culture Today

Social order. Aside from increasing the number of those considering themselves Ndebele, the conquest and absorption of other black African peoples created a hierarchy of social classes. The *Zanzi*, members of the traditional upper class, are descendants of the original band of Zulu warrior families who accompanied Mzilikazi in his breakaway kingdom (see above). The *Enhla*, middle class members, descend from conquered groups of Sotho and Tswana origin (see TSWANA). In the lowest class, the *Holi*, are the descendants of others whom the Ndebele absorbed after they reached Matabeleland.

Family life. In Ndebele marriage, rules have long been stricter for women than for men. Though fewer do so today than in the past, a man may marry more than one wife. A woman, however, may have only one husband. She risks divorce and the loss of her children unless she remains faithful. If the husband is unfaithful, he typically risks only the anger of his wife's family. Ndebele society distributes child-raising duties beyond the family, providing a safety net for the child whose immediate kin are unable to care for it. Every child has two mothers: a natural or "little" mother and a "big" mother, who stands ready to replace her should the need arise. This duo-mother custom seems particularly far-sighted in light of present-day work patterns, which take some parents far from the family home.

Economy. The Ndebele of Zimbabwe work in a nation with a highly diverse economy. Mining of the country's rich mineral deposits remains a leading industry. Aside from gold, the people mine asbestos, nickle, and gemstones such as the prized emerald of Sandawana Valley. Other industries include the manufacture of iron, steel, paint, paper, electrical appliances, and textiles. Most agricultural production remains in the hands of white farmers, many of whom employ black workers. White-owned tobacco farms, which supply about 40 percent of Zimbabwe's agricultural income, are the largest employers of blacks. While most black families farm for themselves, they generally produce only enough to feed their own family. Women, in fact, perform much of the farm work.

Food, clothing, and shelter. In the past, the Ndebele both hunted and raised livestock, in addition to cultivating grains and other crops. The hunters worked in groups, driving their quarry towards men armed with clubs (the *knobkerrie*) or spears (the *assegai*). Confinement to the reserves effectively ended hunting practices. Today the people raise cattle and cultivate grains such as maize, which since colonial times has replaced sorghum and bulrush millet as a staple.

The Ndebele transform their maize into a thick porridge called *isitshwala*. They eat the porridge with vegetables or soured milk drained of whey. Also they grind the maize into cornmeal, then combine it with meat to make a stewlike soup. Other customary foods are raw eggs, roasted turtle, and uncooked meats sun dried or flavored with herbs. In past times, hunting supplied meat. Now the Ndebele obtain it from their cattle, no longer limiting themselves to using these animals only for dairy products or trading.

Change has also affected Ndebele clothing and housing. At one time, Ndebele women were famous for their *iindzila*, stacks of copper and brass rings worn on their ankles, arms, and necks, often in combination with a blanket wrapped tightly over the shoulders. The fashion has changed. Currently many women find the rings cumbersome for everyday wear, and therefore discard them for all but ceremonial occasions. Also fewer women possess traditional iindzila. The weight of these old pieces caused discomfort and could deform a woman's bones. Contemporary women prefer to clip on a plastic choker with lightweight imitations of the customary rings. At the same time European-style dresses and men's clothing are replacing the traditional leather cloaks and robes. Houses are undergoing a similar transformation. The customary thatched roof is disappearing.

Education. In the past, Ndebele men and women taught children skills for daily survival: how to hunt, wage war, or raise food. What little schooling the people had was supplied by white European missionaries or farm schools run by white employers. Today the people actively seek schooling. Over 90 percent of Ndebele primary school age children in Zimbabwe attended classes in 1985. The country, however, suffers from a dearth of teachers and facilities. By the late 1980s, facilities existed for only about 65 percent of the school-age population. Classes are taught to students in English; Shona and Ndebele are offered as language courses. In higher education, the University of Zimbabwe at Harare serves approximately 5,000 students. A major problem has been a teacher shortage, since so few black adults received training when whites governed the country. Therefore, the people instituted teacher training programs. Another high priority is adult education. Through recent literacy efforts, over 500,000 adult Zimbabweans have learned to read.

Religion and tradition. In the past, the Ndebele have resisted efforts at conversion by Christian missionaries. Taking more than one wife, for example, conflicted with Christian values. Perhaps 20 percent of the present-day Ndebele identify themselves as Christians. In these cases, though, Christian beliefs do not preclude traditional ones. The group's original religion, based on a high god called Nkulunkulu, remains widespread among the Ndebele. In this religion, a single priestess (*igoso*) intervenes between the people and their ancestors. These ancestors, in turn, intercede with the god Nkulunkulu on the people's behalf.

Other traditional practices continue to thrive, especially in Zimbabwe. Government health programs bring updated clinics to Zimbabwe villages. While these clinics are frequented by the people, so are traditional healers. These healers rely on age-old practices (involving detailed knowledge of herbal remedies), which have withstood the contact of Europeans and their ways. Such coexistence represents a blending of old and new that Zimbabwe seems to have achieved more successfully than many other African nations.

For More Information

Oliver, Roland and Michael Crowder, editors. *The Cambridge Encyclopedia of Africa.* London: The Cambridge University Press, 1981.

Saunders, Christopher. *Historical Dictionary of South Africa.* Metuchen, New Jersey: Scarecrow, 1981.

TSWANA
(tswa'neh)

A subgroup of the Sotho peoples of southern Africa; called
BaTswana by the people themselves.

Population: Approximately 3,000,000 (1980s est.).
Location: Botswana, South Africa.
Languages: Setswana, English.

Geographical Setting

Although only about one-third of the Tswana live in Botswana (which
means "land of the Tswana"), the republic is the hub of Tswana

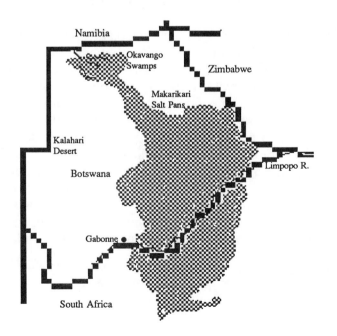

cultural identity. Bounded on the south by South Africa, on the east and north by Zimbabwe, on the north by Zambia and Angola, and on the west by Namibia, Botswana is almost entirely situated in the Kalahari Basin. This basin, a semiarid zone, extends from South Africa to Zaire. Mostly tableland covered with scrub or tree savanna, the Kalahari Desert is really a dry, wooded grassland that supports various types of game and provides some grazing for cattle. Only about five percent of Botswana's land can be farmed effectively. Since much of the land is unsuitable for regular cultivation, the great majority of the population lives in a narrow strip along the South Africa and Zimbabwe borders or in the northeastern region, where rainfall is heavier and more regular. Climate is subtropical, with summer highs reaching above 100 degrees Fahrenheit. Winter temperatures can drop below freezing at night.

In South Africa, the Tswana live in the largest of the "independent" black South African homelands, Bophuthatswana. The reserve is broken into 19 tracts and offers little agricultural potential. Like the other homelands, it is largely rough, dry, and poor in soil quality. Most Tswana who live in Bophuthatswana rely on employment in the wealthier, white-controlled areas outside the homeland.

Historical Background

Southward migration. The various Tswana groups trace their origins to the expansions of Sotho chiefly families who originated in the modern-day central and southern Transvaal. This expansion began, according to their historical traditions, in about the 14th century. The oral traditions recount the breaking up of the original migrating groups, owing both to competition between the sons of chiefs and to outside factors such as drought. In the 17th century, several chiefly lines took up residence with their followers along the eastern Botswana region. One powerful kingdom, the Rolong (BaRolong), known for their iron smelting and blacksmiths, had already emerged by the 15th century in an area extending from near present-day Pretoria westward into Botswana. An interesting social development among some of these people was their coming together to live in large towns.

Time of troubles. In the 1820s and 1830s, turmoil in the High Veld region to the east drove large numbers of refugees to join the Tswana societies and more than double their populations. Already the Tswana had had to deal with raiding groups of mixed race, the Grigua, who settled to the south of them, near the Orange River, at the end of the 1790s. The Grigua continued to be a problem into the 1830s, while a new rising threat was the Ndebele kingdom of Mzilikazi, which seized control in about 1833 of the former lands of the Rolong Kingdom. The Ndebele moved their whole population away north to Zimbabwe in 1838 and 1839, to the great relief of the local Tswana. Also, during the 1830s, white colonists from South Africa began moving north in large numbers (see AFRIKANERS). These whites who, like the Grigua before them, came into the region in small covered wagons, contended for land with both the Tswana and the Ndebele. It was their victory over two Ndebele forces in 1838 that precipitated Mzilikazi's decision, already contemplated for some time, to move north across the Limpopo River. The Ndebele did, however, continue into the 1880s to raid some of the northeastern Tswana areas from time to time.

White settlement. Periodic exposure to Europeans had begun in the early 1800s, when traders, hunters, explorers, and missionaries began penetrating Tswana lands. From the 1820s to the 1840s, mission stations were established in several communities: Rolong, Hurutshe, Kgatla, and Kwena. By 1885, Christianity had become widespread among the Tswana, leading to a decrease in customary religious and social practices, such as rainmaking rites and marriage to more than one wife. At the same time, the whites settled progressively farther north. They displaced some communities (including Rolong, Hurutshe, and Kgatla); a few took refuge to the north in modern Botswana. Other Tswana in western Transvaal came under the control of the white settlers. Of Dutch, German, and French Huguenot descent, the white farmers were called Boers. The Boers attempted to enforce laws that taxed land and cattle and that made it illegal for Africans not to work for the new white landowners. Yet the whites for a long time had little success in subduing the independent chiefdoms and kingdoms. The discovery of gold (1866) and diamonds (1868) in the region just east of Tswana lands prompted further white settlement near the western Tswana. Thus far these Africans had remained independent. Now the revenues gained by the Boers' republics made them increasingly able to dispossess and control local Tswana groups.

The British presence. The Boers accused the missionaries, who were British, of encouraging the Tswana to resist Boer settlement. The Tswana appealed repeatedly to the British government for protection against the Boers. In 1884-5, spurred by a promise of mineral wealth and by a competing German presence, Britain responded to the Tswana petitions and established their control of the western part of Tswana territory still not under Boer control. The portion south of the Molopo River (which is a border of modern Botswana) became part of the Cape Colony of Britain. The area north of the river became the Bechuanaland Protectorate. (*Bechuana* is an old spelling of *Botswana*.) As for the eastern Tswana lands, the Boers, not the British, controlled this territory (an area called the Transvaal). In 1911, though, there was a union. The Cape Colony and the Transvaal were joined in forming the single country South Africa. Modern Botswana remained a British Protectorate until independence in 1966.

Three Tswana leaders. Tswana resistance to white settlement on their territory crystallized around Khama III, also called Khama the Great. Hereditary chief of the Bama Ngwato, one of the eight main Tswana groups, Khama adopted Christianity as a boy. He was educated by missionaries before becoming *kgosi* (chief) in the 1870s. Khama united the Tswana, defeated the Ndebele in the 1880s, and shrewdly played the British off against the Boer settlers. His aim was to preserve the power of the Tswana *dikgosi* (chiefs) in Botswana. With two other dikgosi, he visited London in 1895. They were ultimately successful in preventing the British from turning over Botswana to the developer Cecil Rhodes.

Khama died in 1923. He had a pair of sons; the older son succeeded Khama. Two years later, however, the older son died, himself leaving a four-year-old son, Seretse. Until Seretse came of age, Khama's younger son Tshekedi would act as kgosi in his stead. Tshekedi Khama, like his father, attempted to strengthen the power of the Tswana chief. He led other dikgosi in successful efforts to limit the extent of British control.

Seretse, educated in England and married to a white Englishwoman, entered political life when Tshekedi died in 1959. In 1962, he formed a political party that called for independence from Britain. Seretse's party won a landslide victory in popular elections in 1965, the people preparing for independence. Upon independence in 1966, Seretse Khama became the first President of the new Republic of Botswana.

He was succeeded by Dr. Quett Masire, who won office through a national election. Since independence, Botswana, unlike many other African nations, has enjoyed a stable and democratically elected government.

Culture Today

Population overview. From the earliest days, the Tswana absorbed the people they conquered or colonized rather than merely ruling over them. This custom of adopting others into Tswana society has helped unify the modern nation. While about 90 percent of the population considers themselves Tswana, only about half descend from original Tswana stock.

Most of the Tswana in Botswana inhabit rural areas in the south. Only about 15 percent lived in cities in 1981. The largest city and Botswana's capital is Gaborone. In 1981 its population totaled 70,000. Migration from rural areas to cities increased dramatically during the 1980s, partly owing to a series of droughts. Gaborone's current population numbers about 100,000.

Food, clothing, and shelter. The traditional diet draws on agriculture, herding, hunting, and gathering. Staple crops include bulrush millet, sorghum, and maize. Also eaten are peas, beans, squashes, melons, wild berries, and tubers. The people herd cattle, sheep, pigs, and goats. Particularly the cattle are regarded more as an investment than as food. Only the wealthiest own large herds. Five to 10 percent of the herders own over half the country's cattle. Hunted meat continues to be a popular source of protein, often in the dried form called *biltong*. Many calories consumed by the Tswana also come from the traditional beer. Called *kadi* or *bojalwa*, it is a light, chalky drink made from sorghum or bulrush millet.

Both the missionaries and work done by Tswana laborers in white-controlled agriculture and mining exposed the people to European clothing styles. European clothing had been widely adopted by the end of the 19th century. It remains the popular style of dress among the Tswana today.

The customary dwelling consists of a circular dried-mud wall topped with a cone-shaped roof of thatched poles with protruding eaves. Since colonial times, the people added features such as wooden doors and glass windows to their homes. Many are now rectangular and have larger rooms, showing a European influence.

Family life. The Tswana household operates under the division of labor common to many African societies. Men and boys tend the livestock, hunt, clear fields, and assist in planting or reaping. Women and girls perform most farm labor, collect wild foods, cook, brew the *bojalwa*, build and repair the clay walls of the houses, fetch water and wood, and make pots and baskets. Frequently men and boys spend long periods living at *meraka* (cattle posts) away from the main towns. Women and girls sometimes take up temporary residence near the fields they are cultivating. In recent years, however, the division of labor has grown less rigid. Women, for example, are no longer prohibited from handling cattle. Men continue to have most control in the family. However, a man must accumulate wealth for the family through work in order to justify his position as head of the household.

Economy. Botswana's rich mineral resources, a large part of which are yet untapped, include diamonds, copper, nickel, coal, salt, soda ash, manganese, asbestos, iron, lead, and potash. In the 1980s, mining revenues paid for development in the country. The decade brought water, electricity, telephone lines, roads, and railways to many parts of the nation, meanwhile providing jobs for the people. After diamonds, the country's leading export is beef, much of which is purchased by South Africa, Botswana's leading trade partner. Botswana imports nearly 80 percent of its food, nearly all of it from South Africa, which also supplies goods such as vehicles, medicines, and electrical appliances. In addition, about 50,000 Botswana citizens work in South Africa, many of them in gold or diamond mines. This participation in migrant labor stretches back to the 1870s. Earning small wages, the laborers make just enough to help feed and clothe their families in return for dangerous work and long hours. Frequent beatings by white or black bosses have been common.

Education. The economic growth of the 1980s allowed Botswana to reach a national goal by the end of the decade: almost complete access to free primary education. The main obstacle to education (and other services) was the spread of families to the *meraka* (cattle posts) and agricultural areas. Population increases, however, have made it possible to build schools in more distant areas, as the numbers of children found in these areas have grown. In 1966, Botswana had 251 primary school and only nine secondary schools. By the early 1980s, there were nearly 500 primary schools and 45 secondary schools. The nation had meanwhile mounted an effort to teach adults literacy, or reading and writing. Some 59 percent of the adults lacked these abilities in 1971. The illiteracy rate had dropped to some 29 percent by 1985.

Health. Botswana's dry climate has spared its population many of the tropical diseases prevalent in countries to the north. Droughts, however, have caused undernutrition among the rural people. Having a steady supply of clean water remains a constant concern. In the 1980s, the national government brought health clinics to most rural areas. They join the efforts of medical missions and private companies. Many Tswana also consult their own people's healers. Old methods rely both on magic and the medicinal qualities of various herbs and other plants.

A healer commonly diagnoses an illness through divination, or *go laola.* The healer throws two sets of bones on the ground, and the positions of the fallen bones lead to a definition of the illness. Outside health workers have recently attempted to include the herbal and other non-magical remedies into their newer medical practices.

For More Information

Alverson, Marianne. *Under the African Sun.* Chicago: University of Chicago Press, 1987.

Maylam, Paul. *Rhodes, the Tswana and the British.* Westport, Conn.: Greenwood Press, 1980.

Morton, Fred et al. *Historical Dictionary of Botswana.* Metuchen, New Jersey: Scarecrow Press, 1989.

Schapera, I. *The Tswana.* Plymouth, England: Clarke, Doble & Brendon, Ltd., 1976.

TUAREG

(twa' reg)

Muslim camel-herders and traders in the Sahara Desert
and farmers south of the desert.

Population: 400,000 (1985 est.).
Location: Saharan Africa: Southern Algeria, Mali and Niger.
Languages: Tamahaq, Arabic.

Geographical Setting

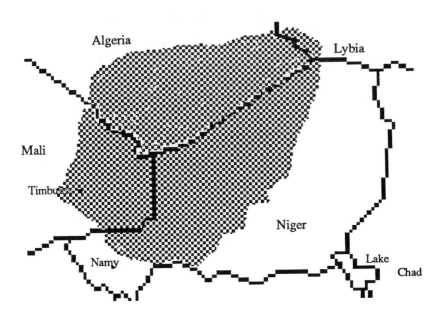

The Tuareg are now clustered in the Ahoggar Mountains of southern Algeria, the Tassili Plateau in southeastern Algeria, the Air Massif of Niger, and the area north and just south of the great bend of the Niger River in Mali. The land is a mix of steppe and savanna in the south. In the center and north, barren desert is dominated by mountain peaks. The south has rainfall of 10–20 inches yearly, which allows for growth of grasslands and regular cultivation of arid-country crops, such as bullrush millet. However, in the northern part of the Tuareg region, rain seldom falls and the desert areas are persistently hot. The mountain areas experience relief from the heat in the evenings, and freezing temperatures are not uncommon in the winter. Strong winds blow the sand in the desert, making traveling difficult. In the past, Tuareg traders and raiders would cover their faces with veils to ward off the blasting sand—a practice that earned them the title "warriors of the blue veil."

Historical Background

Migration. The Tuareg moved from northeastern Africa into the southern desert in a series of migrations. The exact date of these travels is unknown, but they appear to have begun by the 7th century. At first centered around the oasis of Tuat in southwestern Algeria, the Tuareg took control of the Ahoggar and Air regions. From there they spread southwest to the area around Timbuktu by 1100–1300.

Other related Berber peoples had spread south through the western Sahara even earlier. Among these peoples, one group of religious zealots formed a religious retreat near the Senegal River in the 11th century. Known as the Almoravids, they organized the great jihad that carried into Spain. The Tuareg and other Berbers took up camel raising between 100 and 500 A.D., and it was possession of these animals that allowed them to spread far across the Sahara to the northern edges of the West African savanna. From as early as the 4th century A.D. they combined camel herding and trading, carrying goods such as salt and copper from the desert to the southern savannas to exchange for wheat and gold. Long the leading traders of the desert, they carried on an active trade in slaves, gold, and ivory. Merchants in trading centers such as Timbuktu paid them by the camel load to trade goods, and by the head for the delivery of slaves. To the present day, they remain prominent traders in Timbuktu and northern Nigeria.

Tuareg vs. French. When the French claimed the region as a colonial possession and moved into the desert area, the Tuareg resisted. Beginning in the early 1890s and continuing through 1894, they were successful in fighting off French intrusions. By 1899, the Tuareg were at war with the French army. Again they were at first successful, but by 1900 the Tuareg had been defeated and French rule established.

20th century. A religious war erupted in 1917, during which many of the Tuareg were killed and others were driven out of the mountain region. Many fled to Chad and others moved to the area of Darfur in Sudan, where they still inhabit villages such as El Fasher. About 30,000 Tuareg chose a more sedentary life near the villages of Kano and Katsina in Nigeria. Those who continued their nomadic existence were disastrously affected by severe droughts of the 1970s; animals died and more Tuareg were forced to move into shantytowns outside the villages and towns of Nigeria and Niger. Since then, with rains returning to normal, many Tuareg have resumed their herding lifestyles.

Tuareg camel riders near Timbuktu. *Photo by Eliot Elisofon. Courtesy of National Museum of African Art.*

Culture Today

Economy. Their history has resulted in division among the Tuareg. Herders of camels, goats, and sheep, and, in the south, humpbacked cattle still add to their income by carrying trade goods. But, where once their camels were the principle carriers in the region, now trucks and railroads cut through the Tuareg trading area. Today's camel caravans carry goods from the trucks and rails to places where no roads exist. Those Tuareg who have moved closer to villages and towns near the great bend of the Niger River have now abandoned their travels to become farmers in the savanna. These farmers grow grains that are still traded with the desert-dwelling Tuareg for salt.

Social structure. The Tuareg are a highly stratified society of nobles and vassals. Probably resulting from the camel herders' sense of superiority over the sheep and goat herders in the past, Tuareg society has traditionally been divided into castes: rulers (who did little more than wage wars and raid), camel herders, sheep and goat herders, farmers, the low class smiths and leatherworkers, and, in the past, slaves. Even though slavery is now illegal, the lowest caste consists of black servants working for meager pay whom the Tuareg describe as slaves. Today, the Tuareg language refers to four social classes: nobles, vassals, *Inanden* (workers), and *Iklan* (slaves).

The Tuareg are divided into seven groups according to living areas. In the past, members of each area group were led by a separate chief whose symbol was a particular drum. There was and is no central chief of the Tuareg. Each area ruler (*amenskal*) has the ultimate political and judicial authority, but only with the consent of his people. Under this system, the people refer to themselves as *Imuhar* (free men).

In addition to these authorities and castes, there was once a class of religious noblemen. However, the religious war of 1917 eliminated many of these noblemen. Still, the caste system that honors herders over farmers and camel herders over sheep herders persists.

Food and shelter. In accord with the differences in their means of earning a livelihood, Tuareg homes and foods vary. Some of the people continue to herd and are nomadic desert dwellers. They live in tents made of animal skins that have traditionally been tanned and dyed red, and they depend on their animals for food. Camels are suppliers of milk, as are goats and sheep. These small animals also supply some meat for the diet and are traded to nearby farmers for grains such as bullrush millet and dates.

The identical diet is available to the farming Tuareg through this same trade system. These people, settling near established villages, have built homes of mat or grass bound together with ropes, much like those of other savanna dwellers. Still other Tuareg have opted for city life and have become laborers in the port communities of Nigeria, Ghana, and the Ivory Coast.

Clothing. Traditional men's wear is a poncho-style shirt, baggy trousers, and sandals. Women's customary dress includes poncho-style cotton shirts and shawls as well as sandals. Both men and women cover their faces in the company of others. Men traditionally wore a blue veil over their faces; women drew headcloths over their mouths when with strangers or in-laws. Today, these costumes are still practiced among the Tuareg, but their frequency depends upon the area in which the people live and their proximity to other societies. In the villages and towns, Tuareg men now frequently yield to Western style dress.

Religion. Once, the Tuareg herded their livestock and lived at the south edges of the early Arab conquests of the 7th and 8th centuries. They soon adopted the new Muslim religion brought to them by Arab traders. This religion governs many aspects of present-day life. However, the Tuareg reject one behavior allowed by the Muslim religion. They do not accept the right of a man to take more than one wife.

Family life. A Tuareg man and one wife begin a family unit. This unit may extend to include relatives other than husband, wife, and children. In fact, bands of nomadic Tuareg are often made up of extended families. Children in this society can inherit wealth, land, or livestock from either the father or the mother. However, family responsibilities are divided. Men, assisted by their sons, herd the animals, build houses, and farm the land. Women in this society are restricted in their associations with others, but are highly respected. Once leatherworkers, they are now often relieved of economic responsibilities for the family and devote their time to the children and to music and poetry.

Arts. Isolated in the desert area and the southern savanna, the Tuareg developed distinctive abilities. Tuareg learned men created their own

Pounding grain in a Tuareg village. *Photo by Eliot Elisofon. Courtesy of National Museum of African Art.*

alphabet and written characters. These characters (*tifinagh*) became the written language of the Berbers, of which the Tuareg are a southern branch. Societies such as the Kabyles are northern representatives.

The Tuareg have been well known for their leather work. In the past, women crafted products such as decorated belts, pouches (once used for carrying salt), and leather ornaments. However, the drought of the 1970s drastically reduced the available leather and slowed the production of leather goods for market.

For More Information

Englebert, Victor. "Drought Threatens the Tuareg World," *National Geographic*, April 1974, pp. 544–571.

Kirtley, Michael and Kirtley, Aubine. "The Inadan: Artisans of the Sahara," *National Geographic*, August 1979, pp. 282–298.

Imperato, Pascal James. *Historical Dictionary of Mali. African History Dictionaries.* Metuchen, New Jersey: Scarecrow, 1977.

Murdock, George Peter. *Africa: Its People and Their Culture History.* New York: McGraw-Hill, 1959.

TUTSI
(toot' see)

Tall, proud people who form the aristocratic caste in Burundi and formerly in Rwanda; called BaTutsi by the people themselves.

Population: 696,000 (280,000 in Rwanda; 416,000 in Burundi–1987 est.).
Location: Rwanda and Burundi.
Languages: Rwanda and Rundi, Bantu languages of Hutu peoples conquered by the Tutsi.

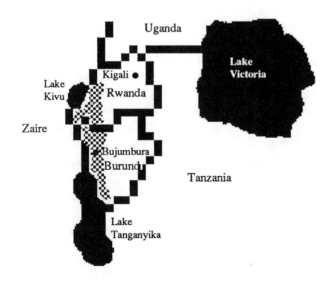

Geographical Setting

The Tutsi (Watutsi) homeland is located in the highland area of east-central Africa, a region of varied terrains, including mountain ranges, lakes, river, and swamps. Elevations range from 4,000 feet in the valleys to 9,000 feet in the mountains. The rugged terrain is difficult to travel over and to live in. The climate changes with the terrain. In the mountains, temperatures can become extremely cold, and the opposite is true in the valleys, which are subject to high temperatures. Although the total rainfall is usually between 40 and 50 inches, the rain is erratic. Heavy rains have in many places eroded the topsoil necessary to keep trees anchored and to nourish crops.

Historical Background

Origin. Many myths surround the origins of the Tutsi, relating them to Egypt, to Ethiopia, and to other peoples. These myths have no basis in known fact. What is clear is that they began as people specializing in cattle-raising and living as neighbors to people who focused much more on raising crops. They probably once formed a distinct ethnic group with their own language, now lost. Around the 14th or 15th century, some Tutsi began to use their wealth in cattle to gain clients among the cultivators, whom they called Hutu, and to seize power from some of the Hutu kings and chiefs.

As the Tutsi subdued the Hutu groups, they began to establish a forced cooperation. Hutu were given some cattle to raise, and protected from other enemies by the Tutsi. In exchange, the Hutu supplied their masters with farm products. This association with the Hutu developed into an interdependent institution called *ubuhake.*

The rewards from ubuhake were balanced much in favor of the Tutsi. Hutu had access to cattle products, including milk, butter, fertilizer, and urine, but they did not own the cattle, and they were still obligated to work the fields. The Tutsi received farm products and labor, while retaining most dairy products and being relieved of hard labor. In addition, Hutu joined Tutsi in payment of taxes to the Tutsi king (*mwami*). Ubuhake eventually gave rise to a caste system, ranking people by birth. Tutsi ranked above Hutu, which in the long run led to Hutu unrest and rebellion.

The colonial period. It was not until the late 1890s that Europeans (Germans) came in contact with the Tutsi. German colonizers met little opposition since they left the Tutsi kingdom in place. This situation remained even though World War I saw the German authorities replaced by Belgians. But for 20 years following the war the Belgian government worked to erode the power of the mwami and to do away with the lord/client ubuhake system. In exchange, the Tutsi assumed new positions of control. Gradually they filled positions in the administration of the Belgian-dominated government and in education and other professions. The increased status of these Tutsi further aggravated the hostile feelings of the Hutu. In 1959, the Hutu revolted against the by then Tutsi-dominated government.

Two years later, the Belgians allowed independence for Rwanda and Burundi. Hutu and Tutsi governments seized power in the two countries. In Rwanda, the Hutu rebelled and threw out the Tutsi, but in Burundi the Tutsi remained in power and have engaged in two reigns of terror, in 1971 and in the 1980s, trying to suppress Hutu discontent.

The system of ubuhake was the means by which the Tutsi subsisted for over 400 years. Taxes in the form of agricultural surplus or cows or milk were exacted to support the monarchy. Each nuclear family and its Hutu dependents was self-sufficient. With the disappearance of ubuhake in the 20th century, the Tutsi in Burundi more and more have found economic survival in the world of business, government, education, and other professions.

In the early 1990s a Tutsi insurgency is attempting to re-establish Tutsi dominance in Rwanda.

Culture Today

Social structure. The social system in which the Tutsi have traditionally lived is very stratified. Divisions between classes were and continue to be of strictest importance. In the past a person born into one group inherited an occupation common to that caste and probably practiced by the parents. If the person wanted to marry, a proper mate would be chosen by the elders from those available in the person's own class.

For the Tutsi, the Hutu, and the Twa (another group, made up of hunters and foragers in the region) the family was the main organizing factor. Families are bonded together in groups called *inzu* containing five or six generations of people who trace their descent to one common male ancestor. The inzu is important because of the rituals associated with marriage, feuding, and taxpaying and because of the political bonds created between members of the group. Historically, kinsmen so bonded were expected to defend one another against enemies or to retaliate if one of their group was wronged. Marriage has the potential for making an alliance with another inzu. Therefore, marriages are often carefully researched.

Family life. Marriage once also involved gifts to the family of the bride. An ideal groom possessed many cattle and was knowledgeable about politics. An ideal bride was a good housekeeper and basket weaver.

From a very young age, Tutsi children learn what is expected for someone of their class and sex. They are taught to be clean, quiet

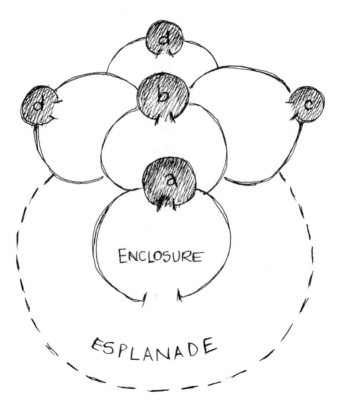

A Tutsi compound—a. reception hall, b. private house, c. kitchen, d. servants' homes.

and obedient. By about age five, they are required to do simple tasks in support of the family. Sex roles are learned by the age of ten, and adolescence brings training needed to become productive husbands and wives. In the past, childhood instruction included the use of weapons and knowledge of folktales. Today this instruction has given way to formal school-based education.

Religion. The Tutsi religion is now a mixture of old Bantu beliefs and Christianity. The Tutsi who live in villages often build a hut for the male ancestor on which the inzu is based. In this hut, members of the family throw beans or peas, or spit as a sign of respect for the ancestor. Sometimes a girl or woman spends time in the hut to give the spirit ancestor company. Spirits of the dead, *bazimu*, are generally considered to be bad tempered. They are believed to need to be calmed daily with offerings to prevent them from harming humans or cattle. It is believed that the spirits of ancestors intercede with the supreme god, *Imana*. Other gods include Ryangombe, god of initiation and afterlife, and Imana/Ryangombe, a god pair representing the lord/client system of the Tutsi.

Historically, power and a reputation for military courage, self-control, trustworthiness, and generosity have been important in the Tutsi value system. Loyalty to the *mwami*, the Tutsi leader, to one's caste, and to one's lineage were, and to a lesser extent remain today, important ethics in Tutsi society.

Art and dance. Tutsi women are makers of beautiful, geometrically patterned beadwork that adorns necklaces, bracelets, and headpieces. Women also produce intricately woven baskets. Tutsi men are noted for their speech making, and for memorizing and creating poems that celebrate their history and conquests. Training for storytelling once played a part in the male's preparation for warrior status, but today is for pleasure and preservation of the tradition. Also excellent dancers, the Tutsi perform many different movements for different occasions. An example is the Leopard Dance, which is performed before a hunt. Another traditional hunting dance re-enacts the successful hunt and glorifies the hunter.

Government. The Tutsi governing body was always very complex and highly organized. Before the monarchies in Burundi and Rwanda were overthrown, the Tutsi were governed by a mwami, the king in a centralized government. That mwami was considered the eye

Tutsi dancers near Lake Kivu. *Photo by Eliot Elisofon. Courtesy of National Museum of African Art.*

Tutsi pipe.

through which God looks upon the land. He was believed to have divine powers. Supported by the queen-mother and the *biru,* a council of advisers, the king taxed smaller districts within the kingdom to sustain the king's court, his administration, and a Tutsi army. A land chief and a cattle chief governed in each of these smaller districts. Lesser chiefs were responsible for tax collection and for settling local disputes. The military was a strong force in Tutsi history. All men belonged to an army unit and warrior training was an essential part of manhood. The army waged war on many neighboring peoples and was known for its aggressive strategy. The Tutsi justified these excursions with religious tenets, believing that they lived in God's land and were given rights to everything by divine power.

Many Tutsi men still belong to army units, even though the army is inactive. While the mwami is retained today as a symbol of Tutsi unity, much of his power and all of his hierarchy of chiefs were abolished in favor of a national government.

Recent change. Since Rwanda has become dominated by a Hutu-led republican government, many Tutsi have emigrated to neighboring countries. The Tutsi homeland, without the servant class of the old Hutu and with environmental destruction, has suffered economic decline. Under the Hutu government, cattle were taken from the Tutsi and distributed to other peoples. No longer does the system of ubuhake govern interactions.

Tutsi-Hutu rivalry remains a problem in Burundi. The issue of a national ethnic unity for the Tutsi persists against the influence of Western cultures. Tutsi living in the urban centers of the Tutsi countries have turned to Western-style clothing and customs.

For More Information

Best, Alan C. G. and Harm J. de Blij. *African Survey.* New York: John Wiley and Sons, 1977.

Davidson, Basil. *A History of Eastern and Central Africa.* New York: Doubleday and Co., 1969.

Maquet, Jacques. *The Premise of Inequality in Rwanda.* London: Oxford University Press, 1961.

WOLOF

(waw' lawf)

A people who established agricultural communities in the river areas of Senegal and Gambia.

Population: 1,375,000 (1985 est.).
Location: Senegal, Gambia.
Languages: Wolof, French, and English.

Geographical Setting

Living in the extreme west of Africa, the Wolof have learned to farm the savanna grasslands southward from the Senegal River to the Gambia River. Here the low coastal area rises gradually to a tropical plateau averaging less than 1,000 feet above sea level. Northward the area spreads toward the Sahara Desert. Here rainfall is a moderate 20 inches a year, while in the southwestern city of Casamance, in a neck of Senegal that reaches around Gambia, yearly rainfall can be 80 or more inches. In the east, rainfall is sometimes scarce. Heavy rainy seasons interrupt long periods of dry weather. Some of the tributary streams dry up, and farmers are in frequent danger of losing crops due to lack of water. Closer to the sea, a chain of sand dunes gives way to a sandy plain and swampland. In this region, the lives of the Wolof are varied. Farmers clear the grasslands and sow their crops, while Wolof merchants trade up and down the rivers; still others are involved in a wide range of activities in the larger cities such as Dakar.

Historical Background

Origin. Traditional stories claim that the Wolof came from the north to settle in an area where another group, the Jola, was already well established. By the 15th century the Wolof had conquered many of the other groups in the area, except those just along the coast, and had created a large empire. The first king of the Wolof Empire, Ndiadiane N'diaye, is reported to have assumed power in the late 14th century. His empire included a number of different states between the Senegal and Gambia rivers, each with its own ruler. Among the states were Walo, Kayor, Baol, Sine, Salum, and his kingdom of Djolof.

The Wolof empire. The rulers formed a college of electors that voted the *burba*, or supreme king, into office, but retained power over their own territories. Their relationship with the burba was loose in that he left them alone to rule their kingdoms and was satisfied if they presented him with annual gifts. From 1444 to 1510, Portuguese merchants entered Wolof country and began to seek slaves, a situation that encouraged greater unity among the people. Prince Bemoi, who ruled the empire during the 1480s in the name of his brother King Birao, received the missionaries of the Portuguese and tried to cement ties in the belief that this would increase trade. However, the rulers of the separate Wolof kingdoms revolted, and their rebellion contributed to the downfall of the empire.

Introduction to Islam. Then in 1673 the Fulani, from Futa Toro just east of the Wolof, waged a *jihad*, or holy war, against Wolof kingdoms to convert the people to Islam (See FULANI). The Wolof kingdom of Walo was subject to constant raiding by the Moors, who had previously converted the nobility among the Wolof to the Muslim religion. They now began to spread Islam in the area.

Trading gum, indigo, and ivory, as well as slaves to the Portuguese, the Wolof built smaller kingdoms along the coast. The most strategic position was occupied by the Wolof kingdom of Kayor, which extended along most of the coast of Senegal. Its ruler reduced the power of local chiefs and recruited professional soldiers who would always be at his disposal in case of need. In the 1600s the Wolof kingdom of Kayor had taken control of several smaller states from its neighboring Wolof kingdom, Djolof, and that state sought to regain control. Citizens of the two large states fled to one of the lesser kingdoms, Baol (near present-day Dakar). The king, or *Teny*, of Baol defeated the Djolof ruler, then began to consolidate his power by arranging deaths of all nobles considered powerful enough to threaten his reign.

Islam and its religious leaders gradually grew more attractive to the common people as their kings' policies became oppressive. This attraction was increased by periodic forrays from Mauretanians, Moors from the north, who made frequent raids in the 1600s and 1700s.

Independence. In the 1800s, the French settled on an island off the coast of Wolof country and proceeded to expand into their territory. The Wolof chief, Lat Dior, objected to their plans to build a railway across Wolof territory, but he was driven out by the French in 1892. After the territory became a colony of French West Africa in 1895, the Wolof and other peoples of the colony were awarded French citizenship and representation in France. One state, Djolof, remained independent until 1880 when its leader was driven out and a government friendly to the French was installed.

In 1960, Senegal won independence from the French, and in 1965 Gambia became independent from Great Britain. In 1982 the two new nations agreed to form a federation. The president of Senegal is also the president of the federation.

Throughout their history, the Wolof have not been a united people and have often been subject to rule by others. That situation remains today. Although the Wolof make up the majority of the population in Senegal, they have not assumed a major political role in the country. However, the Moslem leaders of different Wolof regions have a measure of political power, since their cooperation is necessary for the enforcement of government policies.

Culture Today

City society. City-dwelling Wolof earn livings in a wide range of occupations, as fishermen, merchants, teachers, government officials, and so forth. In descriptions of the Wolof, the term *caste*, which normally means social stratification, actually refers to occupational groups. Craftspeople (smiths, musicians, and leather workers) traditionally occupy the lowest class among the Wolof.

Village society. Ownership of land and influence in the village of the rural Wolof is governed by descent, usually through the father's side of the family, and sometimes through that of the mother. Succession to ruling positions has traditionally been through the mother's lineage. Beyond that, Wolof society in precolonial times was a sort of caste system, with freeborn members of royal lineage in the upper class, followed by freeborn nobles and peasants. As in the city, lower class groups included the craftspeople. The lowest class consisted of slaves, either born in the house or brought in by capture. As the Wolof move to cities and larger towns, this traditional caste system has begun to break down.

Economy. A majority of the Wolof people are farmers who grow bulrush millet, sorghum, and maize for food. They also grow beans, sorrel, tomatoes, and red peppers. In the savannah regions, farmers clear the grass by burning or by using a hand axe and machete. The Wolof handle the fields with such care that the original plant life quickly returns when the land is left untilled. In areas of more moisture, the Wolof have borrowed skills from their Mandinka neighbors to grow rice, which is becoming an important crop both for home use and export (See MALINKE). An important export product is groundnuts (peanuts).

Members of certain castes—the Tigg caste (blacksmiths), for example—have the right to practice a specified occupation. They may choose to labor outside this field (in business perhaps) but others cannot specialize in their fields without the inherited right to do so.

In Wolof society, some of the artisans are griots, or praise singers. They serve as musicians, poets, and speech makers. Among their duties is the recital of family histories. They also announce news and gossip, shuttle written messages back and forth, and distribute gifts. Today's griots achieve widespread fame, performing on Radio Senegal. Yet craftspeople (smiths, musicians, and leather workers) have in the past formed the lowest class of free people among the Wolof.

City-dwelling Wolof earn livings in a wide range of occupations. They labor as fishermen, merchants, teachers, government officials, and so on.

Family life. Marriages can be arranged by the parents of the groom, who sometimes has little to say about the arrangement. Men who find women they wish to marry consult a fortune-teller to determine compatibility, then take gifts of nuts to the potential brides' mothers. If this is accepted, a bride price is established and a Muslim wedding

The Marché Sandaga in Dakar. *Photo by Monica Guylai.*

ceremony is arranged. In strict Muslim weddings, the bride does not need to attend the ceremony. Marriages may also take place by elopement. Such marriages once involved kidnapping of the bride by horsemen hired by the groom. As in other Muslim societies, a husband may have more than one wife. In these cases, the old wives create verses with which to insult the new one and hire a griot to recite the verses as sort of an initiating gift.

Once a family is established in a rural area, the roles of men and women are distinctly defined. Men clear the land, raise millet and groundnuts, build houses, make mats, weave baskets and cloth, play musical instruments, teach religion, and carry on trade. Women help guard the crops, grow rice, draw water, care for smaller animals such as goats, sell excess vegetables at the market, gather plants for medicines, tend the children, and perform a number of household duties. In some Wolof communities, men and women divide religious duties: the men follow the tenets of Islam, and the women practice more ancient beliefs.

Food, clothing, and shelter. Wolof live in their own villages in the savanna or in mixed villages with Mandingo and other peoples along

Shopping for cloth in Dakar. *Photo by Monica Guylai.*

the rivers. In the village, a cluster of houses are grouped around an open square that is often shaded by trees. Fenced alleyways connect the houses. A roofed platform, or *dat,* in the square forms a place for men to meet during the heat of the day, for travelers to rest, and for young people to dance and sing in the evenings. Houses in the compound are made of mud or reed walls with thatched, conical roofs. Wealthier residents sometimes whitewash their houses using oyster shells. Inside are one or more beds and locked wooden boxes for storing clothing and other possessions. There may also be a hammock or a chair, a prayer mat, a kerosene lamp, and various tools for preparing food. The house has no windows, but two doors made of reed or corrugated tin.

Wolof basket weaver. *Photo by Monica Guylai.*

On the east side of the village, there is a mosque. Most Wolof are Muslims. However, a blend of old and new religions persists, as attested by the village streets. The main street to the village is intentionally crooked, because the Wolof believe that evil spirits can only enter the village on a straight path.

A typical city home stands a foot or two above the ground, and has a wide veranda nearly all around it. The floor is cemented, and the roof is made of corrugated metal.

Bullrush millet is the staple food in many Wolof homes. Pounded into flour, the grain is then steamed and mixed with the baobab leaf to make the main dish, *chere*. An evening meal might consist of chere, *base*, made of groundnuts, peppers, pumpkins or beans, and sometimes meat or fish. Other meals also include different dishes made from millet: boiled millet with sour milk, sugar, and baobob fruit for breakfast, and steamed millet with a vegetable soup for lunch.

Wolof women are known for their flowing gowns and sophisticated hairstyles. Typically their ensemble consists of a full shirt and several dresses, one on top of the other and each slightly shorter than

Street vendors of artwork in Dakar. *Photo by Monica Guylai.*

the dress before it. A large shawl drapes over the shoulders, and married women wear wigs covered by headcloths. Makeup completes the outfit. Men wear full, white pantaloons that fall below the knees. On top, they don a *boubou*, or sleeveless shirt, that has inside pockets and extends to the ground. Usually the boubou is white or dark-blue and embroidered. Traditional colors for women are white, blue, or black. However, dress is changing, with many Wolof people wearing European-style clothing in the cities and towns.

Both men and women wear jewelry, which is crafted by the Wolof themselves. Their trade in gold dates back at least to the 17th century, when the metal was acquired from peoples of the interior in return for salt. The Wolof use the gold to manufacture ornaments.

Religion. Since the 11th century, the Muslim religion has been a dominant influence in the area in which the Wolof live, and by the 15th century, Wolof chiefs had begun to claim that religion but did not follow its practices completely. In the 1700s, the teaching of Islam became widespread. Hence, the village mosque is an important landmark in Wolof communities. A large mosque in the Wolof state of Baol attracts hundreds of thousands of visitors for an annual pilgrimage. From the age of seven, boys receive religious instruction, learning passages from the Koran, and how to write Arabic characters.

The Wolof mix the Muslim faith with ancient beliefs. These beliefs involve witches, spirits of ancestors, dwarfs who protect wild animals, and a great imaginary snake, the sight of which causes death. To ward off the evil effects of some of the witches and malevolent spirits, the Wolof wear a wide assortment of amulets. Today these amulets often contain verses from the Koran, combining again the old religion and the new.

Recreation. Recreation among the Wolof includes drumming, dancing, wrestling, and storytelling for which the people have a rich storehouse of fables and riddles. These stories are told by a cast of storytellers, *griots*. It is the griots' responsibility to recite genealogies and histories of local families. Included in their stories are tales of the past when the Wolof were at the height of their power in the great Djolof empire. Wandering troupes often act out these stories. Other stories tell of the wild animals in Wolof territory and their interactions with humans or of daily issues in Wolof life. Often these stories are prefaced by a sort of oath to their truthfulness, like "Our legs are crossed. It happened here. It was so."

On special occasions, especially at the New Year, Wolof communities are entertained with a parade of lanterns. The lanterns are in the shapes of common Wolof objects (ships and houses, for example) and are lighted by candles. In Senegal, these parades were banned in 1954, but they can still be seen in the trading centers of Gambia.

Arts. In addition to singing, dancing, playing musical instruments, and storytelling, Wolof craftspeople create ornaments. They are known for the quality of the fine, filigree gold and silver jewelry created by the men. Women craft water jars, steaming pots, and bowls from clay. Made without a potter's wheel, these containers are sun dried, and baked in piles of straw, wood chips, or cow dung. Leather workers make sandals, sheaths for knives, wallets, handbags, and a number of other items for sale to Europeans. The Wolof also weave colorful cloths made from cotton that is picked, cleaned, and dyed by the women. Other craftspeople make fine baskets and carve objects from wood.

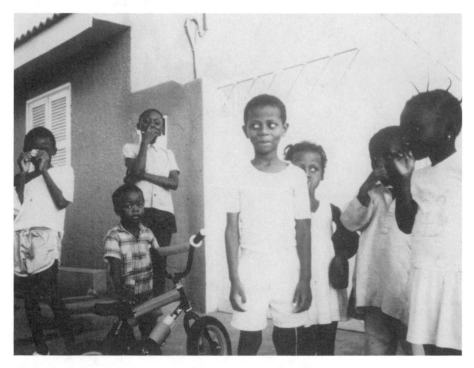

Children of Thies, Senegal. *Photo by Monica Guylai.*

Change. As with many peoples of Africa, Wolof lifestyles are changing. As towns and cities grow, traditional clothing is changing to favor European styles, radios replace drums and other musical instruments, and new dishes enter the diet. And the Wolof, through their religious leaders, are beginning to take a more active interest in the governments of Gambia and Senegal. Also, as in other places in Africa, where wearing traditional clothing was recently regarded as a symbol of backwardness, a reversal is in progress. The old customs have gained new respect and value as identification of Wolof unity. Today both traditional and European-style clothing are accepted.

For More Information

Africa South of the Sahara, 20th ed. London: Europa Publications, 1990.

Gamble, David P. *Ethnographic Survey of Africa: The Wolof of Senegambia.* London: International African Institute, 1967.

Magel, Emil A. *Folktales from the Gambia.* Washington, D.C.: Three Continents Press, 1984.

YORUBA
(yoh' ru bah)

The largest ethnic group in Nigeria, considered the most urban
people of the tropical region.

Population: 17,000,000 (1985 est.).
Location: Southwestern Nigeria, the Republic of Benin, central Togo.
Language: Yoruba, one of the Kwa group of West African languages.

Geographical Setting

Historic Yorubaland, about the size of England, contains many distinct ecological zones. Streams and rivers wind through the dense

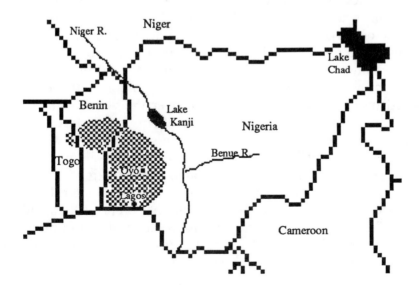

tropical forests in the southern states and the sprawling savanna of the northern states. Along the coast there are both dense forests and swamps. In the forest north of the coast the rainfall is heavy but the soil is poor. Northwest of this area is a belt of deciduous forest that receives moderate rainfall and rich soil and has good agricultural conditions. Deep in this forest sits the spiritual center and traditional cradle of the Yoruba, known as Ile Ife. About 100 miles to the north is the city of Oyo.

The social organizations of the Yoruba are as diverse as their geography. Settlements range from poor and depopulated villages in the savanna to large metropolitan cities like Lagos and Ibadan. Underneath the physical differences lies a unity based on language, custom, and a common historical experience.

Historical Background

Origin. The background of the Yoruba before European encounters is not known through any written material, although blood typing, language studies, and archeology provide much information. Another source of history rests in the myths and legends that make up the Yoruba oral tradition.

The basic myth tells how Olorun, owner of the sky, let a chain down from heaven, allowing Oduduwa, the creator of existence, to reach the ocean. The Yoruba claim to be descendants of the creator Oduduwa. He reportedly threw a handful of soil into the water and put a bird and a palm nut on it. The bird scratched the ground and the nut grew to a tree whose branches symbolize the dynasties founded by Oduduwa, who laid earth over the waters and set foot on his creation at a place called Ile Ife. There, in the west of Africa, Oduduwa founded a large city and left 16 sons on earth who established their own kingdoms. Thereafter, the Yoruba were never united under a single ruler but rather populated separate kingdoms.

Although Yoruba civilization emerged somewhat later than other developed nations, their culture and politics were well established prior to European contact. The Yoruba were divided into numerous independent political units. Some of these units grew into states, while others remained on smaller scales. States developed in the forest despite the climate, disease, limited agricultural conditions, and problems of transport that made life very difficult.

By the 11th century the Yoruba had developed a rich urban and court life. Ife retained fame as the original city. The most powerful kingdom, though, was based in the city of Oyo, and Yoruba culture stems primarily from its people.

Both Oyo and Benin became large empires in the 1600s and expanded their power through military confrontations into the 1700s. Local rulers of the conquered peoples usually remained in power but paid tribute to the *alafin* (ruler) of Oyo by sending such gifts as thatching grass, kola nuts, mats, firewood, European goods, and slaves. Many of the slaves bound for the West came from raids conducted in the empire of Oyo during the 1790s.

Following collapse of the Oyo power, civil wars among the kingdoms of the Yoruba plagued the people in the 1820s. The Yoruba of Ife raided the Yoruba of Owu for people to sell into slavery. Owu retaliated with an attack on Ife, and a long history of civil war began. The feuding over territory and slaves continued until the 1860s when changes to other kinds of commerce reduced the need for slave labor.

Warfare. Traditional Yoruba society was a mixture of kingdoms, each consisting of towns, villages, and surrounding farms and forests. The structure of government in these kingdoms was extremely diverse. They varied from having no kingship, to having several semipowerful kings, to having one all-powerful king and a centralized government. In some kingdoms, officers were elected, while in others their positions were inherited. Often land and rights to political office were held by a group rather than by an individual. In general, however, a balance of power and political process existed between the king, or *oba*, and the chiefs of different villages or descent groups. This balance was sometimes achieved violently, however, as the remains of fortified towns testify. Warfare between kingdoms inhibited trade outside the kingdoms, keeping palm products from the British traders who greatly desired them. So when the British took control of Lagos at the coast in 1866, they developed a peace treaty, which brought an end to inter-Yoruba wars and opened up trading.

Slavery and British involvement. When the British occupied the Yoruba homeland in the late 1800s, they did more than stop intergroup warfare. They introduced Christianity and European education to the Yoruba. Moreover, they added fuel to the slave trade, which had already existed to some extent since the 15th century. Yoruba peoples had been taken as slaves in the 16th century for use on sugar plantations in Brazil, and in the 17th century they were shipped to other parts of South America and the Caribbean. In the 18th century they were taken to North America to work on plantations.

Slavery existed as an institution in many African communities before the coming of a world slave trade. Before British involvement, Lagos was a most important slave market in Yorubaland. Slaves could be inherited like beads and clothes. Some literature even suggests that they were humanely treated. Slaves could buy themselves off from their masters if they saved enough money to pay the original sum. They also had time off each week to themselves.

Expansion. The 19th century was one of expansion and growth for the Yoruba. Industries in their cities thrived, especially the manufacture of cloth. Specialization occurred, with labor divided into spinning, weaving, and dyeing. There was a great deal of agricultural activity as well. Palm oil became a popular export after the slave trade subsided. In the 1880s, the Yoruba farmer began to cultivate cocoa, which became the most profitable crop of all. There were more Yoruba wars from 1877 to 1886 and a continuation of raids for slaves. Until the 1890s, these slaves were used as free labor in the production and transport of palm oil products.

Nigeria, home of large numbers of Yoruba, was created between 1893 and 1903 by the British, and they retained control until the country achieved independence in 1960. With independence came discontent on the part of the Yoruba farmer. Demands for reduced taxes and better prices prompted attacks by cocoa farmers on government offices in the Yoruba city Ibadan. In 1967, the Yoruba of Nigeria played a leading role in winning the civil war fought against the Ibo of the southeast.

In 1986 and 1987 the dominance of the northern peoples of Nigeria again threatened the unity of the nation. Under pressure from the north, the president of Nigeria, Babangida, declared that the country had joined the Organization of the Islamic Conference. Concerned for their religious safety, the Christian Ibos rebelled. Skirmishes and closing of universities followed. Clashes between Christians and Muslims broke out in the north. The continued unrest and subsequent debates in the government led to the planning of a Third Republic, which is still in debate because of a rule banning earlier political groups from participation in the new government until 1992.

Throughout this organization and reorganization, the Yoruba played an important role in the military and in establishing a stable country.

Culture Today

Economy. Yoruba economy is a farm economy. Cultivated crops included yams, plantain, bananas, maize, and cassava. While today hoe agriculture is still the foundation of their culture, the major cash crop in Nigeria has become cacao beans, and the Yoruba produce 90 percent of it.

A crucial factor in the economy of these people has always been trade: sea borne trade across the Atlantic of gold, pepper, spices, and other tropical products, and, also, inland trade between the forest and savanna. The kola nut that grew in the forest and savanna was in great demand in the Sudan, especially after the spread of Islam, because it was one of the stimulants that the religion allowed. Ivory, gold, and some slaves were also traded. Once the trade monies were controlled by kings; today the money from the markets goes to the local governments. The markets in smaller towns are more temporary than those of the large towns, whose markets contain several thousand traders and permanent stalls.

Towns and villages. Towns, or *ilu*, are distinguished from farm villages. Ilu is a name for a permanent settlement with its own government. On the other hand, farm villages called *aba* or *abule* are more temporary settlements where people stay if they are working on farms that are too far from their home town to commute to every day. A town is usually divided into wards, or sections, and includes a ruler's palace. Wards are often clustered around the main road with the farm belonging to each one right behind it. The wards are then further divided into compounds, which are the sites for various separate houses. This pattern characterizes many kingdoms, although settlements do vary widely in their spatial organization.

Shelter. Originally a kingdom of the Yoruba, the city of Ibadan is one of the largest in Africa, with a population that numbers well over one million. Today such cities have contemporary one- and two-story cement homes for individual families. The traditional Yoruba town was centered around a royal palace and a market that stood in front of the palace. Around these central structures were compounds, or living quarters, for families. Each compound might house hundreds of people, all members of related families.

The traditional Yoruba house is rectangular, with a triangular roof that is thatched with palm leaves, and walls made of wattle and mud. Typically the house includes bedrooms, a sitting room, a kitchen, a fireplace, and a family room. Traditional furniture consists of cooking utensils, water pots, a mortar, and mats rather than beds or chairs. In addition, the home has a veranda and yard, and the front posts of verandas are artistically carved with figures of horses and men.

Family life. Women in Yoruba families work independently and control their own incomes. Husbands may have more than one wife, and the custom is for children to inherit property from their father. However, life in the 20th century has affected the nature of inheritance. In the past, a whole lineage owned the rights to property and fruit-bearing trees. Upon the death of a father, the oldest son would assume control of all the related families. Today the traditional rules have been changed as there is a shortage of land and conflict among brothers for crops grown for cash. Land is often divided among the number of adult sons who want to work it, and rights to fruit-bearing trees now belong to the individual landowner.

Food and clothing. Although the Yoruba are known as city dwellers, they are also an agricultural people. Typically, they commute from towns to farmland where they grow a variety of crops: yams, cassava, bananas, plantain, maize, guinea corn, and beans. Their diet includes fish, meat on occasion, soup made from palm oil, and fruits and peppers for relish. As described, the Yoruba produce over 90 percent of the cocoa exported by Nigeria, and it has become their most profitable cash crop. Income from the crop has produced a degree of wealth that has created a need for shopkeepers, builders, tailors, mechanics, and other Yoruba businesspeople. Along with changes in occupations, the traditional dress is sometimes abandoned for Western-style clothing. The customary clothing for men is a long cloth gown worn to the knee or ankle, covering a sleeveless undervest and baggy trousers. The traditional garb for women is a wide piece of cloth from below the neck to the ankles. Over it, a blouse hangs to the waist. A thin veil and tie are worn around the head.

Religion. The Yoruba practice a variety of religious faiths. Most are Christian or Muslim, while some practice the traditional religion, which includes a supreme god and more than 400 lesser gods and ancestor spirits, called *orisa*. Among the practitioners of the traditional religion are members of the *Ifa* cult, which is very widespread. Ifa is the god of wisdom and one of the principal deities of the Yoruba. He is believed to have been sent to Earth from heaven to perform special tasks, such as using his profound wisdom to put the earth in order. Ifa is considered completely informed about the past, present, and future. Yoruba religion, as well as their history, government and art, are all considered roads to Ile Ife, which is the "soul" of Yoruba land.

A separate cult, the *Egungun*, is the Yoruba connection between living and dead. Yoruba believe that the spirit of a person never dies but continues to influence the living. A person experiencing misfortune may believe that one of his ancestors has been offended. Making a mask, the unfortunate one presents it to the Egungun society, who in turn appoint a member to dance with it to appease the ancestor.

Witches, another source of misfortune for women, are appeased by another group of male dancers, the *Gelde*. These men perform

A Yoruba cooking shelter. *Photo by Eliot Elisofon. Courtesy of National Museum of African Art.*

healing dances with movements like those made by women in their daily chores.

Language. The Yoruba language is made up of different dialects. A different one is spoken in each locality, but there are three major groups of dialects that are mutually understandable. They include the dialects of the Oyo empire, the Benin Empire, and that of Central Yoruba. In addition to these is a standardized form called "standard Yoruba," which is developing and is used by the media and in higher education.

Art. Exchange and profit made possible by large scale trading also made possible a class of specialized craftsmen to master art techniques that were supported by the surplus. Of all urbanized African peoples, the Yoruba produce the greatest wealth of art. The ancient bronze castings found at Ile Ife rank among the art masterpieces of the world, including those of the ancient Egyptians, Greeks, and Romans, and from Renaissance Europe. Their artworks include many materials such as stone, wood, lead, iron, copper, bronze, terra-cotta, ivory and brass. But what the Yoruba are most famous for is their use of the lost-wax method of casting metal, which is very complex and requires great skill.

Art was created and used predominantly for religious rituals and other ceremonies. It was also used to create items for other use such as cooking vessels, jewelry, ornaments, and weapons. Woods and metals, particularly iron and bronze, figure prominently in Yoruba art. Woodcarvings illustrate Yoruba lifestyles in detail and give a good idea of their cultural background. The style of these works has not changed much for the last three centuries or so. It remains naturalistic but not historical because it does not generally depict specific events or name individuals. Woodcarving has been called the heart of the people because it portrays life on the farms, in the villages, in the cults, and in the palaces. A typical carving might be a woman sitting at a loom with a baby on her back, a king presiding over an execution, or a warrior riding on horseback. Some of the objects on which these are carved are doors, posts, masks, drums and bowls.

Metalworking in Yoruba culture is the most important tradition in their history of art. The use of metals has been traced back as far as the 8th century when Arab traders passed through the region. The revolutionary role of iron is echoed in Yoruba mythology. For example, there are tales of the legendary relationship between Sango, the *orisa* of thunder and lightning, and Ogun, the *orisa* of war and iron, probably because of the importance of weaponry in defending the homeland and the power it gave them. The Yoruba believed that Ogun was present in the metal, making it active, and so all ironwork for rituals, agriculture, or hunting had to be "virgin," or never previously heated. Aside from providing a means of defense, iron was transformed into tools for agriculture. One important myth underlines the divine origin of the blacksmith. It tells that at creation, people fed on wood and water and that they had long projecting mouths. The bat, which was originally a human, is said to have been a blacksmith by trade and, using its metalworking instrument, it reduced human's mouths to their present shape. For this the bat was condemned to lose its human form and assume that of the beast.

Two Yoruban writers have gained renown outside their own country for their interpretations of the Yoruba folktales—Wole Soyinka, who won the Nobel Prize for Literature in 1986, and Amos Tutuola.

Ceremonies. The traditional Yoruba see their gods as having nervous control of the universe, demanding from humans periodic sacrifice

University of Ile Ife. *Photo by Barbara Neibel.*

to demonstrate their continued loyalty and submission. For traditional Yoruba, no major achievement in the life of an individual, a group, or a community is considered possible without the active support of the supernatural. Ritual is a constant factor of life, as shown by such events as child-naming, marriage, installation of a king, initiation into adulthood, burial rites, and annual festivals of the various communities.

Installation rites for a new king are important because of the monarchical system of government common to many Yoruba towns. The king (*oba*) is the living symbol of the community. He is considered the link between the community and the supernatural, so this

A Timi of Ede drums for dancers in Ede, Nigeria.
Photo by Eliot Elisofon. Courtesy of National Museum of African Art.

event could conceivably have an effect on everyone. Another common ceremony is the presentation of a person's *oriki*, which is a praise-name or nickname. It describes the circumstances of the birth or the development and character of a person. Prominent people, lineages and towns have oriki that are like long poems with many verses. They are sung to the beat of drums. The main purpose of oriki is to glorify, but it has other functions as well. It relates historical events with surprising accuracy and can even be funny or embarrassing to the person. This, however, depends on the orator.

For More Information

Biobaku, S. O. *Sources of Yoruba History.* Oxford: Clarendon Press, 1973.

Eades, J. S. *The Yoruba Today.* Cambridge: Cambridge University Press, 1980.

Fuja, Abayomi. *Fourteen Hundred Cowries, and Other African Tales.* New York: Lothrop, Lee, and Shepard, 1971.

Smith, Robert. *Kingdoms of the Yoruba.* London: Methuen Co. Ltd., 1969.

ZULU

(zoo' loo)

Southern African cattle herders and warriors;
called AmaZulu by the people themselves.

Population: 2,500,000 (1989 est.).
Location: Natal and Transvaal in South Africa.
Languages: Zulu, a Bantu language, Afrikaans, and English.

Geographical Setting

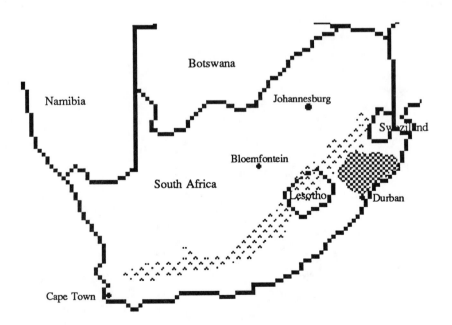

Zululand is a small reserve along the coast of the Indian Ocean in South Africa. Although they once controlled more than half of what is today the Natal Province of South Africa, about 86 percent of the Zulu population now occupies about 10,000 square miles. The land is mostly fertile coastal plain that rises to a semiarid highland in the west. Near the coast, the climate is moist and subtropical. Many streams and rivers wind through the country, draining the Drakenberg Mountains that parallel the coastline 100 to 150 miles inland. Although intensive agriculture is no longer permitted under the reserve system, subsistence agriculture and the production of livestock are practiced in some areas and are successful because of the climate. The coastal South African city of Durban lies on the southern edge of Zululand.

Historical Background

The Zulu people are descendants of the Ntungwa-Nguni peoples who inhabited the southeast region of Africa beginning in the 15th century. A subgroup, the ancestors of today's Zulu, migrated toward Natal, where it settled along the Umhlathuze River about 1700 A.D. Toward the late 1700s Natal became crowded as different small kingdoms grew in population, and the people began to spread out across the land to cultivate, herd, and hunt. Different communities often came into conflict over the land, resulting in wars and cattle raiding. In the period 1810–1818, Shaka, who was then chief of the Zulu, began to establish himself as a powerful and merciless war leader. He adopted certain recently established military tactics used by neighboring kings such as a stabbing spear (*iklwa*) in addition to the old spears that were thrown at the enemy. Shaka also changed the ways of drafting young men at certain ages for military and labor service, housing his soldiers in barracks while they remained in service about 15 years. These young men were drawn from all over the kingdom, and thus, during crucial years in their lives, developed their primary loyalties to each other by fighting, working, and living together. This measure consolidated over the years a sense of Zulu nationality.

Disliked at the royal village, where his father was ruler of the Zulu chiefdom, Shaka had gone as a young man to serve Dingiswayo, the king of Mtetwa, who promoted him to a high position in his court. Zulus were subjects in the Mtetwa kingdom. Around 1810, when Shaka's father died, Dingiswayo, impressed by Shaka's abilities, helped him gain his father's place as ruler of the Zulu. At the time he became ruler, Shaka was 23 years old.

Shaka's rule. Before Shaka became ruler, the Zulus were relatively unknown. Then in 1816 Shaka's patron, Dingiswayo, was defeated and killed by Nawane under King Zwide. Bringing up his forces too late to save Dingiswayo, Shaka crushed and scattered Zwide's army. Rallying the allies and tributaries of Dingiswayo, Shaka reshaped the old confederacy of Dingiswayo into a centralized Zulu state under his rule. He then set in place the military system for which he is famed, and proceeded to the conquest of parts of modern-day Natal.

Zulu warrior of Shaka's army.

European contact. In 1824 the first European traders arrived and took Shaka's attentions away from his subjects. By this time Shaka had succeeded in subjecting most of the tribes in the area and had created many enemies. His relationships with the Europeans were peaceful, but trouble fermented within Zululand. In 1828, Shaka was assassinated by two of his brothers, Dingane and Mhlangane. The brothers then fought for control of the Zulu. While Mhlangane was plotting to kill Dingane, Dingane succeeded in killing Mhlangane and took Shaka's throne. Eleven years later, at the Battle of Blood River, Dingane and his regiment were defeated by European voor-trekkers, Dutch pioneers also known as Boers (See AFRIKANERS), who supported the effort of his half-brother Mpande to gain the kingship. Mpande reigned over a 28-year span of relative peace. Upon his death, his son Cetshwayo became the last king of the independent Zulu nation.

The Anglo-Zulu War. In 1879, British forces invaded Zululand and the king Cetshwayo went into hiding. The British divided the land into 13 kinglets. The division was not well received by the people because the divisions took no account of the already existing tribal boundaries. Three years later, Cetshwayo returned as king of one of the kinglets. There he was succeeded by his son Dinizulu in 1884.

Dinizulu's goal was to reunite Zululand. He obtained help from the Boers for his civil war, for which the Boers demanded land. Dinizulu then appealed to the British in establishing boundary lines with the Boers. The result was a greatly diminished Zululand and a separate area for the Boers called the New Republic. In 1887, Zululand was officially annexed to Natal and protected from further dismemberment. Dissatisfied with the outcome, Dinizulu remained determined to unite the Zulu and win independence. This sentiment was widely held by his people and contributed to an unsuccessful Zulu Rebellion in 1906. Dinizulu died in 1913. Since then the Zulu have been dominated by the white government of South Africa, and have been subjected to the controls of apartheid since the late 1940s. Beginning in 1948, the whites in control of South Africa's government set up separate "homelands" for different African groups. People were forced to resettle in the homelands. The Zulu homeland, KwaZulu was in the province of Natal. In 1973, the Zulu there won some rights to self-government. Still, in the 1980s, Zulu Chief Gatsha Buthelezi strongly opposed the homeland policy, favoring instead majority rule by black Africans in South Africa. Zulu leaders view this as the best way to correct problems created by the government's apartheid system.

Culture Today

Village life. Zulu settlements were traditionally quite large and self-sufficient, but in recent years have become smaller and dependent on outside work. For those living on the reserved land, the arrangement of the village has seen little change. Typically, the village is circular or horseshoe-shaped and surrounded by wood-stake fences, with one public entrance and one or two private entrances. Because the Zulu had a fancy for labyrinths, probably originally stemming

King Cetshwayo.

from military defense needs, there are often several of these fences, one inside the other, with the center setting off the cattle pen, and the huts located between the fences. Zulu houses are traditionally dome-shaped and constructed of reeds, straw, and grass, with the floors shiny from a cow dung plaster coating. The villagers are mostly related to each other by marriage or blood. There is a separate house for the chief, each of his wives, their sons, and their families, and sometimes for adolescent girls and boys.

Other house styles have appeared with the forced move to KwaZulu. Some of the first settlers occupied houses of corrugated iron, which conducted heat poorly. Later they built earthen houses, and still later moved into cement-block homes. All these varieties exist today.

Family life. In Zulu tradition, the father of a family was generally the most respected, feared, and obeyed member. Children were not allowed to speak in the presence of the father unless spoken to. Children's behavior with the mother is often more relaxed since she is seen as less of a threat than the father. She is often disobeyed or talked back to. This variation carries over to a more formal attitude toward the father's family and a more friendly attitude with the mother's relatives.

Women perform the majority of the work. They are responsible for raising crops as well as for rearing the children. Children learn

Zulu village.

proper behavior, their roles in society, and tribal history and folklore from their mother. Women, with the help of the girls, thatch the roofs and carry wood for the homes. They make pots and mats for eating and sleeping. They also cook the food and brew the popular beer.

In the past, men were usually busy settling cases or, when young, fighting. Their at-home duties included cutting trees, constructing

Zulu homes before relocation.

Zulu homes.

houses and fences, and preparing the land for planting. They also tended to the needs of the cattle, assisted by the boys. Much time was spent in the production of weapons, which involved smelting, woodworking, ironworking, and tanning. Today more time is spent visiting other men on the reserve.

Economy. The role of men in family life and in the village is changing as more and more Zulu young men leave the village to work in the cities or in the South African mines. A father may, for example, take a job at a construction site in another province. In this event, he probably lives in a nearby work hotel, and travels home to see his family perhaps once a year.

Food. Zulus are traditionally cattle-herders and hoe-farmers. They subsist on products from their cows such as milk, meat, and blood, and from their fields (kaffir-corn, millet, sweet potatoes, beans, groundnuts, and pumpkins). In recent years the Zulu diet has been more often supplemented by processed foods obtained through trade or products introduced by contact with white civilization. Tobacco, for example, has become a popular item, as have Western-style clothes. On European-owned land bordering the Zulu reserve, cash crops such as sugarcane and cotton are grown, processed, and some of it used by the Zulu who often form part of the work force for the large farms. A few of the women find jobs in factories near their homes, and some women set up booths for selling goods on the street.

Government. The system in which political organizations depend on family ties prevailed until the British took control in the late 1800s. It continued in a less powerful mode after that. A ruling clan (governed by a chief or king) controlled the land. At the head of smaller districts were leaders who reported to the king. Below these district chiefs, villages were headed by their own chiefs. Taxes were collected when and if the king and his advisory council wanted them. A defeat in war meant maintenance of the same structure under a different leadership. Under British control, the king's power was greatly limited and remains so today. Some of today's Zulus occupy positions in the South African administration of black affairs.

Religion. Zulus look to the spirits of their ancestors for guidance in every matter of importance. These spirits are thought to have power over nature. Zulus make offerings and sacrifices before every event to appease the spirits, hoping for protection, good fortune, and happiness. Above the spirits in Zulu religion is a supreme god, *Unkulunkulu*, but this being is believed to exert less power over individual lives.

The ancestor spirits are believed to have a permanent home in the graves; therefore, graves are treated with great respect. They are sacred and cannot be disturbed. If they are, Zulus believe misfortune will fall on everyone involved. Special pains are taken to cover graves and guard them against violation. Sometimes the ancestors (*amaDlozi*) choose to visit the world of the living, which they do in the form of certain snakes. The kind of snake is determined by the status of the individual. Whenever a snake suspected of being an ancestor spirit is noticed, a sheep or goat is sacrificed to ward off evil and guarantee the happiness of the spirits.

Magic. The Zulus believe magic is used for both good and evil purposes. When something bad happens, such as illness or a poor crop, it is attributed to either an unhappy spirit or to bad magic used by an enemy. When sacrifice fails to alleviate the situation, a witch doctor is called to identify the evil-doer among the living. Good magic can be used to create love charms used by many young women. Herbs can be prepared for magic by men or women, but serious medicine can only be performed by the male witch doctors.

Ceremonies. One of the most important events for the Zulus is the Feast of the First Fruits, which is held by all tribes of Natal. It is celebrated before any of the harvest is eaten. The Zulu believe that the crops are the property of their ancestors, who grant permission for their use in exchange for sacrifices. The festival once served a second purpose—strengthening the army and the position of the king. Every warrior was called to the royal kraal to receive special medicines for the occasion. These were supposed to fill them with *nsila*, the spirit aura.

A more common, but no less elaborate, ceremony for the Zulu is the wedding. The customary version begins about a month before the actual wedding day with the bride and groom separately composing songs in honor of the event. On the chosen day, the bride's father sends a couple of cows to announce the arrival of the bride. She follows, adorned in oxtails, beads, and feathers, and completely surrounded by her friends, who hold up mats to keep her from being seen by anyone but the groom. When the party is all gathered, the bride and groom sing songs and hear advice from their relatives. A feast and party follow with much dancing and beer-drinking.

Arts. Almost every ceremony of a social nature is accompanied by music and dance, important for signifying Zulu unity. Stringed instruments made of hollowed gourds or reeds are popular. There is almost no use of drums with these instruments. Singing is characterized by repeated sounds produced by the performers in a constant flow. Songs in the form of praises play another important role. These *Izibongo* songs are used to glorify a person's accomplishments and relate their history. Once most common for warriors, Izibongo remains a way of passing folklore through the generations.

Door carving of a traditional ruler—this one in Benin City. *Photo by Barbara Neibel.*

In recent years, Zulu literature has emerged, inspired by the constant belittling of Zulu people through apartheid, or separation of the races. Albert Luthuli, the elected chief of the Amakholwa tribe echoed the feelings of many Zulu people in his autobiography *Let My People Go*. Luthuli earned the Nobel Peace Prize for his work. Benedict W. Vilakazi wrote two volumes of verse in the Zulu language. His poetry tells of the feelings of the Zulu workers in South African mines and of their pride and hopes.

Change. With the limited land space now allotted to the Zulu, and the increasingly felt effects of European civilization, Zulu identity and unity are fading. Many Zulus find it necessary to leave the villages for work in the mines or elsewhere outside of Zululand. These workers are mainly the young men who were traditionally the most important age group of the society, and who provided the strength and pride so important to the Zulus. They have adapted to the urban areas by keeping their families small and limiting the number of their wives. Although the land they occupy now is protected from exploitation, the Zulus themselves live under the strictly segregated and oppressive system of apartheid. This is felt more strongly by those who live in towns. Here there have been recent outbreaks of violence, some led by spear-wielding Zulu unhappy with their conditions. Once all Zulus and other Africans aged 16 and over had to carry passbooks with photos and directives telling where the passbook holder could live and work. It was against the law to enter an area not named in the passbook. Now passbooks have been abolished, but other practices still exist. In the 1990s, the practice of apartheid has come under increasing international censure and is being phased out of the policy of South Africa.

For More Information

Judge, Joseph. "The Zulus: Black Nation in a Land of Apartheid." *National Geographic*, December 1971, pp. 738–775.

Morris, Donald R. *Washing of the Spears: The Rise and Fall of the Zulu Nation.* New York: Simon and Schuster, 1986.

Samuelson, L. H. *Some Zulu Customs and Folk-lore.* London: The Church Printing Company, 1979.

Smail, J. L. *From the Land of the Zulu Kings.* Durban, South Africa: A. J. Pope, 1979.

The New Africa

African Countries Today

Most of the countries of Africa south of the Sahara are emerging nations, taking shapes from the 19th century boundaries set for European colonies and struggling to accommodate the distinct African societies that have existed for longer than the colonial period. Large cities exist, cities little known outside Africa, but with 500,000 to 3,000,000 citizens. These cities bring together the older societies and help develop national identities. Throughout the area, these national allegiances are in various stages of solidity, depending largely on the size and compatibility of the societies included within the country boundaries.

ANGOLA

Population: 9,220,000 (1987 est.).
Location: Western Africa; between Namibia and Zaire.
Languages: Portuguese (also English, French, Chokwe, Kikongo, Kimbudu, and several other African languages).
Principal cities: Luanda (capital), Huambo, Lobito.

The nation of Angola became independent in 1975. In the 1950s, Portugal claimed as an overseas province this land in which it had traded since the 1570s. Three different groups struggled for independence and fought each other for control of the country after the Portuguese left. The troubles did not stop when the independent government became established because of interference from both the United States and Russia and because Angola supported Namibia in its attempts to free itself from the Union of South Africa. As a result,

South African troups entered Angola periodically throughout the 1970s and 1980s.

Angola is a country largely dependent on agriculture. Before 1975, large plantations owned by the Portuguese grew coffee, sisal, cassava, and sugarcane for export. When the Portuguese left the country, many of these plantations went unattended or passed into the hands of the workers. The result has been a great decline in production on large farms. In addition, most Angolans are subsistence farmers without adequate access to roads and markets and lacking adequate profit incentives to market their crops. Today Angolans must import half of the food they need to eat.

Angola is rich in minerals: diamonds, iron, and oil. These resources are not yet fully developed, and Angola remains one of the poorest nations in Africa. The country has had to borrow large sums from other countries. However, provided peaceful conditions, Angola is more capable of overcoming these problems than many other African countries.

As with many African nations, Angola was carved out of the continent in the late 19th century as a European satellite. This was done with little regard for the people living there, some of whom had their communities and ancestor ties broken as the boundary lines cut through their lands. In Angola, as in many African countries, one attempt to restore the traditions of the people has resulted in renaming the cities to give them African language names. The city of Sao Paulo de Luanda has become Luanda, for example, and Porto Alexandra has become Tombua. In this book the different peoples who live in Angola are represented by the **Chokwe, Herero**, and **Kongo.**

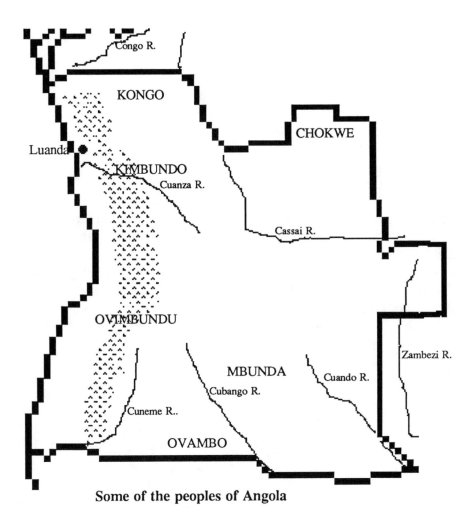

Some of the peoples of Angola

BENIN

Population: 4,000,000 (1988 est.).
Location: West Africa; between Togo and Nigeria.
Languages: French, Fon, Yoruba, Fulani.
Principal cities: Cotonou, Porto-Novo (capital).

The country of Benin, once called Dahomey, was formed in the late 19th century by agreements between the French and British, both of whom claimed territory in this part of Africa. The northern section was once part of the kingdom of Dahomey. Other small kingdoms existed nearer the ocean. Benin bulges in the north and narrows toward the Gulf of Guinea, where the chief feature is the mouth of the Ouémé River, which empties into the gulf in an area of sand banks. Benin has no good natural seaports. Toward the south, the climate is tropical—hot and humid with heavy rainfall. In the north,

the land rises to 200 to 500 feet, and the rainfall decreases a little. Far to the north, a low mountain range crosses Benin and the neighboring nation Togo.

In 1960, Benin became independent politically from France, although it remained dependent economically. The country tried for 12 years to build a working democracy. But in 1972 President Mathieu Kerekou began instead to organize a socialist state, giving the country stability. Still, economic conditions in Benin worsened. In the early 1980s a major part of the economy was smuggling products in and out of the country through Nigeria. When Nigeria closed its border with Benin between 1984 and 1986, Benin began to ask for help from other African countries. More recently the government has

Some peoples of Benin.

been trying to encourage western capitalists to help develop the country.

Once the people of Benin were separated into a number of city-states, and today they are divided between north and south. In the south Fon, Adja, and Aizo people live as farmers. In the northwest, Bariba people grow shea trees and produce kapok, a silky fiber from the fruit of the silk-cotton tree. Yoruba farmers live along the east of the country. Somba people live in the northeast, while Fulani herders are settling down in the north. Benin cultures are represented in this book by the **Fon, Yoruba**, and **Fulani**.

BOTSWANA

Population: 1,200,000 (1988 est.).
Location: Southern Africa; bounded by Namibia, Zimbabwe, and South Africa.
Languages: English, Tswana, Khoisan.
Principal cities: Gaborone (capital), Francistown, Selebi-Phikwe.

The Okavango River enters Botswana from the northwest and almost immediately spreads over a wide region to create the Okavango Swamps. Then it continues southeast to Lake Xau and the Makarikari Salt Pans. In flood times, the water forms a shallow lake over the swamp area. Farther east, the Chobe, Shashi, and Limpopo rivers and their tributaries provide a more stable water supply. It is here that 80 percent of the citizens of Botswana live.

The southern half of the country is a high (3,000 feet) semidesert and steppe, the Kalahari Desert. People who speak languages with

clicking consonants have lived in and around the Kalahari Desert for thousands of years.

Established in 1884 as a British colony called Bechuanaland, this country seemed, in the early 20th century, destined to become a part of the Union of South Africa. However, the people of the country resolutely opposed this idea, and it was abandoned in 1960 when South Africa broke away from the British Commonwealth. Botswana gained its independence in 1966. Its citizens mostly come from societies of Bantu people who formed eight small, independent kingdoms before becoming a British colony.

Except for some mining of coal, copper, and gold, most Botswanans raise cattle and goats, and plant crops needed for food. Only

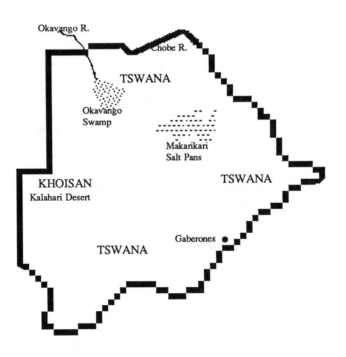

Some peoples of Botswana.

one out of five workers in Botswana is employed outside the family farm. When it became an independent country, Botswana was poor, one of the 20 poorest countries in the world. In 1971, diamonds were discovered in the country. Now Botswana is building a mining industry with mines for coal, copper, and diamonds.

Because most of the population speaks dialects of one Bantu language and the eight major groups are closely related, the people of Botswana are represented in this book by the **Tswana**, the name for their common language.

BURKINA FASO

Population: 8,500,000 (1988 est.)
Location: West Africa: north of the Ivory Coast, Ghana, and Togo.
Languages: French and several African languages: Fulani, Hausa, Mossi, Samo, Mandingo, etc.
Principal cities: Quagadougou (capital), Bobo-Dioulasso, Koudougou.

The traditional land of the Mossi people, whose populations were divided among several old kingdoms, lies in the north-central part of the country which was earlier known as Upper Volta. Once a French colony, the country became independent in 1960. After a period of six years, during which Upper Volta attempted to form a democracy, the military took control of the government. Several army factions vied for power. Between 1983 and 1987 Upper Volta suffered

a revolutionary war. The emerging leader, Captain Thomas Sankara, changed the name of the country to Burkina Faso—"Land of the incorruptible men."

The country is a flat table land that is slightly tilted to the south. It is a region of poor soil and little water. However, three rivers have cut valleys on the plateau: the Black Volta, White Volta, and Red Volta rivers. Even though the rivers dry up considerably in the dry season and flood frequently in the wet season, their valleys provide the best living conditions in the country.

Burkina Faso people are mostly poor subsistence farmers, and there is little employment in other kinds of work. Attempts to form a civilian government have failed several times and the country is ruled by the military. Despite these hardships, Burkina Faso has a rapidly growing population. In the 12 years following 1975, the population almost doubled. The rapid growth in population and the lack of good soil and other natural resources has made Burkina Faso the third-poorest country in the world.

There are representatives of many African peoples in the country, among them Mandingo (Malinke), Mossi, Bobo, Fulani, Hausa, and

Some peoples of Burkina Faso.

Tuareg. For more about the people of Burkina Faso see **Fulani, Hausa,** and **Malinke.**

BURUNDI

Population: 4,100,000 (1988 est.).
Location: East central Africa; between Rwanda, Tanzania, and Zaire.
Languages: Kirundi, French.
Principal cities: Bujumbura (capital), Gitega.

Burundi is one of two African nations that kept the old societal boundaries intact through the claims and divisions of the European countries. In the west, a range of mountains separates Burundi from Zaire. East of these mountains is a high plateau that slopes south and southeast to an altitude of 4,500 feet. The average altitude of the Burundi plateau is 5,500 feet. The tropical climate of the country is tempered by this altitude.

Most of Burundi is high grassland and most of the people are subsistence farmers, growing manioc, bananas, sweet potatoes, sor-

ghum, peas, beans, and corn. In some areas, farmers raise coffee as a cash crop. Burundi people live in small villages. Gitega, the second largest city has a population of only 16,000.

The first people of Burundi may have been a pygmy hunting group, the Twa. Bantu people settled in the region by 500–100 B.C., bringing a farming way of life and skillful ironworking. Between 1000 and 1500 A.D., numbers of specialists in cattle-raising, who are called Tutsi, began to strive for political power with the more farm-oriented people, called Hutu. Gradually Tutsi kings were able to defeat Hutu kings and chiefs and weld the chiefdoms and tiny kingdoms into one large kingdom, Burundi. In the late 19th century Germany took over the region and made it part of its colony of Tanganyika (now Tan-

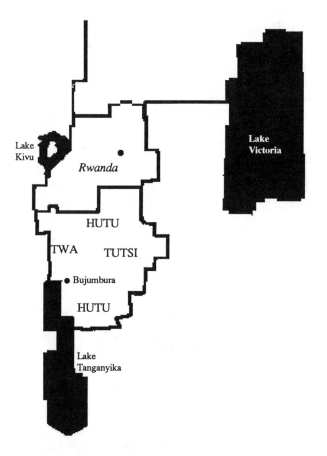

Hutu, Tutsi amd Twa castes of peoples are intermixed throughout Burundi.

zania). After Germany was defeated in World War I, Burundi and its neighbor, Rwanda, were put under Belgian rule. Colonial control left the people of Burundi under the old structure of rule, in which the Tutsi formed the ruling caste. The Tutsi excluded the Hutu from power and wealth while providing them with education and new ideas of equality. In 1962, Burundi gained independence, and the Hutu, who comprised 84 percent of the population, began to demand a greater voice in the government. The Hutu rebelled in 1972 and again in 1988, killing many of the Tutsi. The government, dominated by the old Tutsi aristocrats and with a Tutsi army retaliated both times with great massacres of Hutu. Since then, the Hutu and Tutsi have been in continual dispute.

In this book, the people of Burundi are represented by the **Tutsi**.

CAMEROON

Population: 11,000,000 (1987 est.).
Location: West Africa; southeast of Nigeria.
Languages: French, English, Tiv, Beti, Yaoundé, Bamiléké, Fang, Fulani, and others.
Principal cities: Douala, Yaoundé (capital), each with more than 500,000 residents.

The terrain of Cameroon is highly varied, ranging from southern oceanfront and tropical lowland forest to a forested upland, the central Adamaoua Plateau lies between the Benoué and Sanagra rivers, where the forests give way to the savanna of the north. The north region is a great plain that slopes down to the basin of Lake Chad. Forested mountains with peaks reaching more that 13,000 feet in altitude mark the west. Historically, the land was divided: the west

was controlled by the British and the north and east by the French. The much larger French portion became a United Nations protectorate and began to build its economy while the British section remained neglected. However, in 1961, the British section was divided. Nigeria received one portion and the rest became the new country Cameroon.

Like the terrain, the economy is diversified. Seventy-five percent of the people are engaged in agriculture, much of it subsistence farming to meet the needs of the people living there. However, cocoa and coffee are grown for export in western Cameroon. Bauxite, the ore of aluminum, has been discovered in the southwest, and in 1977 oil was discovered off the coast of Cameroon. In addition to producing oil and bauxite, the country manufactures cement, rubber, and paper.

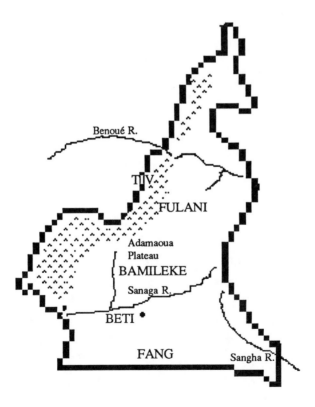

Some of the more than 80 societies of Cameroon.

The societies of Cameroon are equally varied. In the south, Fang and Beti people dominate. In the north there are Bamiléké and Fulani groups. Among the nearly 80 different Cameroon societies are small bands of pygmies in the far southeast of the country.

The same variety is seen in religion. Northeastern Cameroon peoples are Muslim, but in other areas many of the people are Christian. Still, most of the citizens of Cameroon hold to older religious traditions.

For more about the people of Cameroon see **Fang** and **Fulani.**

CENTRAL AFRICAN REPUBLIC

Population: 2,800,000 (1989 est.).
Location: Central Africa; bordered by Sudan, Zaire, Congo, and Cameroon.
Languages: French, Sangho, and several other African languages.
Principle cities: Bangui (capital), Berbérati, Bouar.

Rolling hills on a plateau 2,000 to 2,500 feet above sea level spread over this country and are broken in the northeast and north by higher hills rising to 4,000 feet. The Ubangi River, which flows south to the Congo, marks the south boundary of the country and its tributaries drain the southern and northwestern parts of the plateau. Branches of the Chari River drain the north country toward Lake Chad.

The Central African Republic is tropical, with rainfall from June to October that brings tornados and floods. The land is drier in the

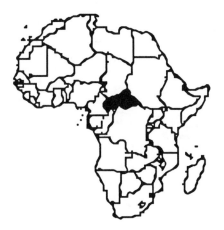

northeast and east, and in the far south a tropical forest provides dense plant life. In the north the forests give way to savanna grassland.

Although only about 9 percent of the land is suitable for growing crops, agriculture accounts for nearly half of the national income. Eighty percent of the people of the Republic earn their living in agriculture as peasant farmers or as workers on the large coffee plantations. The cotton grown in the river valleys is a major cash crop. Diamonds were discovered in 1965, but mining them has not provided the economic help needed by the country. The Central African Republic still depends on France for needed supplies and on neighboring countries such as Zaire for military support of the government.

Under French rule from 1894, the country was known as Ubangi-Shari and included the present country of Chad. The people voted, in 1958, to become an independent country in the French community, but it was not until 1960 that the Central African Republic proclaimed independence from France. The country is now led by an army general André Kolingba, who took command in 1981.

There are many African societies represented in the Central African Republic: Mandjia, Banda, Banziri, Sara, Mbum, Mbuti, Bunga,

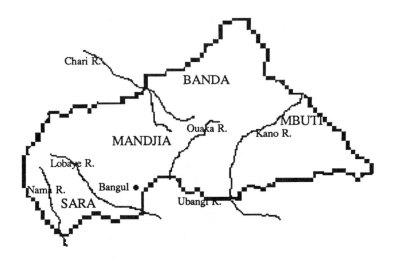

Some peoples of the Central African Republic.

Mbaka, and Zande, among others. For more about the people of this country, see **Mbuti.**

CHAD

Population: 5,000,000 (1985 est.).
Location: Central Africa; bounded by Libya, Sudan, Zimbabwi, Cameroon, Nigeria and Niger.
Languages: French, Arabic, and a number of African languages.
Principle cities: N'Djamena (capital)—once Fort Lamy, Sarh (Fort Archambault), Moundou.

Northern Chad is part of the Sahara Desert. Eastward the land becomes less barren as 4,000-foot rocky cliffs rise to Mt. Tibesti (12,000 feet). The southern part of the country is savanna, dropping as one proceeds north into the Lake Chad basin and Lake Chad, which is nearly 150 miles long and 100 miles wide but in many places only about four feet deep. Most of the people of Chad live in the southern region. Fewer than 150,000 people live in the three desert provinces.

Only about one-third of the country is suitable for cultivation, but more than two-thirds of the working people are farmers. Chad farmers grow cotton and coffee for export, and manioc, millet, corn, peanuts, sweet potatoes, and yams for their own food. There is little industry in Chad. A major obstacle to the economy of this landlocked country is the difficulty of transporting materials without adequate roads or railroads.

Proud and well adapted to the harsh land, the people of Chad, led by King Amoney of Bagirmi, resisted French rule until 1913. In 1960 Chad again became an independent country. Since then, civil wars, political upheavals, and border disputes with Libya have slowed the country's progress.

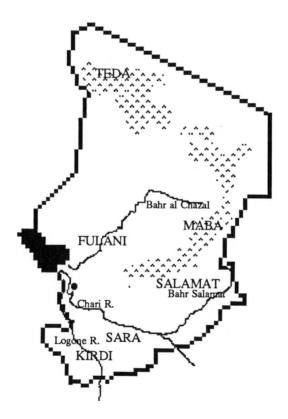

Some of the peoples of Chad.

The people are a mixture of several black societies and Arabs. They include Somrai, Bagirmi, Sara, Masa, and many others in the south and in the center, and nomadic Teda, Bulala, Arabs, and Fulani in central and northern areas. In this book you will read about the **Fulani.**

CONGO

Population: 2,000,000 (1987 est.).
Location: Central Africa; bounded by Cameroon, Central African Republic, Zaire, and the Atlantic Ocean.
Languages: French and several Bantu languages.
Principle cities: Brazzaville (capital), Pool, Pointe-Noire, Bonenza, Cuvette.

At the Atlantic Ocean, the Republic of the Congo is a flat plain cut by fingerlike ridges rising in folds to 2,000 feet above sea level. The hills of this Mayombe Escarpment are covered with forests. Eastward, the land forms a plateau dividing the Zaire (Congo) and Ogowe river basins. This is a hot, dry country where average daily temperatures reach 80-90 degrees Fahrenheit.

In the 14th to 17th centuries, the southern edges of this country were part of the great kingdom of Kongo. At the center of the country

lay the large but loosely organized kingdom of Bateke, while at the coast below the Mayonmbe range lay the commercially important kingdom of Loango. As early as the 16th century, the coast was visited regularly by European ships, while the interior regions along the river had long engaged in an established interregional trade. As trade with Europeans in the 16th century expanded to products other than ivory, these states were also often willing to participate in selling captured neighbors. Pointe-Noire was an important stop for slavers.

Today 40 percent of the citizens of Congo live in towns and cities, seven of which have populations of more than 100,000. The people work as farmers, farm product processors, fishers, miners of lead, zinc, gold, and copper, and oil field workers. Many different groups

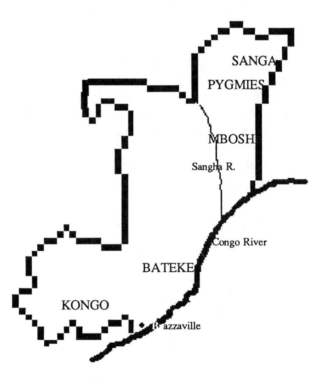

Some of the 70 or more peoples of the Republic of Congo.

of people reside in Congo, among them Kongo, Bateke, Mboshi, Sanga, and Pygmies. All speak Bantu languages. For more information about the people of the Republic of the Congo, see **Kongo.**

DJIBOUTI

Population: 387,000 (1987 est.).
Location: East Africa; on the Gulf of Aden between Ethiopia and Somalia.
Languages: French, Afar, Somali, Arabic.
Principal cities: Djibouti (capital), Dikhil, Ali-Sabieh, Tadjourah, Obock.

Long an important crossroads of trade routes between Arab states and Africa, Djibouti was claimed by the French to counteract British power in that part of the world. At first the French were interested in a small port town, Obock. However, as British competition grew, the French decided to build a new and larger port. Work on the new city-port of Djibouti began in 1887 and was completed in 1917. The French first called their small country French Somaliland and, in the

1970s, the French Territory of the Afar and Issas. Finally, with independence it took the name Djibouti after the principal city.

Temperatures sometimes exceed 120 degrees Fahrenheit. Rainfall is less than 5 inches a year, and except in the highlands of the west, plant life is scarce. Evaporation pools have left large salt deposits in some areas. Along with tending herds of goats and camels, the nomads carried salt and other trade goods inland to exchange with Ethiopians and other Africans. The economy of Djibouti has long been based on trade.

Except for Arab settlements in the larger towns, two peoples, the Afars and the Isaas, a Somali group, divide the country and share places in the legislature. Tensions between rival groups has resulted in bloodshed in recent years. For more information about peoples of Djibouti see **Afar.**

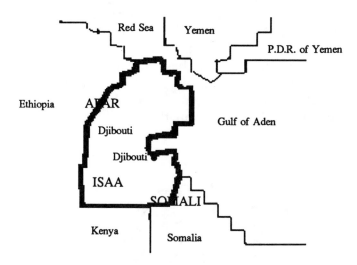

Some peoples of Djibouti.

ETHIOPIA

Population: 46,000,000 (1987 est.).
Location: East Africa; south of Sudan along the Red Sea.
Languages: Amharic, English, Arabic, Ge'ez, and more than 100 other languages.
Principal cities: Addis Ababa (capital), Asmara, Dire Dawa, Gondar.

The history of Ethiopia is so long and its people once so illustrious that early visitors from Greece and Rome called it the land of the "most just of men." Much of the center of the country is a high plateau through which runs a great depression known as the Great Rift of Africa. The high plateau has mild climate and good soil. Southeast of the plateau the land becomes dry and desertlike.

For centuries, most of the highland of Ethiopia was ruled by an emperor who claimed descent from the Queen of Sheba and King

Solomon. The last of these rulers was Haile Selassie, who was deposed in 1974 and replaced by a military government. Several reorganizations led to Ethiopia's becoming a socialist country. The indecisions and oppressive actions of government prompted many different groups to consider dividing the country. The people in the area called Eritrea, along the Red Sea, have been in rebellion since the 1950s, when Ethiopia unilaterally incorporated it under its direct rule. The Afar people who live in Ethiopia near Djibouti have also been fighting for freedom. The unrest has affected the principal industry, agriculture, which has also suffered because of severe droughts in parts of the country. As a result, many Ethiopians have died of starvation or fled the country to try to earn a living elsewhere.

The Amhara people of the highlands dominated Ethiopian government for many years. Other groups such as the Danakils, the Gallas, and the Somalis resented this and have at various times rebelled. There are many other peoples in Ethiopia, including the Falashas, the Tigre, and the Shankili, along with some immigrant Arabs, Armenians, and Greeks.

Ethiopia has been a center of eastern Christianity since the fourth century. However, Arab traders brought the Muslim faith so that now the country is about evenly split between Christians and Muslims.

For more about the peoples of Ethiopia see **Amhara, Falasha**, and **Afar.**

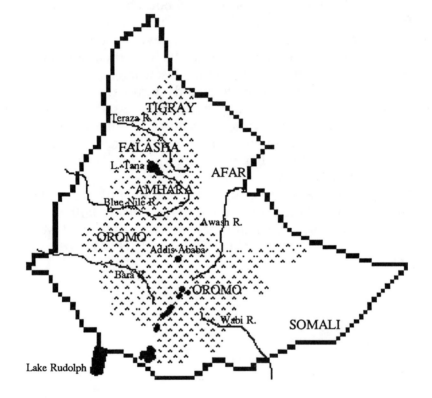

Some of the peoples of Ethiopia.

GABON

Population: 1,000,000 (1986 est.).
Location: Equatorial West Africa; bordered by Equatorial Guinea, Cameroon, Congo, and the Atlantic Ocean.
Languages: French, Fang, several Bantu languages.
Principal cities: Libreville (capital), Port-Gentil.

Lying on the equator, the Gabon countryside is made up of a flat strip near the ocean. More rugged and higher land inland is covered with tropical rain forests or land cleared of rain forests. Almost the entire country lies in the basin of the Ogooué River. This river and its tributaries provide major transportation routes, so most of Gabon's people lived as farmers and fishers along the rivers. This is changing, however. As is the case in many places in Africa, people are moving to the cities to find work. In 1976, Libreville had an

estimated population of 45,000; eight years later it had grown to nearly 250,000. Today this city's population exceeds 300,000.

Portuguese traders and, later, Dutch merchants visited Gabon in the 16th and 17th centuries. But by the 18th century, the major outside influence on Gabon was France. In the days of heavy slave trading, French ships used Port-Gentil as a center of slave trade. Today's largest port, Libreville, was started by slaves who were freed by a slave runner in 1849.

A French colony since the 1880s, Gabon voted to become a separate country in 1960. Since then oil wells have been explored on land and in the ocean near Port-Gentil, and oil has become the mainstay of the economy along with coffee and cocoa. Fishing and harvesting hardwoods are also major industries.

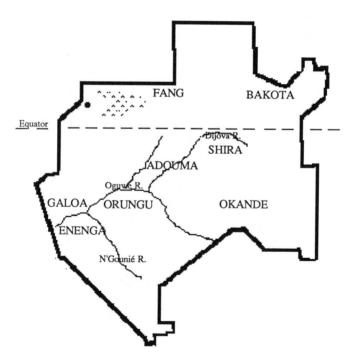

Some of the peoples of Gabon.

Gabon has had the same president since 1971, but not without opposition. There is only one political party allowed in the country, but a major group seeking to open elections to other parties became so strong that by the 1980s its leaders were forced into exile. There are now two governments claiming rule over Gabon, the elected one and the one in exile.

About half the people of Gabon are Christian; most of the rest hold to more traditional beliefs. One-third of the people are Fang, and one-fourth are Eshira people. In addition, Aduma, Okande, Seke, Bakele, and Mbede are citizens of the country.

For more about the people of Gabon see **Fang**.

GHANA

Population: 14,800,000 (1989 est.).
Location: West Africa; between the Ivory Coast and Togo, and between the Atlantic Ocean and Burkina Faso.
Languages: Fifty-six languages of which 7 are official: English, Akan, Dagbani, Ewe, Ga, Hausa, and Nzema.
Principal cities: Accra (capital), Kumasi, Tamale, Tema.

The Black Volta and Red Volta rivers mark the northwestern and northeastern boundaries of Ghana, while the White Volta cuts through the country between them. The three rivers join in the center of the country to form Lake Volta, which runs down along the eastern edge of the country. As the Black Volta River curves across Ghana to meet the other rivers, it provides a boundary between the northern territories and the land of the Ashanti. The southwest is marked by

forests and heavy rainfall. Northward, the forests give way to savanna grasslands. A mountain range, the Togo-Atakora, lies on the east and runs southwest to northeast into Togo.

Under British rule, this land, called the Gold Coast, was a country searching for independence as early as World War II. However, it was not until Dr. Kwame Nkrumah organized a dissenting political party in 1949 that pressure was brought to make it a separate country. Dr. Nkrumah became head of the colonial government and in 1957 succeeded in merging British Togoland and the Gold Coast into one nation. Calling himself *osagyefo,* "the one who is successful in war," Dr. Nkrumah led the country until he was deposed by the military in 1966. Since then several different governments have led the country.

Some of the peoples of Ghana.

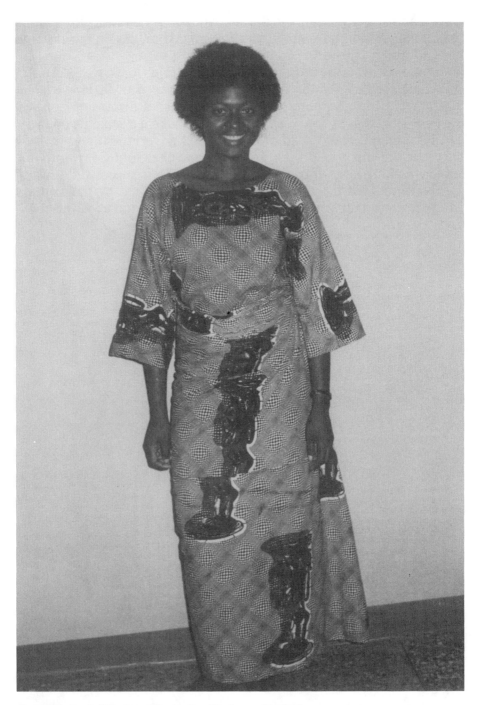

A woman of Ghana. *Photo by Barbara Neibel.*

Agriculture and mining are Ghana's two major resources. Relying mostly on selling cocoa beans, the economy has not kept up with the growth in population. Raising millet and cassava in large quantities for their home market, most of Ghana's farmers are small-scale commercial and subsistence farmers. Once rich in gold, Ghana has now found it necessary to spend government money to manage and support the mines.

In earlier days, Ghana was heavily involved in commerce, trading kola north to the savanna and slaves south to Europeans at the coast. Leaders in this business were the powerful Ashanti who ruled most of the country from their capital at Kumasi, in the south central part of the country. Today, the Ashanti share the economic problems and the government with Nzima, Ahanta, Evalue, Ga, Moshi, Dagomba, Gonja, and many other groups. For more information about the people of Ghana see **Ashanti** and **Ewe.**

GUINEA

Population: 6,300,000 (1987 est.).
Location: West Africa, bounded by Guinea-Bissau, Senegal, Mali, Ivory Coast, and Liberia.
Languages: French, English, Malinke, Susu, Fulani.
Principal cities: Conakry (capital) and Kankan.

One of the most beautiful countries in Africa, Guinea is a land of mountains and rolling high plains covered with hardwood forests. Except for a small section in the northeast which is flat, sandy ocean-front, the land is mostly rugged and forested. Northeast of the flat coast, the land rises to a mountain region called Futa Djalon, the origin of two important West Africa rivers, the Senegal and the Gambia.

In ancient times, northeastern Guinea may have been at the southern edge of the Ghana Empire. In 1725 and again in the mid-

1800s, the region of the Futa Djalon became the base for holy wars. The *jihad* of the 1800s was led by a Muslim leader al-Hajj 'Umar from Senegal, who had moved near the Fulani. When his son Ahmadu became leader he joined in a treaty with the French for protection of the land, although he later refused to recognize the treaty. The French persisted in military operations and took command of the country.

By 1958, France was revising its attitude toward African colonies and offered them some independence under a community of French territories. The people of Guinea voted against this and were immediately cut off from French assistance and leadership. The records of French actions in business and government were destroyed, making it necessary for the new leader, Sekou Touré, to seek help from other sources. Receiving support from the Soviet Union, Touré established an army of 30,000 and used it to rule the country ruthlessly until his death in 1984. Plots to overthrow the government and rumors of plots resulted in raids to exterminate Touré's enemies. Upon the death of Touré, a military government was established that

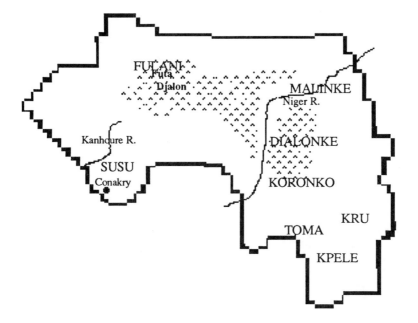

Some of the peoples of Guinea.

proved to be less cruel than the earlier regime. The leader General Lansana Conté has ruled since 1984.

Its mineral deposits and rich farmland make Guinea a potentially rich country of Africa. However, without investments from other countries, the government of Guinea has been unable to develop this potential. Meanwhile, Guinea people have been moving to the cities in search of work. One fifth of the population lives in the city of Conakry.

The people of Guinea include Fulani, Malinke, Susa, Dialonke, Kru, Kpele, Toma, Koranki, and various other groups. In this book, the people of Guinea are represented by **Malinke, Kru**, and **Fulani**.

GUINEA-BISSAU

Population: 940,000 (1989 est.).
Location: West Africa; bounded by Senegal, Guinea, and the Atlantic Ocean.
Languages: Portuguese, and several African languages.
Principal city: Bissau (capital).

Low lying ground covered with mud flats and mangrove swamps, some of which are inundated by incoming tides, make up most of Guinea-Bissau. This low ground rises gradually eastward toward the Futa Djalon of Guinea. In addition, Guinea-Bissau, which owes its separation from neighbors to early claims of ownership by the Portuguese, contains a collection of islands. Meandering rivers provide the major travel routes in the country.

While never seriously settled by the Portuguese, Guinea-Bissau was claimed by Portugal until 1974. Civil war in 1973–74, in which

as many as 40,000 Portuguese troops were needed to suppress re-
bellions, convinced the government of Portugal to abandon its hold.
There followed a civilian government, then a military rule led by
Commander Joao Bernardo Viera, who assumed power in 1980.

Most people of Guinea-Bissau are farmers. They raise rice and
sorghum, along with sweet potatoes, cassava, maize, beans, and other
crops for food. In recent years of drought and locust infestations,
these farmers have not been able to raise enough crops to feed the
people of the country, making it necessary to import thousands of
tons of grain. Fishing is also an important occupation and source of
food, while on higher land near Futa Djalon cattle-herding is an
important business. Guinea-Bissau has deposits of bauxite (aluminum ore) but the terrain makes it too difficult to mine profitably.

About 32 percent of the Guinea-Bissau people are of the Balante
society. Other groups include Fulani, Mandyako, Malinke, and Pa-
pels. The Guinea-Bissau people are represented in this book by **Malinke** (Mandingo) and **Fulani** societies.

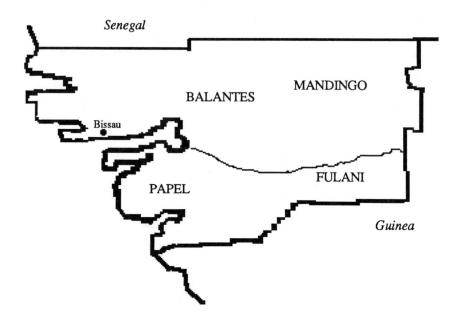

Some of the societies of Guinea-Bissau.

IVORY COAST

Population: 11,500,000 (1988 est.).
Location: West Africa; on the coast between Ghana and Liberia.
Languages: French, Agni (Ashanti related), and more than 60 other languages.
Principal cities: Abidjan, Bonaké.

The Ivory Coast (Côte D'Ivoire), once part of French Africa, has been an independent democracy since 1960. Its one political party has succeeded in electing the same president for six five-year terms. Under the rule of President Félix Houphouët-Boigny, news has been carefully controlled and the economy guided so that the Ivory Coast has one of the most varied economies in Africa.

The country is relatively flat land in most areas, tilting slightly toward the Atlantic Ocean and rising in the northwest to 4,000-5,000-

foot mountains. Four major rivers run parallel north and south through the land. As with other countries in West Africa, the coastline is often hidden by sandbars and lagoons. In order to build a modern port, it was necessary to clear a channel through the sand.

Most of the Ivory Coast is tropical land once covered by rain forests. Today, however, much of the rain forest has been cleared to grow coffee. The Ivory Coast is now the third-largest coffee producer in the world. In recent years, farmers have added cotton as a market crop.

Although 60 percent of the workers are in farm industries, fishing and the manufacture of products such as rubber footwear and cigarettes, are major industries.

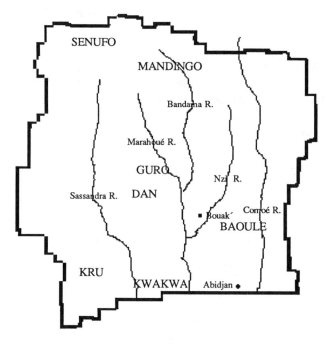

Some of the many peoples of the Ivory Coast.

The people of the Ivory Coast represent many different African societies: Ashanti, Agni, Kwakwa, Kru, Malinke (Mandingo), Senufo, Dan, Guro, and others. For information about the people of the Ivory Coast, see **Ashanti, Kru**, and **Malinke**.

A polychrome-painted house in Cote D'Ivoire. *Photo by Eliot Elisofon. Courtesy of National Museum of African Art.*

KENYA

Population: 21,600,000 (1987 est.).
Location: East Africa, on the equator; bounded by Ethiopia, Sudan, Somalia, the Indian Ocean, Tanzania, and Uganda.
Languages: Kiswahili, English, Kikuyu, Luo, and other African languages.
Principal cities: Nairobi (capital), Mombasa.

Kenya is a land of contrasts. Although the country is near the equator, its highest point, Mount Kenya (17,000 feet), supports small glaciers. Cut by the Great Rift Valley, the western area of Kenya is dotted with lakes, of which Lake Victoria is the most famous. North and east, three-fifths of the country is an arid semidesert. South and west, the country rises to a highland region where 80 percent of the Kenyans live.

Known in the 18th and 19th centuries for its trade routes pioneered by the Kamba people, and later operated by Kikuyu, Luo, and Luyia societies, the land was claimed in the 19th century by the British, who needed these same trade routes inland. They brought in white settlers, built a railroad to Uganda, taxed local Africans to get them to work for Europeans, and excluded Africans from the trade business. However, following World War II, there were actions by many of the older societies to gain a voice in the government. One side-effect in 1953–55 was a fierce Kikuyu rebellion (see KIKUYU) directed against the Kikuyu who cooperated with the British. After this "Mau Mau" rebellion was defeated, politicians and trade unions supported a boycott against the government in 1957. The leader of

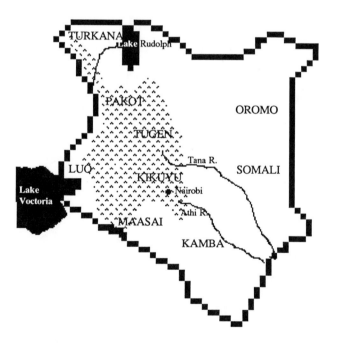

Some of the peoples of Kenya.

the boycott was Tom Mboya, who operated from the trade unions. In 1964, Kenya became a republic within the British Commonwealth and Jomo Kenyatta became president. He was succeeded by President Daniel Arap Moi, the current leader of Kenya.

The people of Kenya are farmers, fishers, and herders. Coffee, tea, cotton, sugarcane, and sisal, about half grown on small individual farms, provide about a third of the nation's income.

In addition, Kenya is one of the most industrial countries in East Africa, with paper mills, auto manufacturers, and cement and other factories. A major part of the livelihood of Kenyans is tourism. Nearly a million people visit the wildlife preserves each year.

Kenya has long had strong societies vying for leadership. Luo, Kikuyu, Maasai, Luhya, and Kamba demand voices in government, as do Galla, Turkana, Somali, Hausa, and others. In this book, the people of Kenya are represented by the **Kamba, Maasai**, and **Kikuyu.**

LESOTHO

Population: 1,600,000 (1987 est.).
Location: South Africa, surrounded by the Union of South Africa.
Languages: Sesotho, English.
Principal cities: Maseru (capital), Leribe, Mafeteng, Berea, Mohale's Hoek.

One far-sighted and immensely skillful king is responsible for the existence of the country of Lesotho. In 1821 and 1822, Moshoeshoe, while still a minor chief, reorganized people of his region after disastrous Zulu and Matabele raids and established Basotholand. Originally much larger than it is today, the country was reduced by land claims of the Boers until the British were asked for protection. After the Boer-Lesotho War of 1865–1868, Basotholand became a British protectorate and in the 1870s was incorporated into the Cape Colony.

But the Basotho, prospering as suppliers of grain to the diamond mines, were able to rearm. In 1878-1880 they fought the Cape Colony, forcing the British to free them from Cape Colony rule and again make them a direct British protectorate.

Nearly a century later, in 1958, another minor chief, Leabua Jonathan, organized the Basutoland National Party. Becoming prime minister, Jonathan met opposition within and outside the country. Moshoeshoe II, king over the house of Basotho chiefs, was attempting to gain power. Meanwhile Jonathan was finding resistance to his development plans from nearby South Africa. He nevertheless led the country until a military coup in 1986.

Lesotho is a poor country whose assets some list as people and water. Rolling hills 6,000–7,000-feet high rise to meet spurs of the Drakensburg Range in the east of the country. Two main rivers of southern Africa originate in these mountains: the Orange and the Tugela. The country is mostly grassland with few trees. Only 10 percent of the land is suitable for farming.

About half the men of Lesotho travel to South Africa to work. For better transportation to work, families gather together in villages

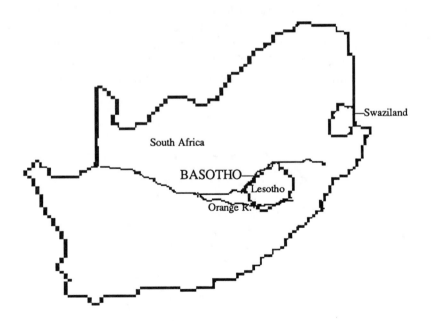

The people of Lesotho.

to use public transportation. At the same time, however, families raise livestock and some plant products on small plots of land. In this grassland, maize is the most important crop. Recently, diamond developments have added to the economy of Lesotho, but the people still remain heavily dependent on South Africa since there is little paid employment in Lesotho.

Basotho, the people of Lesotho, are a single society with many chiefs and subchiefs. However, the land of the Zulu is near Lesotho and some Zulu live in the country (see **ZULU**).

LIBERIA

Population: 2,300,000 (1987 est.).
Location: West Africa; on the Atlantic Coast between Sierra Leone and the Ivory Coast.
Languages: English, Vai, Bassa, Lorna and nearly 20 other languages.
Principal city: Monrovia (capital).

Founded in 1822 by 16,000 freed slaves who returned to Africa under the sponsorship of the American Colonization Society, and who were joined by 5,700 slaves rescued from slave ships by the British and American navies, Liberia has been an independent country since 1847. In the 20th century, the country was led by William Tubman and then by William Tolbert, whose policies were aimed at unifying the more than 20 ethnic groups of the country. However, progress

stalled in 1979, when the government was overthrown by a group led by an army sergeant. Sergeant Doe dubbed himself a general and commander in chief of the armed forces, and ruled Liberia for 11 years until his death at the hands of rebels in early 1991.

The coast of Liberia is a maze of swamps, mangrove forests, and shallow lagoons, in some places extending for 50 miles inland. There the land rises slightly into a dense forest. As the land rises farther inland, it rises to a mountain range near the border with Guinea to the north, and the forest becomes less dense. The coast of Liberia is not suitable for large-ship activity except in a few man-made ports.

The people of Liberia support themselves by subsistence farming and by exporting forest products such as rubber. In addition, small

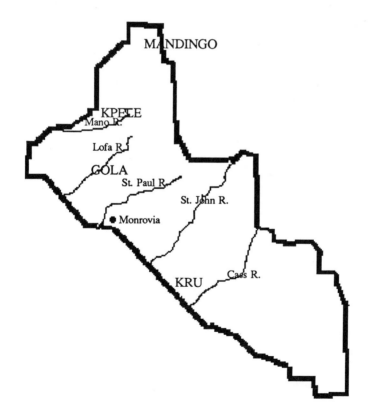

Some peoples of Liberia.

farm animals such as goats, sheep, and pigs are kept. Liberia is, however, dependent on support from other countries, especially from the United States of America.

Despite efforts to unify the country, regional societies still exist. They include the southwest Vai people, the coastal Kru, and the Golla, Kpele, and Mandingo peoples in the center of the country. There are also Fanti fisherman who come to Liberia to fish for a few years and then return to their homes in Ghana. For more about the peoples of Liberia, see **Kru** and **Malinke** (Mandingo).

Inside a home near Robert's Port, Liberia. *Photo by Tom Weir.*
Courtesy of the National Museum of African Art.

Building a home in Liberia. *Photo by Tom Weir. Courtesy of the National Museum of African Art.*

MADAGASCAR

Population: 10,277,000 (1986 est.).
Location: East of the African mainland in the Indian Ocean.
Languages: French, Malagasy.
Principal cities: Antananarivo (capital), Betsimisaraka, Betsileo, Tsimihety, Sakalava, Antandroy, Antaisaka. (All except the capital city have fewer than 100,000 people.)

Hot and humid in the east and northwest and hot and dry in the west, Madagascar has a temperate region in the highland in the center of the island. It is home to people who came in waves from southeast Asia and Africa beginning in the first five centuries A.D. Before then the island was uninhabited. By the 18th century, three major kingdoms ruled the island: Sakalava in the west, Betsimisaraka in the east, and the Merina Kingdom in the central highlands. This central

kingdom had begun to claim rule over all of the island under the great King Andriananimpoina (1787–1810) when the French began to take an interest in the region.

In 1885, the island was proclaimed a French protectorate, and in 1896 Madagascar was annexed to France. It remained part of the French colonies until 1960 when the French granted independence to the country led by Philibert Tsiranana.

Once a large part of the island was covered with forest, but slash-and-burn farming and overgrazing have worn away the forest so that most of Madagascar is now grassland. Two-thirds of the population raise rice on small plots of land. Other farmers grow coffee, vanilla, cloves, cotton, and sisal for export. While the population has been

Some of the many peoples of Madagascar.

growing rapidly, the land devoted to food crops such as rice has been shrinking.

More than 15 ethnic groups cling to some of their old traditions on the island, among them Merina, Betsimisaraka, Betsileo, Sakalava, Antandroy, and Antaisaka, each speaking its own dialect of the Malagasy language. Of these groups, you will find the **Betsileo** in this book.

MALAWI

Population: 8,000,000 (1987 est.).
Location: East Central Africa; bounded by Zambia, Mozambique, and Tanzania.
Languages: English, Chinyanja, Chitumbuka, Yao.
Principal cities: Blantyre, Lilongwe (capital).

Lying in the Great Rift Valley, Malawi's chief feature is Lake Malawi, 1,500 feet above sea level and 360 miles long. The land of Malawi lies west and south of this great lake and rises to a plateau 3,000- to 4,000-feet high, dotted with 8,000- to 10,000-foot mountain peaks, and sloping downward to the south. Mild temperatures and drizzly rains make the area nearly ideal for agriculture. About one-quarter of the land is forest, where pulpwood is harvested and there is a wide variety of animal life.

In the 14th to 16th centuries, much of the country was ruled by the ancient Malawi Empire and the smaller states succeeding it. At that time the area was a major source of ivory and cotton, and cloth weaving had developed into an important local industry.

Taken over by the British, the early moves for an independent Malawi came in 1914 when Reverend John Chilembwe led a revolt in what was then called Nyasaland. This revolt failed, but did demonstrate a growing desire for an independent Africa. Holding firm to their claim, the British made Nyasaland part of the Central African Federation by uniting it with Rhodesia in 1953. African leaders who objected to this arrangement were imprisoned. Upon their release in 1960, these leaders again led an agitation that resulted in self-government for their people in 1963, self-government of Nyasaland as a British protectorate in 1963, and finally renaming the completely independent country with its old name in 1964. Dr. Hastings Kambuzu Banda took charge in 1966 in a political system that has only one political party. In 1971 he made himself president for life.

Eighty-eight percent of the people of Malawi live in the southern half of the country as farmers. Raising maize, cassava, and millet for food, and tobacco and tea for export, these farmers contribute nearly half the income of Malawi.

Only a few thousand Asians and Europeans live in Malawi. The rest of the population is made up of Africans of various groups who are seeking to improve the economic affairs of the country. Projects for building dams to generate needed energy are under construction on some of the waterways. Bantu societies represented in Malawi include Nyanja, Yao, Ngoni, and Tumbuka.

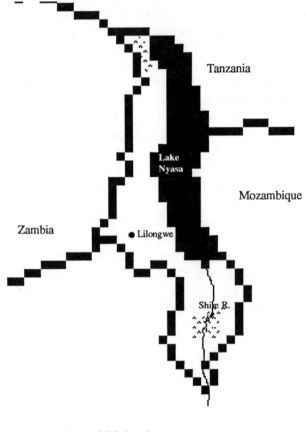

Tanzania

Lake
Nyasa

Mozambique

Zambia

● Lilongwe

Shire R.

Bantu peoples of Malawi:
 CHEWA
 YAO
 NGONI
 NYANJA
 TUMBUKA

MALI

Population: 7,600,000 (1987 est.).
Location: West Africa; bordered by Algeria, Niger, Upper Volta, Guinea, Ivory Coast, Senegal, and Mauritania.
Languages: French, English, Bambara, Wolof, Peulh (Fulani), Sonrai, Sarakolé, Tuareg.
Principal cities: Bamaka (capital), Segou, Mopti.

Home of the Bambara people, Mali takes its name from the Bambara word for rhinoceros, an animal of great strength. It is a land of contrasts, with a desert in the north, and becoming a grassland and fertile area in the south near the Niger River. The land rises to the Futa Djalon in the southwest. Here valleys have been carved in the rising mountains by tributaries of the Niger River. Much of the northern part of the country is loose sand.

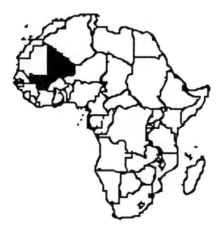

Once the location of the great Kingdom of Mali (See OLD CUL-
TURES: MALI) and then the Kingdom of Songhai (See OLD CUL-
TURES: SONGHAI), southern Mali was the southern end of trade
routes across the Sahara Desert from the north and east. Traders
brought goods and religion to the people of Mali and today about 90
percent of the people are Muslims.

The country gained independence from France in 1959, joining
with Senegal in the Mali Federation. Immediate disagreements between the two states broke the federation and resulted in Malian
independence in 1960 under the leadership of Modibo Keita. Building
a one-party socialist state, President Keita ruled until 1968 when he
was replaced by leaders of the army.

Mali's access to sea transportation is a serious difficulty in any
attempts to improve trade. Landlocked, it depends on seaports in
Senegal for shipping and receiving goods. Because of this difficulty,
and because much of the land is inhospitable, Mali has not developed
a strong economic base. Most Malis are farmers. Only one-fifth live
in cities and large towns, and about five percent of the people are

Some of the peoples of Mali.

still nomadic herders. A long and disastrous drought through the late 1970s and early 1980s has added to their economic problems.

In the past, southern Mali was the center of much movement of societies of Africans and of much travel northward and eastward in trade from such great ancient cities of Timbuktu and Gao. Today these cities have been virtually abandoned as a result of the drought. However, the array of peoples who live in Mali remains: Bambara, long-time leaders in the west, Fulani near Futa Djalon, Marka, Songhai, Malinke, and Senoufo in the Niger River region, nomadic Tuareg in the north, and Dogon, who were perhaps the earliest settlers of the region. In this book, the people of Mali are represented by the **Fulani**, **Malinke** and **Tuareg.**

Loading slabs of salt onto boats at Timbuktu. *Photo by Eliot Elisofon. Courtesy of National Museum of African Art.*

Some granaries near Senou, Mali. *Photo by Eliot Elisofon. Courtesy of National Museum of African Art.*

A mosque in Mali. *Photo by Shiva Rea Bailey.*

Carving an antelope headdress. *Photo by Eliot Elisofon. Courtesy of National Museum of African Art.*

MAURITANIA

Population: 1,800,000 (1987 est.).
Location: Western Sahara Desert Africa; bounded by Western Sahara, Algeria, Mali, Senegal, and the Atlantic Ocean.
Languages: Arabic, French, Wolof, Tukulor.
Principal city: Nouakchott (capital and the only city with a population over 100,000).

Trade winds cool the otherwise warm coastal area and in the south, the desert begins to change to savanna and drops to the valley of the Senegal River. Otherwise, Mauritania is a desert land with little plant and animal life. However, Mauritania is rich in mineral deposits: iron, phosphate, copper, uranium, and gold.

Before the 15th century, invaders from the north, Arabs and Berbers, had entered what is now Mauritania, pushing south the black

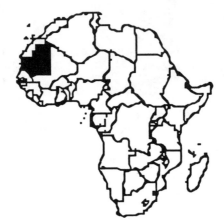

residents of the region who lived north of the Senegal. Berbers destroyed the ancient kingdom of Ghana, which had spread into Mauritania, and occupied the land. However, by the 17th century, Arabs from the northeast had dominated the Berbers. In the early 1800s, French adventurers had signed treaties with Moorish chiefs and began to control the land. By 1909 the French had gained control over the whole region. Mauritania became a separate French unit in 1920 but had its capital in Senegal. By 1958, Mauritania had become a self-governing state still under French direction. Then in 1961, it became an independent nation with a constitution that demanded that the president be a follower of the Muslim faith.

Northern Mauritania is inhabited by nomadic herders of sheep, goats, and camels, who considered their farming countrymen along the Senegal to be inferior. However, this is changing as Mauritania develops its rich mineral deposits.

Nearly half the people of Mauritania are Moors, descendants of the Moors who swept through northern Africa and into Spain in the 11th century. Other peoples represented in the country are Tukulors, Sarakoles, and Fulani. For more about the people of Mauritania see **Fulani**.

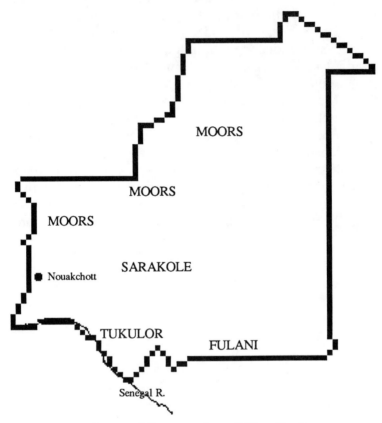

Some of the peoples of Mauritania.

MOZAMBIQUE

Population: 15,000,000 (1988 est.).
Location: East Africa; bordered by Tanzania, Malawi, Zambia, Zimbabwe, South Africa, Swaziland, and the Indian Ocean.
Languages: Portuguese, English, and various Bantu languages.
Principal city: Maputo (capital).

A low coastal land that rises in the west to a high plateau, Mozambique is divided at its center by the Zambezi, one of Africa's largest rivers. Other rivers cut fertile valleys in the south and north: the Limpopo and the Sabi in the south, and the Lugenda in the north. These river valleys and the deltas where they drain into the Indian Ocean are fertile lands; however, in the south and center of the country much of the soil is poor and sandy. Elephants, hippopotamuses, leopards, baboons, and gazelles are examples of animals native to

the country. Cashew nuts grow wild in parts of the country; unfortunately, so do carriers of many diseases, such as malarial mosquitos and tsetse flies.

The Portuguese did not gain firm control over the country until the 1920s. Then in the 1960s a guerrilla war for independence was begun under the leadership of Dr. Eduardo Mondlane. When he was assassinated ten years later, Samora Machel took over the movement. Through these efforts, independence came to Mozambique in 1974. Mozambique has had a continuing history of turmoil because of South Africa's military attacks and support of a rebel group, RENAMO.

Nearly nine of every ten workers in Mozambique are farmers. They raise sugarcane, cotton, tea, sisal, maize, bananas, and rice, also

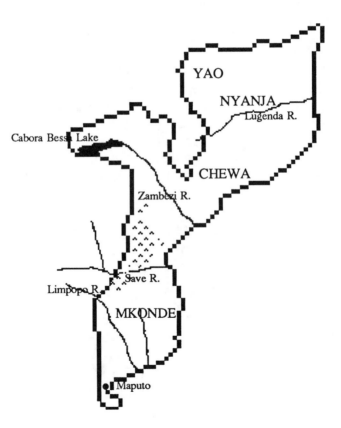

Some peoples of Mozambique.

harvesting wild cashew nuts. Still, many of these farmers have found it necessary to travel to South Africa and Zimbabwe to supplement their incomes by working in the mines. Even this is not enough to offset the difficulties partially caused by drought but greatly increased by the actions of RENAMO, which have kept people from planting crops in large areas. Nearly one-half of the population of Mozambique does not have enough food, and some estimate that as many as 4,500,000 are in danger of starvation.

Forty percent of the people of Mozambique are of the Makua-Lomwe society. North of the Zambezi River live Yao, Nyanja, and Chewa, while the Makonde live on the Rovuma River. In southern Mozambique important peoples are the Tsonga, Hlengwe, and Chopi, all of whom speak Bantu languages.

NAMIBIA

Population: 1,200,000 (1988 est.).
Location: South Africa; bordered by Angola, Botswana, the Union of South Africa, and the Atlantic Ocean, with a short neck of land bordering Zambia in the northeast.
Languages: Ovambo, Herero, Nama, English, German, Afrikans.
Principal city: Windhoek (capital and only city with a population over 100,000).

In the 18th and 19th centuries, Namibia was a land of numerous independent communities, including Ovambo and Herero in the north, Nama and other Khoisan-speaking peoples in the south, and a mixture of Herero and Khoisan groups in the central area. In the 1880s, it was claimed by the Germans. At the beginning of the 20th century, Germany consolidated its rule by virtually eliminating the

Herero of central Namibia, killing around 80,000 men, women, and children. The Germans appropriated most of the best central land and gave it to white settlers, a process that continued after World War I, when South Africa took over the territory under a mandate from the United Nations, and after World War II, when the area became a United Nations trust territory still under South African control. Namibians long expressed their desire for independence but their efforts were unrecognized as South Africa incorporated the country into its own government in 1968. Agreeing to a policy of armed resistance declared in 1966, Namibians fought against its more powerful trustee. Finally, in 1989, after several years of maneuvering involving the United Nations, United States, South Africa, and other countries, Namibia succeeded in establishing its independence.

Along the Atlantic Ocean, Namibia is a coastal desert that rises inland to a plateau area, then falls again to begin the Kalahari semi-desert. Fishing was once a large contributor to the economy. As time passed, the waters became over-fished, but the industry is recovering in the 1990s. Rainfall even in the best-watered high plateau area is no more than about 15–18 inches a year, so that much of the land is only suitable for grazing livestock. Since the early 20th century, much of the farming has been controlled by 5,000 large commercial ranches, so that 20,000 Nama and other black herders were compressed into central and southern reserves, and 120,000 black families lived on about 5 percent of the land in the north. Here the rainfall averages between 10 and 20 inches a year. Today more than half the people live in the northern third of the plateau, and most of them work in the country's major industries: mining for diamonds and uranium. About half of the food needed for Namibians must now be imported.

The African peoples of Namibia include members of the Ovambo, Kavango, Herero, Damara, Nama, and Tswana societies, represented in this book by the **Herero** and **Tswana**, and of other smaller Khoisan-speaking hunter-gatherers.

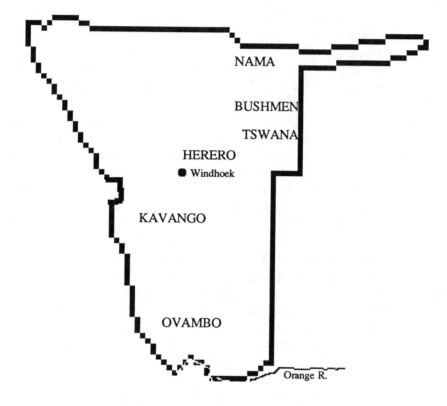

Some of the peoples of Namibia.

NIGER

Population: 7,200,000 (1988 est.).
Location: West Africa; bordered by Burkina Faso, Mali, Algeria, Libya, Chad, Nigeria, and Benin.
Languages: French, Hausa, Arabic, Tuareg, and many other African languages.
Principal cities: Niamey (capital), Zender.

Winning independence from France in 1960, Niger, like many other new African countries, tried a form of democracy. Its people began independence under a president (Hamani Diori) only to have that government fall to a military coup and to be ruled by military leaders.

Trees and shrubs mark the savanna and steppe of the south and give way to the Sahara Desert in the north. The land rises to a mountain range in the center of the country, then slopes down into the

Niger River basin for 180 miles in the south. Lake Chad, a large and shallow lake, forms part of the border in the east. Throughout the changing landscape, Niger has adequate rainfall for agriculture only in its southern parts; large areas are used for raising livestock, while fishing is important along the Niger River and at Lake Chad. Ninety-eight percent of the people earn their living by fishing, farming, or herding. One-fifth of the population consists of nomadic herders, while only one-sixth lives in large towns or cities.

Recently, mining of uranium, tin, and gold deposits has added to the economy, but the mining and trading of copper was carried on as early as the second millennium B.C. Trade is difficult, however, because Niger is landlocked, and its merchants must travel nearly 1,000 miles from its capital through neighboring countries to reach seaports. The poverty of the country is reflected in its schools, which claimed an attendance in 1986 of only 293,000 elementary students.

Like many other African countries, Niger is peopled by many societies. Hausa, Songhai, Fulani, and Beriberi-Manga societies exist in the south, while Tuareg herders roam the north. In this book you will find more about the **Hausa** and **Fulani**.

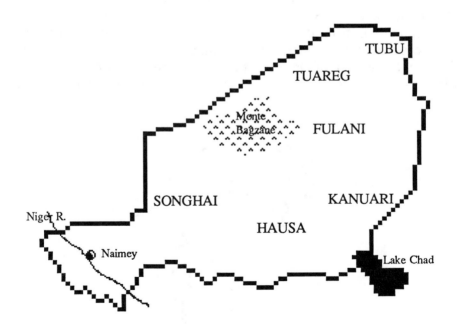

Some peoples of Niger.

NIGERIA

Population: 102,000,000 (1987 est.).
Location: West Africa; bounded by Cameroon, Chad, Niger, and Benin.
Languages: English, Hausa, Kanuri, Fulfulde (Fulani), Bini, Yoruba, Igbo (Ibo), and over 100 others.
Principal cities: Lagos (capital), Ibadan, Ife, Benin City, Kano, Zaria, Katsina, Abeokuta, Port Harcourt, and Nsukka.

The Jos Plateau, a high grassland in the center of Nigeria rises slowly toward the east. Northward, the land becomes a plain covered with the bush and grass of the savanna. Rich soil covers the north and southwest. To the south, the coast is lined with mangrove swamp forests for a distance of 10 to 50 miles inland. Here branches of the Niger River form a delta cut by small rivers and creeks. From the

mangrove forest belt, a tropical rainforest reaches inland for 100 miles.

The Niger River enters Nigeria from the northwest and meets its major tributary, the Benué River, in southeast Nigeria. Several of the ancient kingdoms and present African societies developed along the Niger and Benué. Some of these peoples have had a profound effect on the development of the country of Nigeria.

Today, three large societies form the majority of the population of the country: the Ibo in the east, Yoruba in the west, and Hausa in the north. Along with these groups, a number of other major societies are represented in the country: Ibibio, Fulani, Kanuri, Nupe, Edo, and others.

About 1940 political parties began to drive toward total independence. Three organizations arose representing the three large societies and campaigning for freedom. Initially the western party, mostly composed of Yoruba, led the struggle. However, when independence finally came in 1960, the northern-based party won the largest number of seats in the parliament and led the new government.

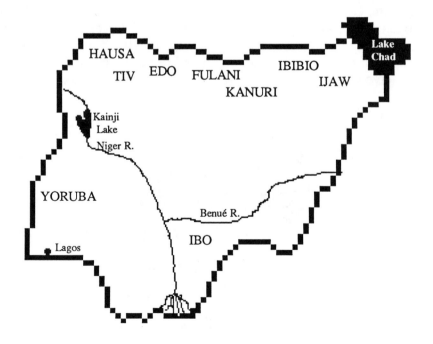

The peoples of Nigeria.

In 1965 a military government seized power and the old political parties were banned.

In the 1970s, petroleum reserves began to supply needed jobs and capital, supplying 70 percent of money for the government by 1987. Even so, 75 percent of the people of Nigeria are tillers of small farms who strive to make Nigeria self-sufficient in food.

As in many places in Africa, the growing cities of Nigeria at first are divided by ethnicity. Benin City, for example, has a city government that operates under the national government, but also has ethnic sections of the city, each of which is dominated by a single group and is led by a chieftain of that group. As the cities develop, these societal isolations tend to disappear. The cities are blending the old African societies and replacing them with national identities.

In this book, the people of Nigeria are represented by the **Yoruba, Ibo, Fulani**, and **Hausa**.

A medicine man practices healing crafts in Benin City. *Photo by Barbara Neibel.*

The office of the medicine man in Benin City. *Photo by Barbara Neibel.*

A housing unit for elderly women in Benin City. *Photo by Barbara Neibel.*

Cooking in the elderly woman housing unit. *Photo by Barbara Neibel.*

A goat market in Ibadan, Nigeria. *Photo by Eliot Elisofon. Courtesy of National Museum of African Art.*

RWANDA

Population: 6,800,000 (1988 est.).
Location: Central Africa; bounded by Zaire, Burundi, Tanzania, and Uganda.
Languages: Kinyarawanda, Swahili, Hausa, French.
Principal city: Kigali (capital and the only city with a population over 100,000).

A land of steeply sloped, flat-topped hills that drop to valley floors that are sometimes marshy, Rwanda is a difficult land. However, for centuries Hutu (Baganda) farmers have worked the hilltops and fertile valleys to raise crops such as bananas. By the 15th century Tutsi herders had begun to tend their cattle among the Hutu farms, and to subjugate the Hutu.

Europeans settlers and traders were little interested in this land except as a route to inland markets. The Tutsi were left to rule and

to exchange dairy products for farm products with their Hutu subjects. In 1946 the land was joined with Burundi to form a United
Nations trust supervised by Belgium. However, African involvement
in World War II had aroused the Hutu, who now wanted a voice in
their own government. Conflicts between the two increased as
Rwanda approached independence in the early 1960s. In 1960 some
Tutsi began to leave the country—including the Tutsi king (mwami).
Then in 1961, 95 percent of the citizens of voting age cast votes in
favor of abolishing the monarchy of the mwami. One year later,
Rwanda became an independent country. A later invasion by Tutsi
who had left the country resulted in Hutu action that killed more
than 10,000 Tutsi.

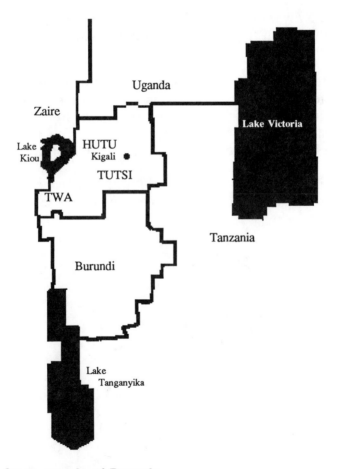

Some people of Rwanda.

Today the composition of the country is 85 percent Hutu, 14 percent Tutsi, and 1 percent Twa. However, the Tutsi periodically stage a revolt attempting to regain the power they once held over the Hutu.

For information about the people of Rwanda see **Tutsi** and **Baganda.**

SENEGAL and GAMBIA

Population: 7,800,000. Senegal, 6,400,000 (1987 est.); Gambia, 740,000 (1985 est.).
Location: On the west coast of Africa; bounded by Mauritania, Mali, Guinea, Guinea-Bissau, and the Atlantic Ocean.
Languages: French, English, Mandingo, Fulani, Wolof, Tukulor and other African languages.
Principal cities: Dakar (capital of Senegal), Thies, Kaolack, Serrekunda, Banjul (capital of Gambia).

The two nations of Senegal and Gambia are excellent examples of the effect of European colonization on country borders in Africa. Gambia was colonized early by the English. In 1816, a British sea captain received the rights to an island at the mouth of the Gambia River from the ruler of the Kombo people. By the late 1800s, the Gambia River and its shores had become a British protectorate.

Meanwhile, France claimed the surrounding territory and developed it as a manufacturing center for African trade goods. Senegal industry grew as a result of its market with Paris. However, the best route for shipping material from inland Senegal was difficult because the British claimed one of Africa's most navigable rivers and about ten miles of land on either side.

Gambia became independent of Great Britain in 1965, and Senegal gained its independence from France in 1960. However, it was not until 1982 that the two nations began to merge so that the Gambia River could come into full use. Senegal and Gambia are still separate nations, but have formed a confederation to share economic development, military preparedness, and international affairs.

Malinke (Mandingo), Wolof, Fula, Serahuli, and Jola people live in small villages along the Gambia River, and spread into Senegal. Toucouleur and Diola are among other large societies in the area. In this book, the people of Senegambia are represented by **Malinke (Mandingo), Wolof**, and **Fulani.**

Some of the peoples of Senegal and Gambia.

Place de L'independence, Dakar, Senegal. *Photo by Monica Guylai.*

Senegal-style art on a restaurant wall. *Photo by Monica Guylai.*

SIERRA LEONE

Population: 3,800,000 (1987 est.).
Location: West Africa; bounded by Guinea, Liberia, and the Atlantic Ocean.
Languages: French, Mande, Limba, Temne, Krio.
Principal cities: Freetown (capital), Koidu.

The typical west African seacoast hidden by mangrove swamp forests and backed by a rain-forested coastal plain marks the Atlantic Ocean front of Sierra Leone. The land rises from this beginning in a series of steps to a plateau where tropical forests give way to brushland and grassland.

In the late 18th century, some British sponsors were looking for a place to settle slaves who had been freed in England and its colonies. Captain John Taylor bought a small piece of land near a mountain

range that ran down toward the ocean and had already been known for 300 years by the name given it by the Portuguese, Sierra Leone (Lion Mountain). Here Taylor began to resettle the freed slaves on land the Mende people had owned. Other settlers came, and the colony expanded until the once friendly Mende began to feel hard-pressed to keep their land. Battles began and continued for many years. In 1808, the Sierra Leone Company, which held the settlement and no longer felt able to protect it, yielded to the British government and Sierra Leone became a British protectorate. The British began to use it as a base from which their navy could enforce the ban on slave trading by British subjects enacted the year before (1807).

Sierra Leone became an independent part of the British Commonwealth in 1961, and dropped its allegiance to the Queen in 1971. By that time, the republic had changed to a one party system under which it has fluctuated between civilian and military rule.

It is a country of declining prosperity. Diamond and iron mining, once mainstays of the economy, are waning, as is the largest industry, agriculture. Sierra Leone farmers grow coffee, cocoa, palms, and fiber crops for export.

Fine soil for farming, and centuries of trade on the Atlantic coast and with the savannas of the interior have attracted many people to Sierra Leone. Today they include such societies as Mende, Temne, Loko, Kono, Sherbro, Susu, Fulani, Limba, Krim, and Mandingo. This book contains information about the **Fulani** and **Malinke** (Mandingo).

MENDE
TEMNE

also

FULANI
KISSI
KRIM
LIMBA
LOKO
MANDINGO
SOSO
SHERBRO
VAI
YALUNKA

Freetown

Some of the peoples of Sierra Leone.

SOMALIA

Population: 6,900,000 (1987 est.).
Location: East Africa; on the coast of the Indian Ocean, bounded by Ethiopia and Kenya.
Languages: Somali, English, Swahili, Arabic.
Principal cities: Mogadishu (capital), Hargeysa, Kismayu, Berbera, Merka.

Northern Somalia is a land of mountains and high plateaus, surrounded by very dry and hot lowland valleys. Southward, the plateau steps down toward the Shabeelle River basin. Good farm land lies between the Shabeelle and the Juba River in the south. On all sides of this farm land lie dry pasture lands, extending south into Kenya, westward into Ethiopia, and in a narrow strip along the coast.

A staging point for religious wars between Christians and Muslims in the early 1500s, the northern part of present-day Somalia, then

under Italian control, was claimed by the British in 1886 after having been a major source of meat for the British garrison at Aden since the 1830s. Meanwhile the Italians continued to establish control over the southern section, and Emperor Minilik of Ethiopia conquered the interior Somali grazing country to the west. It remained divided until 1960 when the British and Italian sections were joined to form the Somali Republic. Since then, Somalia has been in disputes with Ethiopia, claiming Ethiopian land on which Somali people have settled. Somali has also disputed boundaries with Kenya. Beginning as a parliamentary democracy in which a new president was to be elected every six years, the country came under a military rule led by Major General Mohammed Siad Barre in 1969. He remained president until January 1991, when a military coup overthrew the government.

Somali people continue to be herders, raising camels, sheep, goats, and, in the south, cattle. Farmers along the rivers raise bananas, maize, and sorghum. The growing industry in the country is fishing. However, nearly a million people live in the capital city of Mogadishu where the main activity is trade.

Eighty percent of the people of Somalia are Soomaali—nomadic or seminomadic herders. Most of the rest of the country is populated by people of the Jiiddu, Tunni, and Maay societies, many of whom are farmers as well as herders. There are also representatives of Bantu societies in the country, as well as a few Yemenis, Pakistanis, and Indians.

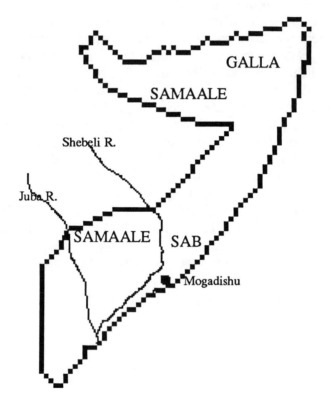

A few of the peoples of Somalia.

SUDAN

Population: 21,100,000 (1984 est.).
Location: Northeast Africa; bounded by the Red Sea, Egypt, Ethiopia, Kenya, Tanzania, Zaire, Central African Republic, Chad, and Libya.
Languages: Amharic, Arabic, English, French, Somali, Tigriaya.
Principle cities: Omdarman, Khartoum (capital), Port Sudan, Wadi Medani, and Al-Obeid.

Sudan is large and flat, as large as California, Arizona, New Mexico, Nevada, Colorado, and Texas combined. Two features distinguish the country—the Nile River Valley and the Kordofan Plateau. The Nile River forms in the Sudan from branches beginning in the mountains of Ethiopia and Uganda. The White Nile from the south cuts its path around a high spot in the landscape, the Kordofan Plateau.

The meandering rivers have left a swamplike region in the south and fertile valleys across Sudan.

The White and Blue Nile rivers converge to begin the long Nile River near Khartoum and Omdarman, cities of 800,000 and 500,000 people, respectively, which lie on opposite sides of the White Nile River. Rivers and railroads are the principal transportation routes in this vast region.

Seized as a colony by the Egyptians in 1821, the northern Sudan under the leadership of Muhammad Ahmad, known as the Mahdi, regained its independence from 1885 to 1898. In 1898, facing competition from the French, the British invaded and conquered the Sudan. Until the 1950s Britain ruled over the country with the co-operation of Egypt, which in those years was a client-state. In 1956, Sudan was granted independence, its government becoming a parliamentary democracy. A rebellion by non-Muslim southerners, who felt discriminated against by the new order, created enough turmoil to allow a military takeover of the government. Though peace was established again in the late 1970s, the old conflicts were not eliminated and in the early 1980s the south began to revolt again. Sudan has had civilian governments for only brief periods since then.

Lack of a good transportation system and a drought in 1984–85 have slowed Sudan's economic progress. This drought and its aftermath have been particularly costly in western and southern Sudan, where many people remain in danger of starvation. The Sudanese people depend on agriculture and herding for their livelihood. Explorations for oil were made in the 1980s and again in the 1990s, but since the best prospects for oil are in the south, exploiting oil resources will be difficult.

Nearly half of the people claim Arabic ancestry. Other societies in Sudan include Beja, Nubians, Nuer, Dinka, 20 or more societies of the eastern region commonly called Nuba, and numerous other smaller societies. The **Baggara** and **Dinka** are described in this book.

Some peoples of the Sudan.

SWAZILAND

Population: 750,000 (1988 est.).
Location: South Africa; bordered on three sides by the Union of South Africa and on the northeast by Mozambique.
Languages: SiSwazi, English.
Principal cities: Mbabane (capital), Manzini.

Situated on the edge of the Union of South Africa, Swaziland was created in the early and middle 19th century by the conquests of its kings Sobuzo I and his son Mswati I. Twice its present size in the 19th century, today it is a small country barely 100 miles across in any direction. However, it remains a kingdom for the Swazi. The present King Mswati III has ruled since 1986. This king has authority over the prime minister, who acts as day-to-day manager of the government.

In the 19th century, the Swazi kingdom was a powerful factor in the eastern interior of southern Africa. Still, the Swazi feared the neighboring Zulu kingdom. In the last two decades of the century, after Zulu power had been destroyed by the British, the Swazi found themselves under intense pressure from the expanding Boer society of Transvaal and from the British. This proved to be costly, since after the Anglo-Boer War of 1902, Swaziland was made part of the British protectorate and a colony of South Africa. British rule kept the country from being swallowed up by South Africa. Not until 1964 did Swaziland again take control over its own kingdom.

One-half of the Swazi people live in a middle belt of the country, where the soil is good for farming. In this area, European and Swazi farms checkerboard the land. In other places forestry and mining are important occupations. Swaziland has deposits of iron, coal, and gold. Diamonds were discovered in the kingdom in 1984. No outsiders, only Swazi, have interests in the mines of Swaziland. Most of the people of the kingdom are Swazi. They raise crops on small farms owned by the Swazi nation. There are few white farmers, and some people of mixed ancestry, called in southern Africa "Coloureds."

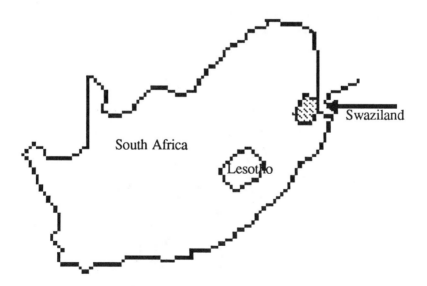

Swaziland is the home land of more than 250,000 Swazi.

TANZANIA

Population: 23,000,000 (1987 est.).
Location: East Africa; bounded by Mozambique, Malawi, Zambia, Zaire, Burundi, Rwanda, Uganda, Kenya, and the Indian Ocean.
Languages: Swahili, English, and numerous African languages.
Principal cities: Dar es Salaam (capital), Zanzibar, Mwanza, Tanga.

The Tanzanian coast runs for 500 miles along the Indian Ocean, with the strip of coastline varying from 10 to 40 miles wide and rising to a plateau that is more than 3,000 feet in elevation. West of the Great Rift Valley in northern Tanzania, the plateau rises above 5,000 feet to form the Serengeti Plain, which borders Lake Victoria. Mountain ranges interrupt the plain in many places. Mt. Kilimanjaro (19,340 feet) rises in the north along the Kenya border and is one of a series of ranges, including the Usambaras, which parallel the border south-

eastward toward the coast. The southern highlands and the Sumbawanga and Mbeya ranges, which reach above 8,000 feet, characterize the southern borderland with Zambia and Malawi. Lying just south of the equator, Tanzania is a tropical land of abundant wildlife. Most of the country is savanna in vegetation, although patches of forest exist at the far west and in the mountains.

More than 100 different ethnic groups live in Tanzania. Some are farmers, raising coffee, cotton, cloves, and sisal, along with staple food products such as banana and manioc. However, many of the people of Tanzania are primarily herders, tending cattle for milk and blood. A few people still hunt and gather food in the dry savannas in north-central Tanzania.

From 1881 to 1916, this land was claimed by the Germans as their colony of Tanganyika. However, African groups and Arab groups in the country did not submit willingly to German rule. Not until the Hehe leader of the resistance, Chief Mkwawa, died in 1898 were the Germans able to make any claim to dominance in the south-

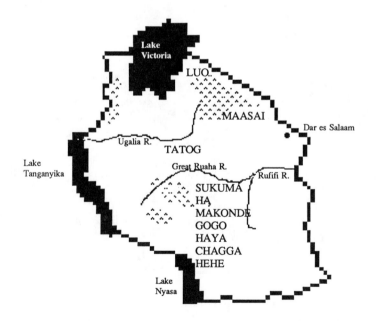

Some of the more than 100 peoples of Tanzania.

ern regions. After World War II, the British took control, under mandate from the League of Nations. In 1945, Tanganyika had become a United Nations trust territory, and then in 1962 it became an independent country after a peaceful struggle led by the country's first president, Julius Nyerere. Zanzibar, at first a separate country, was united with Tanganyika after a revolution in 1964 overthrew the sultan of Zanzibar. The united republic took the name Tanzania, its name today.

South of Lake Victoria, the Sukama and Nyamwezi people reside across much of western Tanzania. Maasai, Gogo, Haya, Chaga, and Hehe are major peoples through the central portions of the country, while notable groups in eastern Tanzania are the Shambaa, Zigula, Zalamo, Mwera, Makonde, and Yao. For more about the people of Tanzania, see **Maasai.**

Houses of Africa: Chaga of Tanzania.

Houses of Africa: Mangbetu of Zaire.

Houses of Africa: Dogon of Mali.

TOGO

Population: 3,400,000 (1989 est.).
Location: West Africa, bordered by Ghana, Benin, and Burkina Faso.
Languages: French, Ewe.
Principal city: Lomé (capital and the only city with a population over 100,000).

The flat sandy coast of Togo, an area covered with coconut trees is set off from the mainland by salt-water lagoons and small lakes. Thirty-two miles wide at the ocean, the country widens to nearly 100 miles in the center, where low mountains run southwest into Ghana and northeast into Benin. Beyond these mountains, savanna is cut by the Oti River Valley. Dense tropical forests once covered the land from the coastal sand to the savanna, but the forests have been destroyed except for patches along the rivers, leaving soil that is poor

in plant nutrients. In spite of this, the Togo agricultural economy is strong enough to supply the country's food needs.

Established as a "model" German colony in 1884, Togo remained under German control until 1914. It was ruled by the French and British during World War I. Under all these rules, the dominant Ewe people worked for independence. In 1956, as independence was imminent, the people of British Togoland voted to join the Gold Coast (now Ghana), and French Togoland voted to become independent. However, independence was not granted by the United Nations and France until 1960. As with many other African nations, the new country first attempted an elected civilian government, but in 1967 a military coup installed Lieutenant Colonel Étienne Edydema as president. He established a civilian National Reconciliation Committee of advisers and has been the leader of Togo ever since.

Represented in Togo are more than 40 ethnic groups, of which the Ewe society is the largest. The Ewe in the southwest are joined in the east by the Kotokoli and Chamba and in the north by Kabrai, Wati and Loso, and at the far north by some Hausa. Other groups include the Moba, Gurma, Ana, Akposo, Lamba, and Fon. These people are represented in this book by the **Ewe, Hausa,** and **Fon.**

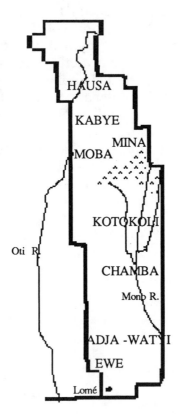

The many peoples of Togo have little common language or history.

UGANDA

Population: 15,900,000 (1987 est.).

Location: East Africa; bounded by Tanzania, Kenya, Sudan, Zaire, and Rwanda.

Languages: English, French, Swahili, Luganda, Gang, and a variety of Bantu languages.

Principal city: Kampala (capital and the only city of more than 100,000 people).

The 4,000-foot-high plateau that covers most of Uganda rises in the east to mountains of 14,000 feet and in the west to the Ruwenazori Mountains with heights of over 16,000 feet. The Great Rift Valley runs along the western edge of the country and holds Lakes Edward, George, and Albert. It is at Lake Victoria, on the southeastern side of the country that the White Nile River begins its course through

Sudan. The high altitude tempers the heat of the equator. Once mostly tropical forest, the southern half of the country is now, for the most part, cleared farm land.

Most people of Uganda are farmers who raise cotton and coffee for export, and plantain (cooking bananas), cassava, and other vegetables for food.

Turbulence marks Uganda's recent history. In the 1890s, the British began a colonial conquest, partly with the assistance of Buganda, the strongest kingdom of the region. The Buganda areas, from which Uganda gets its name, became the center of government and of economic development during the colonial era (1890s to early 1960s).In the early colonial decades many different African peoples feared that Britain would join them with a bigger and stronger Kenya, a colony run by white settlers. The people of Buganda desired their own separate state. When the country finally became independent in 1962, the king of Buganda was made the nation's president, with Dr. Milton Obote as prime minister. This government was overthrown by Major General Idi Amin, who ruled the country tyrannically, finally invad-

Some of the peoples of Uganda.

ing neighboring Tanzania to distract attention from problems inside the country. The Tanzanian army quickly turned back Amin's forces, swept through Uganda to the capital, Kampala, and forced Amin to seek asylum in Lybia and then in Saudi Arabia in 1979. There followed a series of governments until a new nationalist movement, led by Lieutenant General Yoweri Museveni took control in 1986. Museveni became president and has vigorously set about trying to reestablish democracy and restore the once prosperous economy.

Nearly a dozen groups count populations of more than one-half million: Baganda, Iteso, Basoga, Banyaruanda, Bakiga, Lango, and Bagisu among them. Of these, the **Baganda** are described in this book.

UNION OF SOUTH AFRICA

Population: 37,500,000 (1988 est.).
Location: The southern tip of Africa; bordered by the Atlantic and Indian oceans, Mozambique, Swaziland, Zimbabwe, Botswana, Namibia, and Lesotho.
Languages: English, Afrikaans, Zulu, Vasha, Sotho, Tswana, Tsonga, Venda, Ndebele, Xhosa.
Principal cities: Capetown (capital), Durban, Johannesburg, Pretoria (capital), Port Elizabeth, Bloemfontein (capital), and Verienging.

Much of South Africa is a plateau with eastern turned-up edges forming mountain ranges: the north-south Drakensberg Range, the northern Roggeveld Mountains, and the southern Cape Ranges. The Orange River drains the interior basin westward to the Atlantic Ocean.

Bantu farming peoples settled the eastern half of the country 2,000 years ago, gradually absorbing the earlier inhabitants, the Khoisan

hunters and the pastoral Khoikhoi, into their societies (see KHOISAN). In the 1650s, the Dutch East India Company, seeking to better supply its ships, made a small settlement at Cape Town among the Khoikhoi cattle-raisers living there. Between then and the early 19th century, white settlers spread east, depriving the Khoikhoi of their grazing lands and turning them into servants. From 1779, the whites, known as Boers, came into conflict with the Xhosa people, and then with the Zulu and Sotho.

Diamond discoveries in 1867 led to more white immigrants, industrial development, and a new kind of prosperity in South Africa.

A British colony since 1806, South Africa became independent in 1911. Then, in the 1950s, the government began to replace earlier segregation rules with a stronger and more systematic separation of races called apartheid. Under this policy, blacks were restricted in travel and in the locations of their homes. The black people have continuously struggled against this policy and, after initial losses from the 1950s to the 1970s, began to make slow progress against apartheid. Student demonstrations violently suppressed by the police, recognition of rights to belong to trade unions, and an international boycott

Some of the societies of South Africa

has finally resulted in the dismantling of apartheid laws in the late 1980s and early 1990s.

A large number of black societies live in South Africa, many of them on reservations called "homelands." The population includes Xhosa, Zulu, Sotho, Tswana, Tsonga, Swazi, Ndebele, Venda, Khoisan, and others. The societies described in this book include the **Zulu, Tswana, Swazi, Khoisan, Cape Coloureds,** and **Afrikaners.** The Ndebele described in this volume are from the country of Zimbabwe.

WESTERN SAHARA

Population: 104,000 (1980 est.)
Location: Northwest Africa; bounded by Morocco, Algeria, Mauritania, and the Atlantic Ocean.
Languages: Arabic, Spanish.
Principal city: El Aaiún (capital).

This region of sand and rock, with little agricultural land, few roads, and no appreciable trade, was of little interest to its Spanish claimants or to its neighbors until the 1950s. Then interest in the capability for a fishing industry, along with movements by the residents of the area prompted Spain to establish a formal Spanish Sahara province in 1958. Still the residents agitated for independence, and the area became more important when phosphate deposits were found there. Then in 1974, the Portuguese interest in Africa collapsed. Spain be-

came concerned about its ability to hold African territory, and began to set up an independent but friendly government. Immediately, representatives of Mauritania and Morocco agreed to divide the land among themselves.

The struggles between the two countries caused many citizens of the Spanish Sahara province to flee to Algeria, where they found sympathy from the government. Armed and trained by this country, the Spanish Saharans then returned home and immediately began to drive the Mauritanian invaders out. This accomplished, the Saharans turned on Morocco, and in 1979 succeeded in becoming an independent nation under a request that had been made by the United Nations as early as 1966.

So small is this country that the capital city has only about 20,000 residents. There are fewer than 5,000 students in elementary and high schools. Most of the people of Western Sahara fish and dry fish for export or herd camels, sheep, and goats. These people belong to four major groups: Arabs, Tecna, Chorfa, and Znaga.

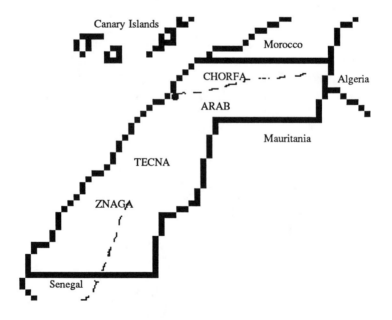

Some of the peoples of Western Sahara.

ZAIRE

Population: 33,500,000 (1988 est.).
Location: Central Africa, astride the equator; ringed by Angola, Zambia, Tanzania, Rwanda, Burundi, Uganda, Sudan, Central African Republic, Congo, and the Atlantic Ocean.
Languages: French, Swahili, KiKongo, Lingala, and many other Bantu languages.
Principal cities: Kinshasa (capital), Lubumbashi, Mbuji-Mayi, Kisangani, Bukavu.

Kinshasa, on the Zaire (Congo) River in western Zaire, is a city of more than 2,000,000 people. It is the seat of government in a country shaped like a large bowl. Carved by the giant river and its tributaries, this bowl has an eastern edge that rises to more than 6,000 feet. The eastern border of the country lies along the Great Rift Valley and is

marked by a series of lakes, the largest of which are Tanganyika, Edward, Albert, and Kivu. Lying on the equator, much of the land is covered by rain forests. Tropically steady temperatures average in the 70-degree Fahrenheit range. In the central regions of the rain forests, rain falls through much of the year. In the savannas it falls over a long rainy season—November through May in the south, and April through November north of the equator.

Several important precolonial kingdoms, among them the Kuba, Zande, Luba, and Lunda states, along with many smaller units, were conquered by the Belgians during the late 19th century. Formed into a colony called the Congo Free State, the region later became the Belgian Congo. In 1960 this territory became independent as the Republic of Congo. Almost immediately, the mineral-rich province of Kantanga (today called Shaba) tried to secede. Other rebellions followed, and struggles between leading politicians led to changing the command of the army. Joseph-Desir Mobutu was named commander of the armed forces and rose to the rank of general. In 1965 he took command of the government. In the 1970s, Mobutu launched a campaign to change the name of the country to Zaire, the old Portuguese version of an African name for the Congo River, and to require everyone in the country to use only African personal names. Now named Marshall Mobutu Sese Seko Kuru Ngbendu Wa Za Banga, President Mobutu has ruled Zaire for more than 25 years.

The first inhabitants of the Congo Basin were probably Pygmies. But beginning about 3000 to 2000 B.C., Bantu-speaking farming communities began to settle the Congo Basin. Their numerous modern descendants include the Kongo, Chokwe, Bopgandi, Mongo, Lunda, Luba, Songe, and Bwaka. In this book, the people of Zaire are represented by the **Kongo,** the **Bemba,** and the **Chokwe.**

BWAKA

ZANDE

Zaire R.

ALUR

MONGO

KONGO   Kanai R.

Kinshasa

BEMBA

Lake
Tanganyika

CHOKWE

SONGE

Some of the peoples of Zaire.

ZAMBIA

Population: 7,000,000 (1986 est.).
Location: Southern Africa; bounded by Botswana, Zimbabwe, Mozambique, Tanzania, Zaire, and Angola.
Languages: English, Nyanja, Bemba, Lozi, Luvale, Lamba, Ila, and Tonga.
Principal cities: Kusaka (capital), Kitwe, Ndola, Kabwe, Mufulira, Chingola, Luanshya.

A flat land rising to mountain areas in the northeast, Zambia is a mostly savanna region sloping toward the west. Altitudes rise above 4,000 feet, except in the Luangwa and Kafue river valleys and the lake regions (Bangweulu, Mweru, and Tanganyika). The high altitude keeps the temperatures moderate. A national parks system attempts to conserve the wildlife, which includes giraffes, zebras, rhinoceros,

elephants, more than 600 kinds of birds, and more than 150 species of reptiles. On the south edge of the country, the Zambezi River tumbles over the Victoria Falls to Lake Kariba. In the north center of the country, hills rise to form the Copperbelt, Zambia's chief source of income.

From 1891 to 1924, the land, then called Northern Rhodesia, was ruled by the British South Africa Company. When this company's authority ended, the territory became a British crown colony. In the early 1950s, the British forced Northern Rhodesia to form a federation with Nyasaland (now Malawi) and Southern Rhodesia (now Zimbabwe. This federation was opposed by the African peoples because it gave white settlers, who controlled Southern Rhodesia, greater power over the lives of Africans. Increasing nationalist agitation followed, with the federation breaking up in 1963. What had been Northern Rhodesia became the newly independent country of Zambia. Dr. Kenneth David Kandua was elected president and has been reelected every five years since Zambia became independent.

Although most of Zambia's people are subsistence farmers, the country's economy is tied to the value of copper mined in the Cop-

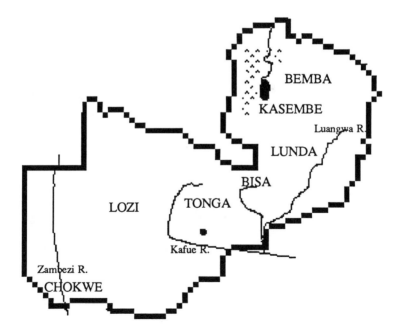

Some of the peoples of Zambia.

perbelt. Corn, sugar, and tobacco are grown for export and many grains and vegetables for food. In addition to these activities, power plants built along the Kafue, along with coal mining, have made Zambia one of the few African states with sufficient energy.

Zambia also is an African country which has successfully united a number of African societies under a mostly national identity. The major groups include the Ila and Tonga in the south, Chokwe, Lozi, and Luvale in the west, Bemba and Lungu-mambwe in the northeast, and the Ngoni in the southeast. The **Chokwe** and **Bemba** are described in this book.

ZIMBABWE

Population: 8,600,000 (1987 est.).
Location: Southern Africa; bounded by Botswana, Zambia, Mozambique, and South Africa.
Languages: English, Shona, Ndebele, Kalanga, Venda, Tonga, and Chewa.
Principal cities: Harare (capital), Bulawayo, Chitungwiza.

One of the newest African states, Zimbabwe is a plateau between the Zambezi and Limpopo rivers. Highest in the northwest, a high veld drops in steps toward the west and south, through middle veld, low veld—rolling hills of various altitudes and with varying soils. In the east, higher hills and mountains mark the boundary with Mozambique. The country is generally good agricultural land and also contains gold, asbestos, copper, nickle, tin, and platinum ores.

Zimbabwe was the home of the famous gold and ivory-trading medieval kingdoms of Great Zimbabwe, Mutapa, and Rozvi. Conquered by the British in the 1880s, it became a self-governing colony, then joined other regions in a short-lived confederation. With the demise of the confederation, Northern Rhodesia became Zambia, Nyasaland became Malawi, and Zimbabwe was formed from Southern Rhodesia.

Although the white population of the country was much smaller than the black population, white interests were protected from 1930 until 1980 by a system of land division that gave unequal "pyramids" of land to the two groups. As the cities grew in trade and mining areas, separation of ethnic groups resulted in separate towns for blacks. In the 1940s and 1950s this system met with increasing resistance from the black people. Finally, in 1980, the new Zimbabwe was formed under the leadership of Robert Gabriel Mugabe, who vowed to eliminate racial differences by establishing a socialist state. He chose to do this gradually, so as not to disturb the economy of Zimbabwe.

Some of the peoples of Zimbabwe.

Most of the black people of Zimbabwe belong to two language groups. The Shona, who were early gold traders in the area, make up 70 percent of the population, and include Karanga, Zezuru, Ndau, Korekore, and other smaller groups. The second group, the Ndebele, are an offshoot of the Zulu people. Today the Ndebele represent about 20 percent of the population, yet once they dominated the larger Shona group. The **Ndebele** are described in this book.

A town in Zimbabwe. *Photo by Eliot Elisofon. Courtesy of National Museum of African Art.*

Bibliography

Achebe, Chinua. *Hopes and Impediments*. New York: Doubleday, 1989.

Africa South of the Sahara 1990. 19th edition. London: Europa, 1988.

Awogbade, Moses O. *Fulani Pastoralism: Jos Case Study*. Zaria, Nigeria: Ahmadu Bello University Press, 1983.

Balandier, Georges and Jacques Maquet. *Dictionary of Black African Civilization*. New York: Leon Amiel, 1974.

Basden, G.T. *Among the Ibos of Nigeria*. London: Frank Cass and Co., 1966.

Callaway, Barbara J. *Muslim Hausa Women in Nigeria: Tradition and Change*. Syracruse, New York: Syracruse University Press, 1987.

Davidson, Basil. *The African Slave Trade*. Boston: Little Brown and Company, 1980.

Drewal, Henry John and Drewal, Margaret Thompson. *Gelede: Art and Female Power Among the Yoruba*. Bloomington: Indiana University Press, 1983.

Dunn, D. Elwood and Svend E. Holsoe. *Historical Dictionary of Liberia*. Metuchen, New Jersey: Scarecrow, 1985.

Ezeomah, Chimah. *The Work Roles of Nomadic Fulani Women: Implications for Economic and Educational Development*. Jos, Nigeria: University of Jos, 1985.

Gamble, David P. *The Wolof of Senegambia*. London: Inter-African Institute, 1967.

Hahn, Lorna. *Historical Dictionary of Libya*. Metuchen, New Jersey: Scarecrow, 1981.

Leach, Graham. *The Afrikaners: Their Last Great Trek.* London: Macmillan, 1989.

McFarland, Daniel Miles. *Historical Dictionary of Ghana.* Metuchen, New Jersey: Scarecrow, 1985.

McKenna, Nancy Durrell. *A Zulu Family.* Minneapolis: Lerner Publications, 1984.

Murray, Jocelyn. *Cultural Atlas of Africa.* New York: Facts on File, 1981.

MacGaffey, Wyatt. *Religion and Society in Central Africa: The Bakongo of Lower Zaire.* Chicago: University of Chicago Press, 1986.

Nelson, Harold D., editor. *Zimbabwe: A Country Study.* Washington, D.C.: American University, 1983.

Ndet, K. *Elements of Akamba Life.* Nairobi, Kenya: East African Publishing House, 1972.

Quinn, Charlotte A. *Mandingo Kingdoms of the Senegambia: Traditionalism, Islam, and European Expansion.* Evanston: Northwestern University Press, 1972.

Rasmussen, R. Kent. *Migrant Kingdom: Mzilikazi's Ndebele in South Africa.* London: Rex Collings, 1978.

Reisman, Paul. *Freedom in Fulani Social Life: An Introspective Ethnography.* Translated by Martha Fuller. Chicago: The University of Chicago Press, 1977.

Speake, Graham, editor. *Cultural Atlas of Africa.* Oxford, England: Equinox Ltd., 1989.

Wall, L. Lewis. *Hausa Medicine: Illness and Well-being in a West African Culture.* Durham: Duke University Press, 1988.

Glossary

apartheid The separation of South Africans into racial categories: white, Asian, black, and Coloured people of mixed races; an official system for granting or denying privileges.

bilharziasis Tropical disease caused by a type of worm that invades the bloodstream.

Boers The Dutch colonists, and their offspring, who settled in South Africa.

bulrush Grasslike plants that grow in wet environments.

calabash A utensil used in cooking or drinking made from the fruit of a calabash, a vine that bears hard-shelled gourds.

cassava A starch from the root of the cassava plant; also called manioc.

compound A household or group of households set off and enclosed from the others in a community.

ghee Purified butter in semiliquid form.

Great Rift Valley A great depression of the earth in East Africa.

griot A bard; a singer-poet who records and communicates historical events or delivers messages through song.

groundnut The underground nutlike part of several plants; the peanut.

insurgency Uprising.

jihad A Muslim holy war against nonbelievers.

kraal An enclosure for cattle or other livestock; also the term for a village of native people in southern Africa.

Koran The holy text of Islam, believed to hold revelations made by Allah, the supreme being, to the prophet Mohammed.

maize Corn.

manioc See *cassava.*

matrilineal Traces descent through the mother's family line, in contrast to patrilineal descent through the father's line.

millet A grass whose seeds are used as a food grain.

nomad A member whose group does not live in a permanent home but moves around within a certain region in search of food, water, and grazing land.

passbook A book with its owner's photograph that specifies where that person may live and work.

pirogue A canoe crafted from a hollowed tree trunk.

plantain A bananalike plant of the tropics, used in some areas as a main part of the diet.

polygyny Having more than one wife at a time, in contrast to *polygamy*, having more than one wife or husband at a time.

Pygmy A member of African groups, whose adult height measures from four to five feet; the general term *pygmy* refers to someone of unusually small size.

savanna Vast grassland that is treeless and flat.

seminomad An individual whose people are nomads in many ways but also plant some crops at a "home" location.

shea butter A fat that is whitish or yellowish in color and is derived from the nut of a shea tree.

sorghum A grass that is cultivated as a grain or source of syrup.

steppe A large, lightly wooded, semiarid grassy plain.

subjugation Bringing one group under the rule of another, or making one group subservient to another.

Sudan A region of Africa that is south of the Sahara desert and north of the equator; also names a country in Africa.

subsistence farming Raising crops for survival, or to provide for one's own needs.

tableland A raised, flat region, or plateau.

teff A grain, or cereal.

wattle Poles interlaced with twigs, reeds, or branches and used for building material.

Western-style Refers to customs practiced in Europe and the Western Hemisphere.

Index